For some reason, we thought Electronic Medical Records (EMR) would solve all of our healthcare problems. So we misapplied computer solutions to solve problems of bad processes and rigid cultures. Lean Management can help by engaging people in improving processes, identifying their real information needs, and making EMR truly value added.

Jeffrey K. Liker, PhD
Professor Emeritus, University of Michigan
Author, The Toyota Way

Kurt, Ron and Susan have a message: The Electronic Health Record (EHR) can help or hinder the healthcare delivery system. By following the proven methodology detailed within *The Lean Electronic Health Record: A Journey toward Optimized Care*, the EHR can be the enabler of better and coordinated care. A must-read for doctors and administrators truly interested in putting the patient in the heart of healthcare.

Helen Zak
Chief Development Officer
Catalysis, Inc.
Boston, MA

From defining requirements to realizing optimization to incorporating Lean concepts, *The Lean Electronic Health Record* presents an amazing amount of solid, practical advice related to electronic health record implementation and use. This is a must read for those looking to achieve more value for patients and better clinical and operational performance from their EHRs.

H. Stephen Lieber, CAE
President and CEO, Emeritus
HIMSS (Healthcare Information and Management Systems Society)
Chicago, IL

The Lean Electronic Health Record is a clear, concise description of the use of Lean principles in a real-world setting. Written in a relaxed, personalized writing style, the authors successfully guide the reader through a detailed Lean process for a very complex project. It is an excellent resource for those teaching Lean principles in academia, as well as healthcare teams planning to implement a new EHR.

Gail Bullard, DHEd, MSHA, RN, LBBH
Lean Healthcare Program Coordinator
Ferris State University

Organizations that do not consider the workflows and processes for their EHRs will never optimize or achieve highly reliable outcomes. HRO organizations align and invest in their informatics and Lean teams. These teams collaborating together can achieve the triple aim and effective use of the EHR, and happiness of users and patients alike. This book is an important demonstration of these methodologies.

Michael J. Kramer, MD
SVP and Chief Quality Officer
Spectrum Health System

The Lean Electronic Health Record

A Journey toward Optimized Care

The Lean Electronic Health Record

A Journey toward Optimized Care

Ronald G. Bercaw
Kurt A. Knoth
Susan T. Snedaker

CRC Press is an imprint of the
Taylor & Francis Group, an **informa** business
A PRODUCTIVITY PRESS BOOK

CRC Press
Taylor & Francis Group
6000 Broken Sound Parkway NW, Suite 300
Boca Raton, FL 33487-2742

Printed on acid-free paper

International Standard Book Number-13: 978-1-138-62658-4 (Hardback)
International Standard Book Number-13: 978-1-3152-2671-2 (eBook)

Library of Congress Cataloging-in-Publication Data

Names: Bercaw, Ronald, G., author.
Title: The lean electronic health record : a journey toward optimized care /
Ronald G. Bercaw, Kurt A. Knoth, Susan T. Snedaker.
Description: Boca Raton : Taylor & Francis, 2018. | Includes bibliographical references and index.
Identifiers: LCCN 2017037862| ISBN 9781138626584 (hardback : alk. paper) | ISBN 9781315226712 (ebook)
Subjects: LCSH: Medical records--Data processing.
Classification: LCC R864 .B46 2018 | DDC 610.285--dc23
LC record available at https://lccn.loc.gov/2017037862

Visit the Taylor & Francis Web site at
http://www.taylorandfrancis.com

and the CRC Press Web site at
http://www.crcpress.com

Contents

Foreword

It's an honor to write the foreword for the book *The Lean Electronic Health Record*, as I have an appreciation for the issues addressed in this book and empathy for those who deal with them. The problems and challenges with EHR systems not only affect patients and providers greatly but also create a great financial drag on healthcare systems around the world.

In a recent trip to my primary care provider, a medical assistant had me step on a scale at the end of a hallway. She wrote my weight down on a sticky note and carried it with her. I asked why she had to write it down. "They won't put a computer there [by the scale]," she said with a sigh. Once in the room, she logged in and entered my weight in the EHR system. It's possible that if the clinic had placed a computer by the scale, she might then say, "It takes too long to log in, so I write it down and enter it in the room since I have to log in there anyway." I wouldn't fault her for doing that.

Lean thinkers always try to focus on the process and the system, asking "Why?" instead of blaming the individual for "being resistant to change." It's unfair (and most likely unhelpful) to blame doctors or other providers for being resistant to technology or other new approaches to providing care. We should ask why they seem resistant or why they are complaining.

The M.A. seemed to feel unsupported. She wasn't miserable, but things could be better (and making things better is at the core of Lean thinking). Imagine she had been commanded by an office manager to not write patient information down on sticky notes. But how else can she do her job, given that we can't expect her to have perfect short-term memory. This would be especially true if she were also instructed to be warm and welcoming to patients, with friendly chit-chat then leading her to forget the patient's weight.

EHRs are helpful and necessary—they are not going away—so the best alternative is for everybody to work together, with empathy for others, so we can improve. Blaming others and telling them what to do might feel good, but doesn't really help over time. There might seem like a huge gap between today's "current state" and "ideal EHR" (contributing to ideal care). So, if we can't radically redesign what we currently have, we can at least make small improvements to the software, workflows, and management system. That might buy us some time until we can try again with the next generation of technology selection and implementation process. That's right, "process." We should view everything we do as a process, including the work involved with EHR adoption.

These are many situations and problems in healthcare that can and should be addressed by technology. This book, thankfully, does more than point out the problems we all might recognize. This book paints a picture, and creates a practical path forward, for creating healthcare IT systems that better serve patients and the providers.

Normally, new technologies are supposed to increase productivity and provide other benefits. Robots in a car factory save people from doing jobs that would be unsafe or cause injury from repetitive motion. As a car gets welded, there are some parts of the body that can be welded more consistently by a robot and others that require the flexibility and judgment of a human.

In a Lean-thinking organization, people displaced by (or saved by) automation would be redeployed and retrained to do work that best utilizes their creativity, whether that means programming and repairing robots or using their brains to continuously improve the organization and its work (something robots are not currently able to do). Even without laying people off, robots and automation increase productivity (not to mention safety and quality) when they are integrated into a well-designed process and a well-managed organization.

Healthcare often struggles with technology, as I've seen many instances where new technologies make work more difficult or time consuming. The authors share many examples of this in the book. It's not just "an EHR problem" or even "software problems," more broadly.

More often than not, these are more accurately described as workflow issues, technology issues, training issues, and leadership issues (and that same list applies to scenarios involving paper, phones, and faxes). The phrase "EHR system" usually refers just to the technology, but perhaps we should talk about the broader system around the technology. An ideal EHR system would be an optimized system of hardware, software, training, support, workflows, and management practices that lead to better safety, quality, patient flow, cost, and staff satisfaction.

I believe this book will be a helpful addition to the literature on Lean, healthcare improvement, and EHR adoption. I have known Kurt Knoth for almost a decade through our involvement in a collaborative called the

Healthcare Value Network. I know Kurt's commitment to healthcare is strong, being built upon a solid foundation of Lean practice in various industries and settings. The breadth and depth of his knowledge and experience make him well positioned to help the reader translate the spirit and practice of Lean in a way that allows you to develop your own best solution instead of just copying someone else's practices.

His coauthors, Ronald G. Bercaw and Susan Snedaker, are the perfect collaborators for this book. Ron has received two Shingo Research and Professional Publication Awards for previous books about Lean in healthcare. Susan is an experienced healthcare IT executive and an author of six technical and project management books. As a reader, you're in more than capable hands of these accomplished authors who are all committed to learning, sharing, leading, and improving.

Principle #8 of The Toyota Way says to "Use only reliable, thoroughly tested technology that serves your people and processes." Does the modern EHR system meet that test? Is it reliable and thoroughly tested, or have vendors and buyers rushed something to market or into use? Does the EHR system serve your people by increasing their productivity and reducing their frustrations? Does the EHR system serve your patients by reducing the risk of error and delay in their care, while making it less frustrating to interact with the healthcare organization and providers? Does the EHR system serve your current state and ideal processes and workflows, or are you forced into supposed "best practices" or workarounds that cause irritation and poor results?

Leaders can use the methods and concepts in this book to support the healthcare providers so they can better help the patients, which then leads to better results for the organization. This book has many answers. But, more importantly, it raises many challenging questions. As the reader, you don't need to have all of the answers yourself. Engaging and working with more of your colleagues, providers, and staff will lead to better solutions that are better embraced by your organization.

There are no formal government guidelines for this, but I am certain you will get meaningful use out of this book.

Mark Graban
Author of *Lean Hospitals*
Coauthor of *Healthcare Kaizen*

Acknowledgments

When Ron approached me about writing this book, my first thought was "Yeah, I can do that. How hard can it be?" Turns out that writing a book in your spare time is really difficult, particularly when you don't have much spare time... All kidding aside, I do have a particular interest in this topic. What a great application of Lean: to make the EHR more efficient and effective for patients and providers alike. Witnessing the waste and frustration firsthand, while working with clinicians, as well as seeing it from my own perspective as a patient, I couldn't resist doing my part to help.

I'd really like to thank my coauthors, Ron and Susan. Ron and I go way back and we are fellow Lean nerds, but this was my first time working with Susan. This book would not have happened without Susan's deep knowledge of IT and EHR systems. We wrote most of this book virtually, save for a two-day writing marathon in Denver, so it meant that we all had to depend on each other and trust that we'd get our work done. I hope that the final product reflects all this hard work, and I also hope that you find value in the words that we've published.

I also owe a debt of gratitude to Dr. Terri Osborne for letting me shadow her in the clinic and for her candor about all the things wrong with the current EHR. Thanks also to Dr. Mike Kramer for sharing his vast knowledge of clinical analytics, modern EHR systems, and for being a friend. Thank you to all of the Lean masters with whom I've had the privilege to work over the years, and I am also grateful to the dozens of physicians, nurses, and administrators who have helped me learn what healthcare is all about. Thank you to my father, Gene, for teaching me the value of hard work and showing me that everyone has value and deserves respect. I am also so grateful to my lovely wife, Wendy, for believing in me and supporting everything that I've ever done, and to my children, Addy and Ben, for enduring all the time that I was on the road gaining the knowledge to write this book. I am truly standing on the shoulders of giants.

Kurt A. Knoth

I was encouraged to write this book three years ago. The need for a "Lean" approach to deploying and optimizing an electronic health record is apparent. It is one of the largest lightning rods we see in healthcare. Patients, clinicians, and administrators all have some type of frustration with the EHR. I am humbled by the opportunity to discuss this topic and approach it from a Lean perspective.

Interestingly, upon completing my second book, I swore retirement from future book writing. (This is the same retirement oath I took following the completion of my first book.) Like Michael Jordan, I unretired, and was fortunate to collaborate on this book with two great people, Susan and Kurt. You would have never known we hadn't worked together before. It's easy to do magnificent work when the team you work with has no ego. While Kurt and I share a history and some Lean expertise, this book wouldn't have gotten off the ground without Susan's technical expertise. I think the reason this story hasn't yet been told is that a technical person wouldn't likely have the Lean expertise to write the book, and vice versa.

Thanks to the hundreds of clinicians, management, staff, leadership teams, board members, volunteers, and patient and family members of healthcare organizations, systems, and clinics that I have had the honor to work with over the last 15 years. I think we all continue to learn how to best serve patients together. The countless hours of improvement work with these stakeholders provided the core material for this body of work.

I specifically want to thank Terry Newell and Jane Jones for their contributions to this work, and a big thank you to Heather Wood for her editing contributions. Finally, I want to give a special thanks to my family and to Darlene. My family grounds me with great values and keeps me from taking everything too seriously. Darlene never lets me settle for mediocrity and inspires me to "achieve my potential."

Ronald G. Bercaw

I was approached by my publisher about writing this book on the heels of completing my prior book (*Leading Healthcare IT*, also with CRC Press), and she introduced me to Ronald G. Bercaw to be the Lean expert on the project. After talking with Ron, he suggested pulling in Kurt Knoth, and I'm glad he did. We each contributed our unique knowledge and perspectives in exploring new territory with respect to Lean and EHRs.

I'd like to thank my coauthors, Ronald G. Bercaw and Kurt Knoth, for teaching me so much about Lean as we were writing this book. I learned a tremendous amount and enjoyed the journey.

Thanks also go to my long-time collaborator and colleague extraordinaire, Chris Rima, for providing insightful comments and feedback on content. I'd also like to thank Lisa Mainz for reading, challenging, editing, and redlining my drafts. All four of these individuals helped make my contributions to this book far better than they would have been otherwise.

Susan T. Snedaker

Authors

Ronald G. Bercaw is the president of Breakthrough Horizons, LTD, a management consulting company specializing in delivering world-class improvement through the application of the Toyota Business System, more commonly known as "Lean." With over 30 years of experience in operations, his Lean management experience was gained through multiple enterprise improvement transformations in different industries, including custom packaging, power reliability electronics assembly, and test and measurement products.

Ron has consulting experience in the healthcare sector (US and Canada Health Systems, including primary care, acute care, and community applications of both clinical and back shop improvement); the commercial sector (administration, manufacturing, distribution, supply chain, engineering); and the public sector (Veteran's Health Administration, US Army, US Navy, and US Air Force including MRO, Pentagon, and Surgeon General Assignments).

Educated at Purdue University, Ron learned the details and disciplined applications of Lean principles, habits, and tools from both the Shingijutsu Sensei and their first-generation disciples. Ron is twice published with two Shingo Research Award winning books: *Taking Improvement from the Assembly Line to Healthcare* and *Lean Leadership for Healthcare.*

Kurt A. Knoth is the vice president of the System Supply Chain Services for Spectrum Health, a not-for-profit, integrated health system based in West Michigan. He is an experienced leader in Lean transformation efforts in large, complex organizations.

Kurt joined Spectrum Health in 2012 as Vice President, Process Improvement, bringing more than 20 years of Lean transformation experience in a wide variety of industries and sectors. He has led transformation efforts in the automotive, aerospace, high tech, military, and healthcare sectors spanning eight countries. Kurt began his Lean journey with Donnelly, a tier one automotive supplier in Grand Haven, Michigan. This transformation was featured in Chapter 8 of Dr. Jeffrey Liker's *Becoming Lean—Inside Stories of U.S. Manufacturers.* At Donnelly, Kurt worked under the tutelage of the Shingijutsu Consulting Group and had the opportunity to study kaizen in Japan. He also consulted for firms including Simpler Consulting—an IBM Watson Company, Optiprise (Liker's Lean consulting firm), and KPMG Consulting. His clients included The Boeing Company, US Air Force Surgeon General, ThedaCare, USAF Air Combat Command Headquarters, Lockheed Martin, and Harvard Vanguard.

Kurt received degrees in industrial electronics, plastics engineering, and operations management from Ferris State University. He is also working toward a master's of science degree in management, with a concentration in healthcare, at Southern New Hampshire University. Kurt is a certified Lean Six Sigma Blackbelt, US Air Force AFSO21 certified Sensei, and a certified private pilot.

Susan T. Snedaker, MBA, CISM, CPHIMS, CHCIO is a senior IT director of Infrastructure & Operations at Tucson Medical Center (TMC), a 600-bed community hospital in Tucson, Arizona. TMC is a HIMSS Stage 7 organization and has been a "Most Wired" hospital continuously since 2012. Her expertise spans IT infrastructure, clinical engineering, and information security. During her tenure at TMC, she has worked closely with clinical leaders in the development, deployment, and optimization of the EHR, which went live on the enterprise Epic EHR platform in 2010. Prior to joining TMC, Susan worked in leadership positions in IT in a number of industries and has focused on improving operational IT effectiveness in these roles. She is the author of numerous IT and leadership books including, *Leading Healthcare IT: Managing to Succeed* and *Business Continuity and Disaster Recovery for IT Professionals, Second Edition*, as well as the bestselling *IT Project Management.* For more about Susan visit her website at http://www.susansnedaker.com. Susan is a member of CHIME, HIMSS, ACHE, and ISACA.

Chapter 1

Always Start with the Patient

What's in It for the Patient?

Patients: The only reason that any healthcare system exists, yet so often considered merely as an afterthought. As healthcare providers, we sometimes get so caught up in our day-to-day activities that we completely forget that we are there to serve our patients. Those same patients that are the lifeblood of the healthcare system are beginning to act more like consumers. It's partly being driven by the proliferation of high-deductible health plans that put more of the cost burden on the patient in exchange for lower monthly fees. We have also become a nation seeking instant gratification, information at our finger tips and options to do things where and when we want to do them. The millennial generation is known as "digital natives," meaning they've never known a world without computers and the Internet. They are inherently tech-savvy, seeking services on their own terms and are quickly becoming a significant consumer of health services. It's fair to say that millennials will demand the same types of services offered by other industries; healthcare systems that can provide that type of experience will thrive and those that can't, well…they won't.

Technology has been able to satisfy the needs of patients in just about every other industry. Remember paper airline tickets? How about calling to schedule a dinner reservation? Deposit a check into your bank account? Buying CDs in a music store? Heck, most people don't even get a newspaper anymore. All of these activities can now be accomplished with the phone in your pocket. Why would our patients expect anything less of their local health system?

The current state of affairs within the healthcare system is far from the accessibility patients experience in other parts of their lives. While most health systems now have an Electronic Health Record (EHR) system, it was frequently implemented modeling an existing paper system. Oftentimes health systems implemented their EHR to take advantage of US government incentives for "meaningful use" of electronic health information. (We will explore the financial ramifications of this later in this book.) You would be hard-pressed to find many health systems today that allow you to schedule an appointment online, have access to your medical records, or get your test results electronically. And if you want to do some research to find out how much a test or procedure will cost you, you'd be out of luck as well. A physician's survey conducted in 2012 concluded that 63% of physicians still preferred to communicate using a fax machine,[1] as shown in Figure 1.1.

The fact that we are still using a dinosaur (fax machine) to send mission critical documents like referrals and prescriptions (often printed off and scanned back into an EHR) should give anyone who interacts with the healthcare system pause. When patients realize how far behind the times their healthcare provider really is, they begin to question the competency of the system as a whole.

If you are still using technology from the 1980s, how can I trust you with my health?

How can we leverage an EHR system to create a better experience, with better outcomes? Let's explore some of the ways that a modern EHR system can help bring the US healthcare system into the twenty-first century and bring value to the most important part of the healthcare system: patients.

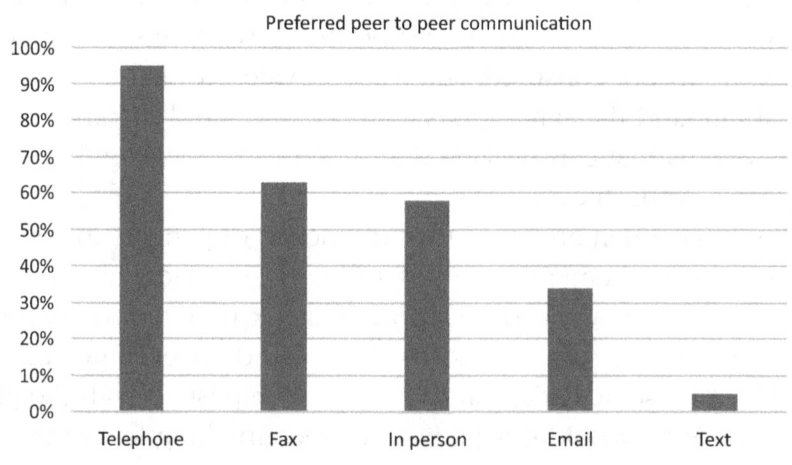

Figure 1.1 Fax machines continue to live on in many healthcare settings.

A More Seamless and Safer Experience

Have you ever had an encounter with a healthcare provider and have been asked the same questions about your demographics and health that you *just* answered in another setting within the same health system? Has it ever happened in the same office? I think we have all had an experience like this! Sometimes these checks are performed as part of a protocol to ensure safety and accuracy (Are we working with the correct patient?), but a lot of times, they are done because there is not a common EHR, and the systems don't "talk." This reminds me of a story from a colleague who brought his son into a health system for treatment of a broken arm. He was admitted into the emergency room and asked the typical battery of questions upon check-in: What is your name? What is your birthdate? What brings you to the emergency room today?, etc. Enter the nurse: What is your name? What is your birthdate? What brings you to the emergency room today?, etc. Enter the physician: What is your name? What is your birthdate? What brings you to the emergency room today?, etc. Then on to radiology, and so it continues. After the fourth set of questions, his son looked at my colleague and said "They don't have very good memories, do they dad?" This was a rather harmless example, and some of the questions are part of the safety protocol. Imagine, however, this was an 85-year-old man who was taking 24 different medications and he had to answer the question "What medications are you currently taking?" multiple times in multiple settings. This is where an EHR can really help.

Adverse drug events (ADEs) are usually caused by conflicting prescriptions or overdoses that lead to patient harm. It has been labeled a serious public health problem by the Centers for Disease Control (CDC),[2] who list the following key facts:

- 82% of American adults take at least one medication and 29% take five or more.[3]
- 700,000 emergency department visits and 120,000 hospitalizations are due to ADEs annually.[4]
- $3.5 billion is spent on extra medical costs of ADEs annually.[5]
- At least 40% of costs of ambulatory (nonhospital settings) ADEs are estimated to be preventable.[5]
- Studies have estimated that 2.4–3.6% of hospital admissions are caused by ADEs, of which up to 69% would have been preventable.[6]

A study at Boston Children's Hospital found that by using EHR medication reconciliation tools, the providers were able to reduce medication errors by 58%.[7] Since the EHR had a list of the patient's preadmission medications already in the system, the providers could display the existing medications list on a split screen while generating a new list on the other screen so that they could see any conflicting prescriptions at a glance. Reducing or eliminating ADEs is a very complex and daunting task for the healthcare system.

Having an EHR in place is a step in the right direction, but there are also many process-related changes that need to be in place to completely error-proof the system for patients. The Agency for Healthcare Research and Quality (AHRQ), a division of the United States Department of Health and Human Services, has proposed the strategies shown in Table 1.1[8] to reduce ADEs.

A fair number of the above strategies require a health system to have a modern EHR system in place; otherwise, they will not be able to take full advantage of these strategies.

Table 1.1 Strategies to Prevent Adverse Drug Events

Stage	*Safety Strategy*
Prescribing	• Avoid unnecessary medications by adhering to conservative prescribing principles • Computerized provider order entry, especially when paired with clinical decision support systems • Medication reconciliation at times of transitions in care
Transcribing	• Computerized provider order entry to eliminate handwriting errors
Dispensing	• Clinical pharmacists to oversee medication dispensing process • Use of "tall man" lettering and other strategies to minimize confusion between look-alike, sound-alike medications
Administration	• Adherence to the "Five Rights" of medication safety (administering the Right Medication, in the Right Dose, at the Right Time, by the Right Route, to the Right Patient) • Barcode medication administration to ensure medications are given to the correct patient • Minimize interruptions to allow nurses to administer medications safely • Smart infusion pumps for intravenous infusions • Patient education and revised medication labels to improve patient comprehension of administration instructions

Source: Patient Safety Network. "Medication Errors." Psnet.ahrq.gov. https://psnet.ahrq.gov/primers/primer/23/medication-errors

Let's explore another way that an EHR can be used to help prevent an ADE related to a drug interaction. Suppose that my surgeon just prescribed ibuprofen for pain, which is standard protocol. What he doesn't know (and I've forgotten to tell him) is that I'm already taking warfarin as a blood thinner. In this instance, the EHR should alert the surgeon that there is a problem; it can also be programmed to alert my primary care physician that I may have been prescribed another drug that may have a negative interaction. This is an example of a *poka-yoke*, which is a Lean term that roughly translates to "error proof." We are all human, and humans make mistakes. The more "guardrails" that we can put in place within the EHR system, the safer the experience will be for our patients. As more and more "simple" errors are designed out of the daily lives of our providers, they can turn their attention to more complex aspects of care and not focus on the mundane.

More accurate, up-to-date information from all of your healthcare providers makes for a better patient experience, especially during a crisis. Image that you are brought to the emergency department in an ambulance and are unable to answer even basic questions about your health. A fully integrated EHR will have all of your pertinent data on file. Your medical history, current medications list, and even an advance care plan will all be at your healthcare provider's finger tips. We don't typically like to think about this, but there are many instances each day when a patient shows up in the emergency room with no evidence of an advance care plan or a healthcare power of attorney (HCPOA). If that same patient is unable to speak, and no one is there to advocate for them, how can we know their wishes? The EHR can store this information and share it with multiple points of access within the health system. Imagine the horror of a family member that makes it to the emergency department just in time to find a Code Team performing chest compressions on a family member who is a hospice patient with "do not resuscitate" (DNR) orders. By taking advantage of the simple tools available within a modern EHR, a situation such as this can be prevented from ever happening again. This is another example of a *poke-yoke*.

A common practice in an inpatient unit is a nurse, doing his best to keep up with daily duties, printing off multiple labels to attach to blood draws for the lab. (This is an example of one of the seven wastes, Over Production, which will be explored later in this book.) This innocent and well-meaning approach to efficiency invariably leads to mislabeled lab specimens. This not only delays care, but also potentially leads to adverse safety events if the wrong patient is treated for the wrong ailment (or not treated at all). This is also a major patient dissatisfier as it leads to additional needle pokes, which are totally non-value-added in the eyes of the patient. Modern EHR systems can interface with scanners and bar codes that can help limit the chance of mislabeling a lab sample. In addition, the price of small label printers has been steadily declining, which makes having a printer in every room a practical reality. There are also small handheld printers that can be kept with the nurse, not unlike the rental car attendant at the airport. This helps improve the efficiency of the care team, as they are not walking needlessly back and forth to a centralized printer.

Reduce Unnecessary Tests and Procedures

Suppose you've recently had an MRI that was ordered by your primary care physician and that you also have a high-deductible health plan. Now you visit the orthopedic surgeon to see what he can do to relieve the pain and discomfort that you are experiencing that led your doctor to order the MRI in the first place. Without an EHR that can "talk" across specialties, that surgeon may order *another* MRI, which will be coming out of your pocket. Not to mention the time required to get the scan scheduled, waiting for the radiologist to read it, waiting for her to communicate the results back to the surgeon, and *then* getting back on the surgeon's schedule. From the patient's point of view, this is wasteful on many levels. It's a waste of their time, a waste of money, and prolongs their suffering. From the health system's point of view, it does enhance the revenue of the radiology department, but ultimately leads to access problems and the threat of further government interventions, since they are usually footing the bill. If the health system also has a health plan, then it's a losing proposition.

An integrated EHR system eliminates the scenario described above. Once the MRI is ordered by my primary care physician, I can go directly to the radiology scheduling portal and pick the time that I would like to get my scan. After my scan is complete, the radiologist reads the study and the results are available to me on the healthcare app on my phone, which is integrated with the health system's EHR system. It may be true that unless I'm a radiologist or healthcare provider, I won't necessarily know what the results of my test are, but if I'm technologically savvy I can search the Internet for clues of what his analysis means so that I can ask questions of my primary care physician or surgeon. If at this point my primary care physician decides that I should schedule a visit with the surgeon, he'll already have everything that he needs from the MRI that was ordered from the primary care physician when I show up at the surgeon's office. Less time, less waiting, better care, and a happier patient.

Self-Service Options

Think of any service industry today, then consider how many of those industries allow you to schedule or order their services online—your favorite restaurant, hotels, Uber, and even your veterinarian. It wasn't that long ago that you still had to make a phone call to your favorite airline to book a plane ticket. Many hours were wasted waiting on hold to work with a scheduler to go through different options to get from point "A" to point "B." As the Internet became more than just email and discussion boards, it didn't take the airlines long to figure out that people were willing to do the scheduling *themselves*, either at self-serve kiosks or via the Internet. Imagine that; the customer will do the work that we used to do, we will charge them the same amount, and they will like it! It didn't hurt that the airlines could eventually do the same amount of work with fewer people, which helped them become more competitive during an extremely difficult financial period for airlines. As we discussed earlier in this chapter, patients are starting to act more like consumers and expect simple things like online scheduling for their healthcare. Let's explore some ways that this is now possible.

If you've ever had a loved one who had to spend at least one night in a hospital, you understand the frustration that comes with physician rounding schedules. You are there to be the advocate for your loved one and you are continually told things like "The doctor will be here soon" or "We will be taking the patient to radiology in the next hour or so." It's just as maddening as the classic "We will be there between 8am and 2pm" announcement that we've all gotten at one time or another from the cable company. It drives cable customers to hate the cable company, and similarly, it drives patients and families to hate healthcare providers.

Invariably, you'll wait hours to speak with the doctor to fulfill your duty as the patient advocate, but your hunger finally forces you to find the cafeteria. Upon your return, the unit nurse informs you that "You've just missed the doctor." This scenario plays out regularly in hospitals across the country. What if there were a better way?

There *is* a better way: Modern EHR systems have the ability to create schedules in the inpatient setting. This means that it is possible to provide patients and families with their own "itinerary" of care while in the hospital. Patients and families can schedule things like radiology studies, occupational or physical therapy appointments, and even order meals using a tablet or smart phone! It's even possible to request a time slot to see your specialist or hospitalist, so that you can ensure that family members are present when they visit.

At this point, anyone that knows anything about healthcare may be rolling their eyes and thinking "Yeah, right. Doctors allowing patients to schedule them?" How would that work? It wouldn't be easy, to be sure. This is one example of where an EHR may have the ability to accomplish a certain task, but the complexity of this outcome is really the change management and process improvements outside of the electronic system. The later chapters of this book will explore how Lean tools can be used to improve patient flows, or more accurately care flows, to optimize the full capability of the EHR system. We will also discuss "bells and whistles" within EHR systems and the importance of choosing these options wisely during your implementation. Patient itineraries are the types of services that patients are going to start demanding, even if it is not possible in the current state. If you are not able to deliver this type of service, eventually a competitor will, and patients will begin to leave your health system to get real customer service. Necessity is the mother of invention, and you'd be surprised what can be accomplished when there's a crisis.

Easy Access to Medical Records

Do you own your health record? You may be surprised to know that only one state, New Hampshire (as shown in Figure 1.2),[8] has a law that designates the patient as the owner of their own medical records.[9] Twenty-one states have laws that *specifically* name the physician or the health system as the owner of patient records. The remaining states have no specific laws regarding ownership. Based on our earlier discussion about patient consumerism and the desire for greater transparency, these laws and attitudes seem antiquated.

To find out if patients really care to see their medical records and (more importantly) if doctors would agree to such an arrangement, the "OpenNotes" experimental study[10] was commissioned by The Robert Wood Johnson Foundation, the Drane Family Fund, the Richard and Florence Koplow Charitable Foundation, and the National Cancer Institute. The study engaged primary care physicians and their patients at Beth Israel Deaconess Medical Center (BIDMC) in Massachusetts, Geisinger Health System (GHS)

http://www.healthinfolaw.org Who owns medical records: 50 state comparison

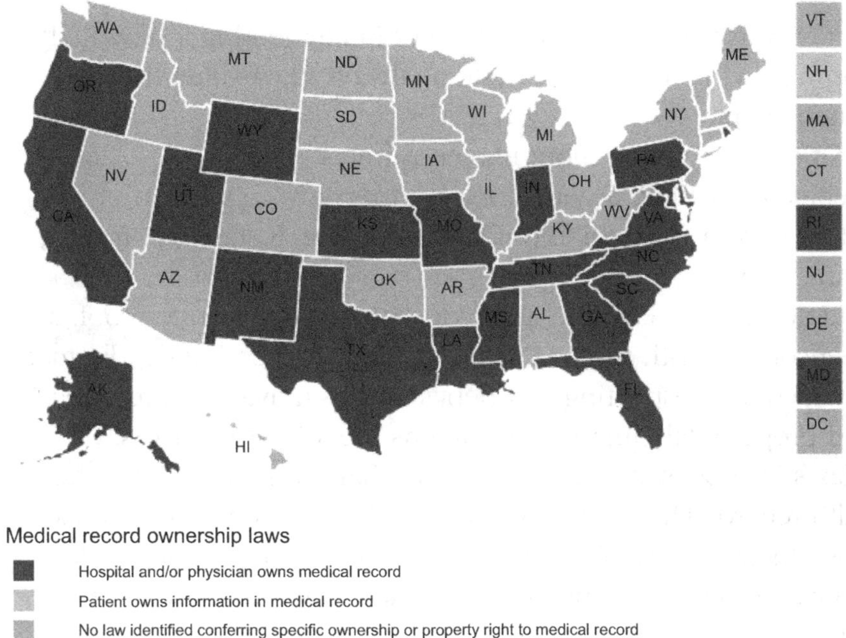

Figure 1.2 Who owns medical records: 50 state comparison. (From Health Information and the Law, http://www.healthinfolaw.org/comparative-analysis/who-owns-medical-records-50-state-comparison.)

in Pennsylvania, and Harborview Medical Center (HMC) in Washington. The objective of the study was "to evaluate the effect on doctors and patients of facilitating patient access to visit notes over secure internet portals."

One fear expressed by physicians included causing patients undue stress due to their lack of medical knowledge and privacy concerns. Doctors were also fearful that they would be required to "dumb down" their visit notes so that a layperson could understand them as well as eliminate the use of popular acronyms common to healthcare. One oft used example is that "SOB" translates to "shortness of breath" in doctor-speak, but means something entirely different to most patients. The results of this study proved that patients really valued the opportunity to read their doctor's visit notes and didn't add undue burden to the physicians. Incredibly, this study also showed that patients who read their visit notes actually had *better* outcomes. "60% to 78% of those taking medications reported increased medication adherence; only 1% to 8% reported that the notes caused confusion, worry, or offense."[10] In the end, 99% of patients wanted to continue to have access to their notes and not one physician chose to go back to the old way.

Chapter Summary

- The patient always defines value. Whether implementing a new EHR system or improving an existing system, always view value through the eyes of the patient.
- Today's patients are acting more like consumers. Healthcare systems must leverage their EHR systems to serve this new generation of patients that expect things like online scheduling, instant test results, and transparency.
- Modern EHR systems have the ability to *poka-yoke,* or error-proof, a patient's encounter with the healthcare system. Preventing deadly medication interactions, respecting a patient's wishes (advance care directives), and properly labeling lab specimens are a few examples.
- Current laws in most states do *not* specify that the patient owns their own health record. The OpenNotes project has proven that patients want to see their physician's visit notes, it doesn't add undue burden to the physician, and the patients that read their notes actually have better outcomes.

Further Reading

1. McCann E. "Getting the fax straight." *HealthcareITNews*. http://www.healthcareitnews.com/news/getting-fax-straight
2. Centers for Disease Control and Prevention. "Medication Safety Basics." cdc.gov. http://www.cdc.gov/medicationsafety/basics.html
3. Slone Epidemiology Center, Boston University. *Patterns of Medication Use in the United States*, 2006.
4. Budnitz DS, Pollock DA, Weidenbach KN, Mendelsohn AB, Schroeder TJ, Annest JL. "National surveillance of emergency department visits for outpatient adverse drug events." *JAMA* 2006 October 18; 296(15): 1858–66.
5. Institute of Medicine. Committee on Identifying and Preventing Medication Errors. *Preventing Medication Errors*, Washington, DC: The National Academies Press, 2006.
6. Roughead EE, Gilbert AL, Primrose JG, Sansom LN. "Drug-related hospital admissions: A review of Australian studies." *Med J Aust* 1998; 168(8): 405–8.
7. Bresnick J. "Study: EHR medication reconciliation reduces errors by 58%." Healthitanalytics.com. https://healthitanalytics.com/news/study-ehr-medication-reconciliation-reduces-errors-by-58
8. Patient Safety Network. "Medication Errors." Psnet.ahrq.gov. https://psnet.ahrq.gov/primers/primer/23/medication-errors

9. Delbanco T, Walker J, Bell SK, Darer JD, Elmore JG, Farag N et al. Inviting patients to read their doctors' notes: A quasi-experimental study and a look ahead. *Ann Intern Med* 2012; 157: 461–70. [PMID: 23027317] doi:10.7326/0003-4819-157-7201210020-00002.
10. Health Information and the Law, http://www.healthinfolaw.org/comparative-analysis/who-owns-medical-records-50-state-comparison

Chapter 2

Take Care of Ourselves before We Take Care of Others

While flying, you've likely read the safety briefing card in the seat back in front of you: "Place oxygen mask on yourself first before helping small children or those around you." While this is a universal truth when it comes to aviation safety, it's not quite the case when it comes to healthcare culture. Those who have dedicated their careers and lives to healthcare tend to always put the wellbeing of their patients above all else. This isn't an entirely bad thing. I want my doctor to be passionate and dedicated to my health. When I get my 20 minutes of his attention for my annual checkup, I want his full uninterrupted attention on me. It's irritating as a patient when the doctor has to turn his back to me to type into his computer. This guy spent at least 11 years in school and training to become a doctor, and here he is doing what boils down to clerical work. In the acute setting, nurses are also spending more and more time interacting with the electronic health record (EHR) and less time at the bedside. It's estimated that a typical bedside nurse only spends about 35% to 46% of his time actually *at* the bedside.[1] The rest of the time is spent looking for supplies, tracking down physicians, or entering data into the EHR.

That's the paradox of modern medicine. As we explored in Chapter 1, patients are acting more like consumers and are becoming more and more demanding. At the same time, physicians and nurses are working in a field that is becoming much more complex and much more demanding than it was even 5 years ago. One element of that complexity that we will explore in this chapter is the EHR and its related work flows and how that has negatively affected the art of medicine.

There is no secret that nursing shortages are already being felt across North America. Think quickly about your organization; how many open position requisitions exist for nursing positions right now? To be fair, the nursing shortage problem is multifaceted, and we cannot blame all nursing shortages on burnout. Nonetheless, one of the largest nursing dissatisfiers is the time spent documenting in the EHR.

On the physician side, the work load has been steadily increasing. Not always from increases in patient workload, but also from the documentation and clerical requirements necessary to run the business and maintain compliance, and the ever increasing documentation required to satisfy insurance requirements. A recent study found that 49.2% of an average ambulatory physician's time in the clinic was spent on EHR and desk time.[2] This same study found that only 27% of the physician's time was spent face-to-face with the patient delivering care. The EHR alone is not to blame for all of this extra work (and rework), rather a poor underlying process that was not that great to begin with. A well-functioning and streamlined EHR process flow can alleviate some of this workload. I do not believe it is a stretch to declare that a well-functioning EHR process flow can automate some of the clerical functions, simplify communication, eliminate some documentation redundancy, and help doctors, nurses, and the rest of the clinical staff improve their work/life balance.

Because healthcare providers are high achievers and have a passion for taking care of people, they naturally drive themselves harder than other professionals. However, by neglecting their own well-being, they are putting patients at risk, their job satisfaction is negatively affected, and it puts undue strain on the staff. Unfortunately, the incidence of "physician burnout" is increasing at an alarming rate. According to a recent survey of over 2,000 physicians, 66% reported higher levels of stress and burnout than 4 years ago, and 46% reported severe stress and burnout.[3] Burnout is a syndrome defined by three components: emotional exhaustion, depersonalization, and diminished feelings of personal accomplishment.[4] Unlike other depressive disorders, burnout is strictly a work-related syndrome.[4] Roughly 80% of physician burnout can be attributed to workflow issues.[5] Poorly designed and implemented EHRs are a major contributing factor to these workflow issues as well as adding additional workload.

There are many factors that play into the current epidemic of physician burnout, including loss of autonomy as physicians join larger health systems and medical groups, the continued problem of too few physicians to meet ever increasing customer demand, as well as compensation issues. Another factor that is relatively recent is the US government requirements around reporting of electronic health information. This has helped fuel the conversion to EHRs and has many physicians saying to themselves (and out loud) "I didn't go to medical school for this!"

The physicians and nurses are not the only ones that are negatively affected by a poorly designed EHR. In a poorly designed EHR, schedulers have more work due to variability from office to office and provider to provider. Some health systems have multiple EHRs for things like specialty clinics and radiology. In such cases, the scheduler has to be trained in multiple systems and will have to jump back and forth between systems almost constantly. Add in the complexity to actually use the system to schedule a patient and a typical scheduler will long for the days of paper and pencil.

Registration personnel may have to ask patients the same questions over and over again, due to poorly designed workflows. When it comes time to check out in an ambulatory clinic setting, the registration personnel are likely to be responsible for After Visit Summaries (AVSs), which now have the potential to end up with the wrong patient, causing a HIPAA violation. All of this "front-end" work of the patient encounter must be perfect; otherwise, the revenue cycle folks end up cleaning things up at the back end, typically after the payer has rejected the charge. I've witnessed entire revenue cycle *departments* that do nothing but this type of rework, which in Lean terms is pure waste.

Another challenge for health systems with multiple EHR systems are transitions of care across different care settings. This sets up the classic multiple questions about the same thing that was discussed in Chapter 1, but it's also a potential failure point from a patient safety perspective when a medication list or test result does not flow along with the patient as they transition across the system.

Provider Burnout Is Exasperated by Today's EHRs

The idea of collecting and recording patient data electronically instead of manually is not a new concept. Dr. Larry Weed introduced the idea of the electronic medical record way back in the late 1960s.[6] His concept made it possible for third parties to independently verify physician diagnoses, which would lead to better outcomes. It was hailed as a major advancement in clinical practice, but implementation outside of a few innovative health systems was very slow. Even after EHRs started to become ubiquitous, physicians never really followed the methods developed by Dr. Weed. Problem lists were not used and since there were no standards for interoperability, it was very difficult to truly share a patient's longitudinal health record. To make matters worse, EHR vendors did not, nor were they incented to, meet even basic informatics standards.

Interest in electronic health records did not really take off until the American Reinvestment & Recovery Act (ARRA) was enacted on February 17, 2009. In short, this act gave physicians and health systems financial incentives to "meaningfully use" electronic health record data. During the early phases of this government program, physicians and health systems were incentivized to engage patients electronically, and the idea was that Larry Weed's vision would finally become a reality.

If nothing else, this act created a cottage industry of consulting firms that made a career of helping physicians and health systems "attest" to the government that they were, indeed, providing "meaningful use" of the EHR. It turned out to be a pleasant surprise for hospital CFOs, as most of them didn't budget for such windfalls that were provided by the US government. Not unlike most other things that the government touches, this well-intended, but poorly executed process became a bureaucratic money grab that layered on more and more work for the physician who seemingly had fewer and fewer hours in the day to actually see patients. Rather than spending the majority of their time caring for their patients, more and more time is now reserved for typing data into the patient's health record. By one physician's estimate, the modern EHR has added at least 1.5 hours to her day, every day that she sees patients.

While I was doing some healthcare consulting work in Boston (including a project to help them streamline their EHR processes), the CEO of this health system would write a weekly update of whatever topic was on his mind. As a seventy-something cardiologist, he was a wealth of knowledge and always had a thought-provoking message. I'll never forget the time that he reflected on his high school experience in the 1960s. He had started a typing class at the beginning of the year and when his father heard of this (a surgeon himself), he told him that "You will be a doctor someday, son. Why do you want to learn to type? You'll have a secretary who will take care of that for you, so that you can take care of more important things." In hindsight, the CEO reflected on his decision (at his father's insistence) to drop typing class and take advanced biology. "It was likely the worst academic decision of my career."

Older physicians (in general) have been more reluctant to adopt EHR systems[7] likely due to being less familiar with technology as well as limited typing skills. Younger providers are more likely to be "digital natives" that grew up with technology and are more likely to embrace the new system as it feels more natural to them. As technology continues to advance, voice-to-text applications like Dragon® Medical Practice and M*Modal® are getting much more capable and easier to use. Many providers are still uncomfortable talking into their EHR with a patient present, thus negating some of the advantages of this technology. There are also traditional scribes (which are sometimes medical students, wishing to learn more by working in the gemba), as well as advanced remote scribes and other technologies, by the time of this writing, that will most certainly help automate some of the EHR documentation.

The Promise of a Simplified User Experience Has Not Materialized

By any measure, today's EHR systems are *not* user friendly. The interfaces are just plain ugly by modern standards. Providers that are used to the feel of polished and easy-to-use consumer websites are forced to log into an EHR system that seems like a trip to back to the 1980s, like that shown in Figure 2.1. Truth be told, some of the leading EHR system interfaces have not been materially updated since the 1980s. For instance, a leading EHR's interface was written, using C++, a computer language that first appeared in 1983,[8] during the Reagan administration.

Regardless of how capable these "modern" EHR systems are, when you are used to using a product that was designed last year, versus one that was designed in the 1980s, it doesn't exactly elicit feelings of confidence. It would be like someone substituting your modern smart phone for an old-fashioned flip phone. Sure, the old phone can do a lot of the same things that your smart phone can do, like calling and texting, but it's much more clunky and frustrating. Remember how texting used to work? To get the letter "C" you would have to press the number 2 button three times. The letter "O" required a press of the number 6 button three times, and so on.

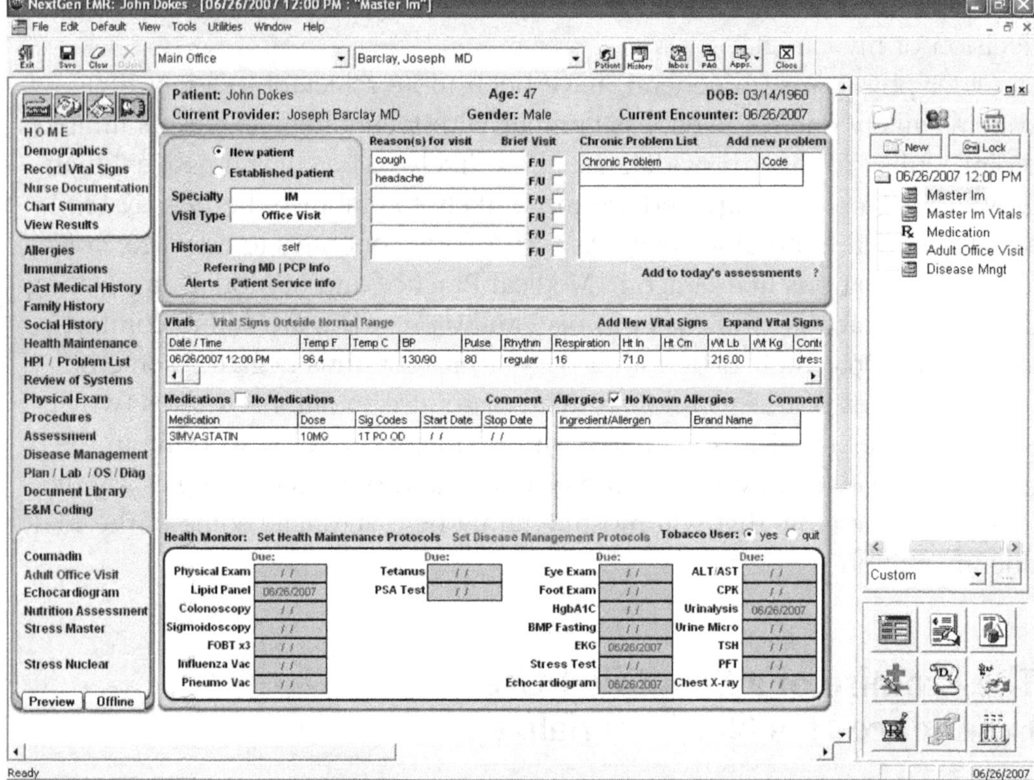

Figure 2.1 Typical modern EHR interface. (Photo courtesy of Technologyadvice.com.)

Keep this analogy in mind as I share the frustration of one provider at a large health system:

> The biggest thing that drives me crazy is the fragmentation of the record, and thus the patient story… into a jumble of poorly formatted documents that I have to manually search through to find the clinical information I need. For example: If I am looking at a radiology report, key clinical information is often hidden at the end of the note; I must spend time scrolling through a bunch of technical details to get to the impression. If I am looking at a lab test, the result might be found at the end of the document as well. Clinical encounter notes are often created by aggregating a bunch of discrete data fields that lack flow and context. The best description

> I have heard of the problem is that EHRs are great for getting *billing* data, bad for aggregating clinical data.
>
> **Terri Osborne, M.D.**
> *Spectrum Health System*

Furthermore, mountains of "indirect" work that used to be invisible to the provider are now right in the middle of their workflow. This indirect work may or may not be clinically relevant, but must be reviewed, regardless. For example, a primary care doctor may get copied on every test ordered by a specialist and then is required to review these results along with everything else in their in-basket. Very important test results can (and have) been buried underneath other "For Your Information" messages to the point where it can jeopardize the safety of the patient. There have even been cases where an important test result was missed, resulting in a lawsuit that included the primary care physician, even though they hadn't even ordered the test.

Other important messages, such as prescription refills, may also be missed, requiring the patient to call the office, which has a negative effect on their experience. There is not typically an easy way to bring important messages to the top or flag them; thus, the provider just has to go through them all, usually after hours, or at the very least, after their normal shift.

Thrown on top of all of this, to make matters worse, training for a new EHR system is usually underinvested. The math looks really good in the short term because, well, providers are busy and to be frank taking them offline for training is very expensive and can negatively affect patient care if not executed carefully. When it comes time to flip the switch, nurses and physicians may have only a rudimentary understanding of the software, and it can be extremely clunky and frustrating. In the long term, this can lead to many other hidden costs and inefficiencies, but when looking at the short-term financials, this reality gets lost in the decimals.

To be struggling with technology right in front of the patient is not a situation that most providers (especially doctors) are used to or comfortable with. This sometimes leads to undesirable behavior, such as batching all patients record updates until the end of the day. This is bad in a number of ways, not least the potential safety issues with relying on the physician's memory about a patient encounter at, say, 8am that is documented at 8pm. Stating the obvious, it also adds stress to a physician by blending together her work life with her home life. The choice is either to stay at work later than your regular shift or take your laptop home with you and do the work at home.

Sometimes, just the way that the EHR is configured makes it vexing to use. For instance, when a primary care physician needs to refer a patient to a cardiologist, the pull-down menu of choices may be a random sounding list of physical clinical locations that were based on billing data from the revenue cycle system. It made perfect sense to someone, but it totally stopped the referring physician in his tracks, and now he must ask his medical assistant to help out. The other option is to just pick the location that "sounds" right and hope someone else picks it up on the back side. Sometimes it gets caught, and oftentimes, it falls to the patient to fix the problem. As mentioned in Chapter 1, there are wonderful things that an EHR can do to improve the patient experience as well as make healthcare safer for our patients, but it can also have the opposite effect if it is not properly designed.

Getting a Day's Work Done in a Day

One tangible reminder of an inefficient EHR process, particularly in an ambulatory setting, is the fact that providers struggle to complete all of their work within their "regular" shift. Since a good percentage of physicians are still paid according to the number of patients that they see (like piecework in manufacturing 40 or 50 years ago), they are incentivized to minimize the time between visits. If they struggle with the EHR, especially in front of the patient, they may choose to batch all of those entries until either mid-shift or the end of the day. This means that their day gets extended and since they are paid to see patients, it feels like this work is being done on their own dime. It's not unheard of for providers doing the math on their overall workload and backing into an hourly rate that is much lower than what it would be for just seeing patients. This adds to a feeling of burnout and wondering if the health system really has their best interests in mind.

There is a better way. In Lean thinking, there is a concept called "one piece flow," which is the opposite of batching. Flow will always beat batching when it comes to efficiency, quality, and safety. When starting an improvement effort, it's always best to get those closest to the work engaged, and get some quick wins. In an ambulatory setting, like the one described above, pick something that drives the physicians crazy and work to minimize or eliminate it. In this case, the goal could be to eliminate work done at home (or after hours). It's easy to measure, as most EHRs automatically time-stamp all transactions, and if you can pull it off, you'll have the physicians hooked. In later chapters, we will explore Lean tools and methods that you can use to make improvements to your workflows.

Additional Thoughts

By many measures, EHR systems are the number one frustration that is voiced by physicians and one of the main factors leading to burnout. Thus far, it doesn't seem as though the EHR vendors are taking any accountability for their part in provider burnout, nor are they putting much effort into creating a more user friendly experience. They are making billions of dollars on their product, and it would seem that funneling some of that money into research and design for a more useable product would gain them more than a little goodwill from their users. As we'll explore in the next chapter, the sales presentations are still focused on the bells, whistles, and other shiny objects that tend to fascinate procurement committees. It's more fun to talk about the new functionality and the whiz-bang features, but maybe the big vendors should start focusing a little more on usability. In the meantime, this book is intended to help you design a more user friendly experience, which will keep your patients safer and provide a better customer experience, regardless of what the software looks like.

What most providers are struggling with today is a system that basically overpromised and underdelivered on so many levels. Can you image what it would feel like to have such a seismic shift thrust upon the very thing that you do for a living? Something that can be extremely frustrating and perceived to be preventing you from doing what you were trained to do: take care of patients? Our aim is to help you find ways to give providers more time with their patients as *well* as their families. It *is* possible and we will show you how.

Chapter Summary

- Poorly designed EHRs lead to inefficient workflows, which exasperate provider burnout.
- There are many employees of a health system that can be negatively affected by a poorly designed EHR system. Scheduling, Registration, and Revenue Cycle employees can be subjected to rework and inefficient processes.

- Modern EHRs are ugly. Compared to other modern electronic interfaces, they feel like a trip back to the 1980s, which does not elicit confidence and trust from their users.
- Many providers cannot keep up with their EHR entries, forcing them to catch up at home, which blurs the line between work and home life.
- EHR vendors continue to focus on additional and more advanced capabilities, but refuse to invest in basic usability improvements that could help reduce provider burnout.

Further Reading

1. Hurst K. How much time do nurses spend at the bedside?, *Nursing Standard* 2010; 24(52): 14. CINAHL Complete, EBSCOhost (accessed June 14, 2017).
2. Sinsky C, Colligan L, Li L, Prgomet M, Reynolds S, Goeders L et al. Allocation of physician time in ambulatory practice: A time and motion study in 4 specialties. *Ann Intern Med.* 2016; 165: 753–60.
3. hVital Work Life. 2015 Physician Stress and Burnout Report. http://info.VITALWorkLife.com/stress
4. Maslach C, Schaufeli WB, Leiter MP. Job burnout. *Annu Rev Psychol.* 2001; 52: 397–422.
5. Strongwater S, Lee T. Are EMRs to blame for physician burnout? *NEJM Catal.* http://catalyst.nejm.org/electronic-medical-records-blame-physician-burnout
6. Weed I, Lawrence MD. Medical records that guide and teach. *NEJoM.* 1968; 278: 593–600, 652–7.
7. Xierali IM, Phillips RL, Green LA, Bazemore AW, Puffer JC. Factors influencing family physician adoption of electronic health records (EHRs). *J Am Board Fam Med* n.d.; 26(4): 388–93. Science Citation Index, EBSCOhost (accessed June 14, 2017).
8. Wikipedia. C++. https://en.wikipedia.org/wiki/C%2B%2B

Chapter 3

Dollars and Cents

How Much Does This New Electronic Health Record Cost?

Regardless of dollars and cents, there are some compelling reasons for both acquiring an electronic health record (EHR) and improving how to deploy an EHR. Patients, family members, and care givers are demanding better care and more transparency. In the previous chapters, we discussed that healthcare customers want more control over their healthcare and more options and input on how the care is delivered. We also discussed that healthcare staff, and physicians, are requesting better electronic tools to make care safer, to streamline communication, to improve workflow, to reduce wait times, to reduce redundancy, and to provide better, real-time information to improve outcomes. The requests for better tools and applications are coming in a work environment where many healthcare staff and physicians at best are complaining and at worst are experiencing burnout. Workdays are becoming longer to keep up with the administrative needs that are required to ensure compliance, medical necessity, pre-authorization, insurance verification, meaningful use, administrative tracking, etc. However, in addition to the patient demands and the staff frustration and burnout, there is a third call to action. Healthcare organizations need to improve how they develop and deploy the EHR to minimize the dollars spent on the deployment and maintenance of the system and maximize the return on investment.

Stating the obvious, EHR development and deployment has a substantial price tag associated with it. Implementation costs vary greatly by vendor. Items included in start-up and deployment can include software fees, licensing fees, start-up fees, integration expenses, annual maintenance costs, hardware and infrastructure costs, and training fees. For large healthcare systems, a *Becker's Health IT and CIO Review* article from June 2015 titled "8 EPIC EHR Implementations with the Biggest Price Tags in 2015" reported the implementation costs in US dollars (see Table 3.1).[1]

Becker's also reported that Duke Medical Center in Durham, NC, spent $700 million in implementation costs in 2014.[1] In a time when healthcare costs are continually rising, healthcare personnel resources are coming up short in numbers, and decreasing reimbursements, it is more important than ever to manage capital resources diligently. Lean approaches in deploying an EHR can help ensure that value is maximized and costs are minimized.

To get an understanding of how "healthy" the bottom lines of US healthcare currently are, the trend of US hospitals with a negative operating margin and negative total margin from 1995 to 2014 is shown in Figure 3.1.[2]

With somewhere between 20% and 30% of *all* US hospitals running a negative margin, it will be difficult, if not completely impossible, to fund a multimillion dollar EHR implementation without large amounts of capital and a substantial return on investment. Even for the profitable hospital organizations,

Table 3.1 Eight EPIC EHR Implementations with the Biggest Price Tags in 2015

Organization	*Implementation Cost*
Partners Healthcare Boston, MA	$1.2 billion
Lehigh Valley Network Allentown, PA	$200 million
Mayo Clinic Rochester, MN	Hundreds of millions
Lahey Hospital and Medical Center Burlington, MA	$160 million
Lifespan Providence, R.I.	$100 million
Erlanger Health System Chattanooga, TN	$97 million
Wheaton Franciscan Healthcare Glendale, WI	$54 million
St. Francis Medical Center Cape Girardeau, MO	$43 million

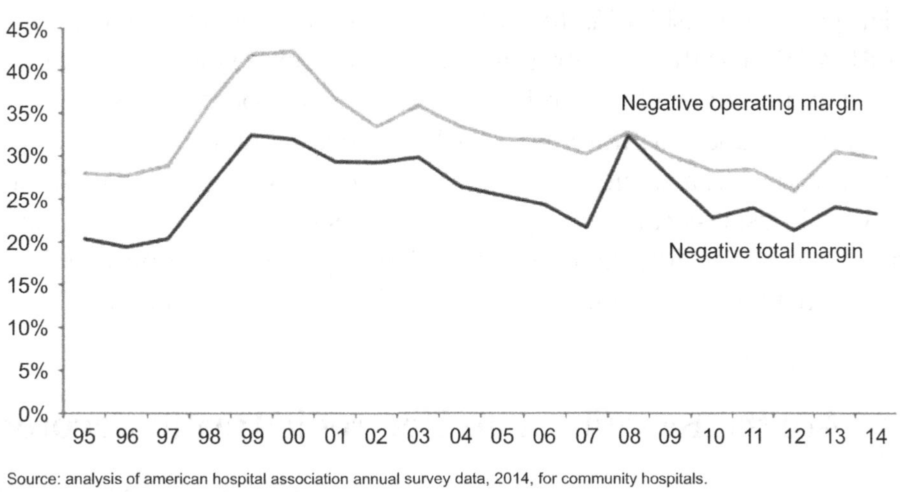

Figure 3.1 US hospitals operating with a negative margin.

the average operating margin is currently running at ~3.1%. Assuming you can live with $0 operating margin going to anything except paying off your EHR for several years, a new EHR with an expense of a $50 million and annual revenues of $200,000,000 will take a few years to get to a positive margin.

Let's review some payback scenarios (see Table 3.2).

Not every healthcare organization is a hospital system or even associated with a hospital system. Many organizations are clinic lead practices or rehabilitation centers. So what does it cost to establish an EHR in a clinic practice? An August 16, 2015 article in the *American Action Forum* titled "Are Electronic Medical Records Worth the Implementation" reports that based

Table 3.2 Sample Payback Scenarios

*Annual System Revenues**	*Margin $ at 3.1% Operating Margin**	*EHR Cash Expense**	*Years to a Positive Margin***
$100,000,000	$3,100,000	$15,000,000	4.8 years
$500,000,000	$15,500,000	$48,000,000	3.1 years
$1,000,000,000	$31,000,000	$100,000,000	3.2 Years
$2,000,000,000	$62,000,000	$270,000,000	4.4 years

* Revenues, margin dollars, and EHR expense dollars are fictitious and for illustration purposes only. Note the operating margin could go down if the EHR has to be financed.

** Assumes 100% of operating margin would go toward paying back the EHR expense.

on research by Dr. Neil Fleming et al. the average cost for an independent physician practice transitioning to EMR use between 2009 and 2011 has a total cost of $163,765, and the cost for a practice of five physicians has a total cost of $233,765. On a cost per physician basis, because many of the costs are fixed, such as software and hardware, it is much cheaper to share the costs among multiple providers in a single practice.[3] This kind of expense to a small, privately owned business can be very painful unless there is a return on that investment. So it isn't difficult to conclude that implementing a new EHR can be very costly to a small clinic in a world of thin or negative margins.

Where Are the Benefits of an Electronic Health Record?

Before we answer the question of whether or not there is an ROI for deploying an EHR, understand, there are many benefits to implementing an EHR. The US Health Information Technology for Economic and Clinical Health (HITECH) Act was signed into law in 2009. Part of this act included a multibillion-dollar incentive for adopting an electronic medical record and reporting key clinical information. The reporting requirements were more commonly known as "meaningful use." Unfortunately, the incentives have long expired. Now the opposite situation is in place. Instead of an incentive, there is a penalty for not adopting an EHR, although the penalty only applies to Medicare patients assuming you are accredited as a Medicare biller.

Penalties aside, there are many other important aspects of operating with an EHR. Earlier in this chapter, there were some compelling discussions around maximizing value to the patients that are served each day in your organizations. Improving transparency to patient appointment schedules, securely delivering patient outcomes and test results, providing a medical reminder of follow-up appointments and diagnostics, and streamlining communication among the circle of care are but a few of these benefits.

More than anything else, when speaking with clinicians, the common theme is that the EHR can and does improve clinical outcomes. One meaningful clinical outcome that is impacted, and an excellent source of return on investment, is the enhancement of patient safety afforded by the EHR. Electronic physician order entry has greatly reduced medical errors. A study published on the Institute for Healthcare Improvement's website cites one organization reduced errors associated with pharmacy medicine order entry by 50% through the use of a commercially available computerized physician order entry system.[4] The results of this study are shown in Figure 3.2.[4]

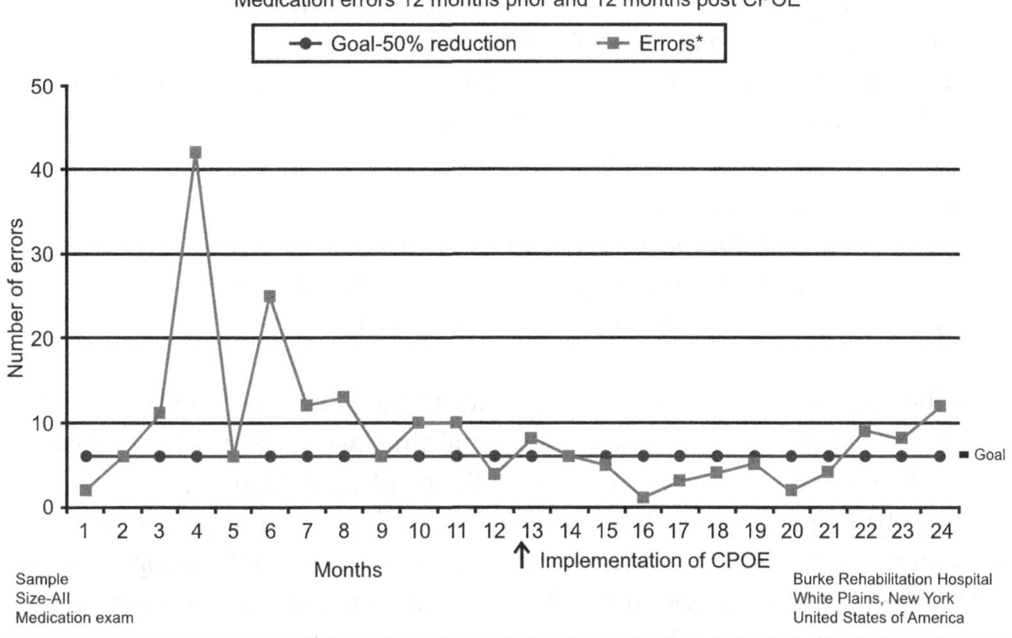

Figure 3.2 Medication errors post physician computerized order entry implementation.

The Institute of Medicine (IOM) has published several books and letters about the EHR. Ironically, this work started in the mid-1990s, and an important letter was written over a decade ago. In their work *Key Capabilities of an EHR System: Letter Report* (2003), the Institute of Medicine outlined eight core functions all EHRs should have.[5]

1. *Health information and data*: In order for the medical profession to make evidence-based decisions, clinicians need a lot of accurate data, and this is accomplished much better with EHRs than paper charts.
2. *Result management*: Physicians should not have to search for lab, x-ray, and consult results. Quick access saves time and money, prevents redundancy, and improves care coordination.
3. *Order management*: CPOE should reduce order errors from illegibility for medications, lab tests, and ancillary services and standardize care.
4. *Decision support*: Should improve overall medical care quality by providing alerts and reminders.
5. *Electronic communication and connectivity*: Communication among disparate partners is essential and should include all tools such as secure messaging, text messaging, web portals, health information exchange, etc.

6. *Patient support*: Recognizes the growing role of the Internet for patient education as well as home telemonitoring.
7. *Administrative processes and reporting*: Electronic scheduling, electronic claims submission, eligibility verification, automated drug recall messages, automated identification of patients for research, and artificial intelligence can speed administrative processes.
8. *Reporting and population health*: Healthcare needs to move from paper-based reporting of immunization status and bio-surveillance data to an electronic format to improve speed and accuracy.

Of the eight core functions an EHR should have, six of these functions directly impact patient outcomes. The remaining two core functions improve the efficiency and effectiveness of the delivery of healthcare.

The EHR helps support clinical decision making (including order sets and care pathways) and reduces errors. Everyone can agree that having standard, evidence-based information available will lead to better care and better outcomes. Everyone can also agree that electronic information is generally easier to read than handwritten notes. The electronic legibility factor enhances patient safety by reducing interpretation errors. Safety can further be enhanced by standardizing abbreviations and vocabulary to again eliminate interpretation errors.

Another benefit of the EHR is the improved organizational efficiencies gained from being an integrated system. Operational benefits can be gained through electronic exchange of information. Moving information electronically is faster, and if protected properly, safer than faxing (or mailing) information. Moving information is less labor intensive, and data are easier to store. And information is easier to access and view regardless of location.

One of the big drivers of the EHR from the beginning was the ability to exchange health information. We all know stories of the critical result lost on the fax machine, or the holdup waiting on an order, result, or referral caused by the needed fax being mixed in with a "100" other faxes. Electronic communication makes it easier than ever for clinicians to share information between members of the circle of care.

In a Lean environment, seconds matter. Any activity that takes time, space, or resources but does not directly meet a customer need is considered waste. Waiting on orders, results, and information all negatively impacts the patient and the clinicians. The EHR makes waiting on available information almost negligible. Reduced waiting means less space is needed to "warehouse" patients and family members. Wait times in clinics, imaging areas, labs, emergency departments, and in-patient units should all be reduced by rapid movement of electronic information.

Lead times for billing and coding will also be reduced. No more waiting on the paper chart to be hand-carried from the clinical areas to the billing office. Information moves in real time. In a large organization, this time can add up to a major cash flow gain. For a $1 billion healthcare organization, one day of cash equates to $2.7 million. So if you only lose one day of time transporting charts to the billing office, your organization has to float $2.7 million in cash.

There are other financial benefits to the electronic medical record. Since information is retrievable from almost anywhere, resources do not always need to be on site. Jobs can be combined and resources can be shared between remote facilities and offices. In an electronic world, repetitive transactions can be automated. A common example of this is automating the billing directly from the electronic coding that resulted from a primary care or specialty office visit.

Because information can frequently be shared between parties, redundancy in information capture can be eliminated. Again, we all know the experience of patients repeating demographic information and clinical information over and over again. Besides being frustrating for the patients and caregivers, it is time consuming for the staff to ask and capture this information at multiple steps along an episode of care.

Access to information that can be aggregated and disaggregated is also extremely helpful and has a financial return. Most healthcare organizations have multiple people that perform required (but not necessarily value added) external reporting. Reporting can include public reporting required by the government, public health, and CMS. Reporting from manual records requires chart audits that take many hours. A well-designed EHR has report writing capability that generates finished reports in seconds. This allows the people resources that do this work to stretch a lot further than in the past. Of note though, the report quality of an automated report is only as good as the data that are entered.

The automation of reporting benefits also applies to internal reporting. Internal reporting can include quality, wait-time, access, and productivity reporting as well as financial and operational reporting that lead to financial statements, board reports, and reports that assist in managerial accounting.

Reporting resources are able to accomplish more than ever due to information readily available in the EHR and better and better report writing functionality.

A final benefit of the EHR is the societal benefit of recorded and stored information. One way the EHR helps society (and businesses and individuals) is by providing invaluable information toward research. One of the big challenges with research is finding an appropriate and properly sized panel for study. Identifying the correct patient types and finding sufficient numbers of qualified patients that can participate in the research often end many research projects before they ever get started. This time-consuming and costly practice was extremely difficult prior to the adoption of the EHR. Parameters can be set for the type of patients, conditions, ages, etc., and reports can be generated quickly to identify research candidates.

As the research unfolds, outcomes can be monitored in aggregate through information available in the EHR. The electronic information of results and outcomes can be exported into spreadsheets where statistical tools can be used to evaluate the research. Research that leads to great results can be translated into best practices and evidence-based care. Recovery times can be made shorter and safer. Pharmaceuticals and therapeutics can get through trials faster and on the market faster to improve both symptom management and outcomes.

A second societal benefit to the EHR is the information provided to assist and optimize population-based health. Long used in other countries around the world and gaining popularity in the United States, population-based health refers to assessing the healthcare needs of a specific population and making healthcare decisions for the population as a whole rather than for individuals. Populations being treated are made up of individuals who have one or more personal or environmental traits in common.[6] Aggregated data are the key to identifying patient populations, assessing their needs, and delivering the best possible care. The EHR makes this possible.

Can an EHR Have a Return on Investment?

The costs of the EHR have been discussed and the benefits of the EHR have also been discussed. So the million-dollar question is, do the benefits outweigh the costs? Is there really a return on investment for the purchase and use of an EHR?

Should you operate a clinic practice, there is a great tool for you to help you do your own analysis. *4MED Approved* has a return-on-investment calculator that a physician practice can use to determine the payback on the investment in an electronic medical system. The website is located at http://www.4medapproved.com/research_tool_ROIcalc.php. Data for your specific operation can be entered into the fields, and the program will automatically provide you with the financial benefits of the investment.

If you choose not to calculate your own return for your clinic operations, you can reference a 2013 article in *MedCity News* by Alok Prasad. He cites: "A 2009 study by the Medical Group Management Association probably best puts it into perspective. Of the over 1,300 medical professionals surveyed, the independent practices reported revenue increases averaging around 49,916 dollars per physician after switching over to EHR from a paper-based practice. That is strictly revenue and doesn't take into account the reduction in operating costs. Clearly, EHR implementation is a cost cutting, practice building solution for even small medical offices."[7] There is enough evidence that after "all in" costs, there is a return on investment for an EHR at a physician or multiple physician practice.

The return-on-investment determination for a hospital or healthcare system is obviously more complex. Internet research on great case studies of return on investments for EHR implementation of hospitals, healthcare systems, and post-acute facilities is fragmented. There are many articles on cost savings from various aspects of the electronic medical record including reduction in prescription errors, meaningful use savings, less transactional costs, higher coding recovery, etc., but few studies on the entire rollup of the ROI.

One study found, however, was a 2016 Davies Award Summary by MetroHealth in Cleveland, OH. "Since 1994, the HIMSS Nicholas E. Davies Award of Excellence has recognized outstanding achievement of organizations that have utilized health information technology to substantially improve patient outcomes while achieving return on investment. The Davies Awards program promotes EHR-enabled improvement in patient outcomes through sharing case studies and lessons learned on implementation strategies, workflow design, best practice adherence, and patient engagement."[8]

Metro Health reported the following: "Analysis shows a positive ROI for the EHR in every year of 2010–2014, on average just over $20 million per year, with ongoing estimated positive ROI of just under $20 million per year."

Other highlights of this analysis include

- Federal incentive programs (Meaningful Use, PQRI/PQRS, e-prescribing) provided over $36 million in hard financial benefits related to EHR ROI.
- Hard financial benefits began being realized at the time of implementation.
- Soft financial benefits accrued slowly after implementation and were not fully realized at the time of implementation.
- Soft financial benefits increased by almost an order of magnitude.
- Soft financial benefits increased from ~10% of total benefits to ~30% of total benefits.
- Even without the soft financial benefits (and federal incentive programs), net EHR ROI is positive."[9]

There is plenty of great evidence from the MetroHealth of Cleveland and other Davies Award winners that a positive return on investment is possible when deploying an EHR. More exciting than the financial return, Davies Award winners also have to provide demonstrated improvement in patient outcomes. So we find that it is indeed possible to have great patient outcomes and a positive ROI with the deployment of an EHR.

What Can Be Done to Minimize Expenses?

Regardless of the financial returns and the benefits to patient outcomes, implementing an EHR is still just plain expensive. It requires tremendous upfront capital that has to be either on hand or financed. It disrupts the organization on multiple fronts including resourcing the design work, resourcing the setting of standards, library creation, training, disruption to existing patient care, etc. The emotional capital consumed by staff and clinicians oftentimes also has a negative financial consequence. How many organizations have lost personnel, management, staff, and physicians through an EHR implementation or optimization deployment? Having already spoken of the challenges of clinician burnout, a new EHR or work to optimize your existing EHR isn't going to simplify anyone's life in the short term.

There are a couple of best practice activities that should be strongly considered to minimize the expense of the EHR. The two basic principles of containing cost for implementation of an EHR include the following: Keep it simple and minimize the urge to engineer.

Having had the opportunity to sit through many sales presentations on EHRs or applications that bolt on to EHRs, I continue to be completely amazed by the amount of functionality that systems have today. To give you a sense of how much functionality exists in a commonly used application, step outside of healthcare and think about Microsoft Excel for a moment. How much functionality is available in that application? If you use your mouse and click on the formula button you will discover you can create averages, sums, counts, maximums, and standard deviations. You can graph and plot and make trend lines. How many different things can you do with data in Excel? Thousands of things.

But the next question is, how much functionality do you actually use on a daily or weekly basis? If you are like the majority of people, of the thousands of choices to pick from, you use roughly a maximum of 5 to 10 formulas. There are some super users that can and do work with all the statistical and analytical functionality, but the typical user neither needs nor uses this capability.

So here's the secret. The EHR system you are using, or soon to be deploying, acts the same way. There are *all* kinds of bells and whistles that can be added or activated within your system. Hundreds of reports can be created from this functionality.

But to get all the reporting and information from the use of these bells and whistles, someone needs to enter all the transactions necessary to extract these data. The "someone" implied here is the clinical staff and physicians or administrative staff. No information from an IT system is free. More information invariably requires more clicks, more questions asked, more time, etc. Using your Lean mind, ask yourself when evaluating which pieces of functionality to purchase and deploy, "Do any of these pieces of information create value, or are they required from a legal or compliance perspective?" "Does the functionality remove waste?" Does it enable flow, create pull, eliminate defects, or create transparency to enable visual management?" "Does the transaction or the information improve outcomes?" If you can't answer yes to one or more of these questions, then you should give very careful consideration to adding a bell or whistle. Once the decision is made to operationalize a piece of functionality, you have made the decision to capture and report on this information for many years. The costs to deploy the functionality are fixed, but the resources to capture and report on a day-to-day basis are not, and you are committing to thousands of transactions at a cost of thousands of resource hours.

Aside from the cost of utilizing the bells and whistles once the system is operationalized, there also is a cost to designing and testing, and training, and activating this functionality. One of the best ways to keep the costs of your EHR system down for both implementation and ongoing maintenance is to avoid any unnecessary bells and whistles. This seems like pretty straightforward advice and common sense.

The challenge is that in viewing the sales presentations and demonstration webinars, you will be completely dazzled with the functionality. It is critical to understand, upfront, what is available in the base software package and the base hardware package. As an example, tablets and smart phone capability is common for many day-to-day applications and personal use. Many of us would be lost without this functionality. When used in conjunction with an EHR, however, the added hardware capabilities increase expense and, in some cases, design cost. I am not advocating that you avoid this technology; just understand that with each added capability, there is an expense. Sticking with core functionality and basic hardware minimizes expenses. Aside from decisions made by staying within your project budget, select and use the enhanced functionality and hardware based on understanding which of those choices adds value.

Another approach to keeping costs down is to leverage as many "out of the box" workflows as possible. One of the common approaches healthcare organizations take, and a Lean organization will tell you this is a mistake, is to map their current state workflows and then "design" the new software into these workflows. Inevitably what happens is the current system is replicated in an electronic environment. This creates a couple of problems. First, the cost of the implementation increases since the software has to be changed/configured to meet the current workflows. Second, you are almost assured of no improvement since you are simply replicating what you currently do. One of the big advantages of designing a target state with the new EHR software is the opportunity to improve process quality and patient safety, reduce lead times for services, reduce cost, and improve the patient experience. Reconfiguration of new software into your old workflows negates all of these advantages.

To minimize the cost of an implementation, try to use as many of the software vendor recommendations and process workflows as possible. The challenge will be that not all vendor workflows are designed with Lean thinking, so it is likely some configuration will be necessary to optimize your EHR. But many times, organizations *chose* to configure their software based on personal preference or legacy workflows. Software, in its most simple form, is a combination of policy plus procedure. Using the baseline workflows of the software helps create a standard for the organization. This standard essentially helps formalize your policies and procedures. By using tested workflows from the vendor, your organization can move toward standardization quickly while simultaneously minimizing the configuration costs.

Chapter Summary

- Implementing an EHR is an expensive endeavor. Careful thought should be given to which platform to use, how fast you want to adopt or optimize the new system, and how to time this body of work with the cash flows for your business to maintain fiscal viability.
- There are many, many meaningful benefits to implementing an EHR. A primary benefit is using the system, and information from the system, to enhance patient safety and enhance the patient experience.
- Done well, there are many important organizational benefits to implementing an EHR. These include but are not limited to the following: easier accessibility to information, decreased paper storage and retrieval costs, improved productivity, easier transmission of information, better security and privacy, and better data for improving evidence-based care and research.
- There is evidence to support that organizations can show a positive return on investment for deploying an electronic medical record at both the physician practice level and the system level.
- Costs can be minimized during an EHR deployment or optimization by minimizing the bells and whistles of the applications and leveraging the standard workflows of your purchased software. Minimizing the start-up or upfront optimization expenses helps with the return on investment by reducing the initial expenses and reducing the ongoing maintenance costs of the functionality.

Further Reading

1. Jayanthi A. 8 EPIC EHR implementations with the biggest price tags in 2015. *Becker's Health IT and CIO Review.* http://www.beckershospitalreview.com/healthcare-information-technology/8-epic-ehr-implementations-with-the-biggest-price-tags-in-2015.html (July 1, 2015).

2. American Hospital Association. Trends in hospital financing, Chapter 4. Chart 4.1, Percentage of hospitals with negative total and operating margins, 1994–2014. In *Trends Affecting Hospitals and Health Systems*. http://www.aha.org/research/reports/tw/chartbook/ch4.shtml
3. O'Neill Hayes, T. Are electronic medical records worth the costs of implementation? *American Action Forum*. https://www.americanactionforum.org/research/are-electronic-medical-records-worth-the-costs-of-implementation/ (August 5, 2015).
4. Winifred Masterson Burke Rehabilitation Hospital, White Plains, New York, USA. Impact of computerized physician order entry on medication error rate. Institute for Healthcare Improvement. http://www.ihi.org/resources/Pages/ImprovementStories/ImpactofCPOEonMedicationErrorRate.aspx
5. Hoyt R. Benefits of an EHR—Reduce costs and errors. practicefusion.com. http://www.practicefusion.com/health-informatics-practical-guide-page-2/
6. Loyola University New Orleans. What is population-focused health care. http://elearning.loyno.edu/masters-nursing-degree-online/resource/population-focused-healthcare
7. Prasad A. ROI vs. EHR implementation costs—Is it really worth it? MedCityNews.com.
8. HIMSS. HIMSS Davies Award. http://www.himss.org/library/davies-awards
9. HIMSS Davies Committee. The MetroHealth of Cleveland--Davies Enterprise Award. HIMSS. http://www.himss.org/metrohealth-cleveland-davies-enterprise-award (January 11, 2016).

Chapter 4

What Is Lean and How Does It Apply to the EHR?

What Is Lean?

Lean healthcare is a management system, predicated on the Toyota Production System, which is used to deliver world-class quality and customer service to patients, caregivers, and their surrounding communities. The Toyota Production System (yes, the same Toyota that makes personal transportation in the form of cars, trucks, and sport utility vehicles) is the comprehensive business approach and corresponding culture Toyota embraces toward continuous process improvement to deliver compelling value to their customers. The words "Lean" and the "Toyota Production System (TPS)" are used synonymously. Technically these two terms are not identical, but both are recognized as being one in the same, so we will use the term Lean going forward. Before describing what is meant by continuous improvement, it will be helpful to better understand a few essential Lean terms. After we understand these Lean concepts, we can better define Lean healthcare. From our definition of Lean healthcare, we can define the Lean electronic health record (EHR).

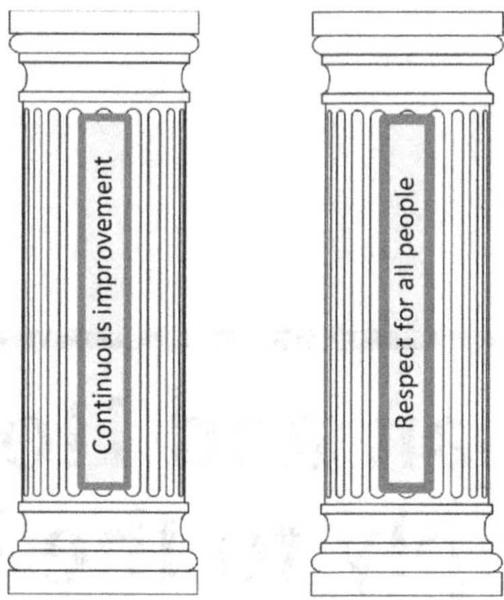

Figure 4.1 Themes of Lean Improvement.

Value Added

Lean improvement is based on two themes: continuous improvement (a different way to state elimination of waste) and respect for all people, as shown in Figure 4.1.

To understand the first theme, continuous improvement, it is necessary to understand the value added/non-value added principle. Every activity that occurs in any organization falls into one of two categories: value added or non-value added. A non-value added activity, when producing a physical product, is easy to grasp. Activities that change the form, fit, or function of the product would be considered value added. Another definition of value-added activity is any action (either product or service related) that a customer is willing to pay for. An industrial example of a value-added activity might include drilling, painting, heat treating, or assembly of a product. For IT services, a value-added activity might include help desk services offered on the telephone. Within healthcare, a value-added activity is defined as any activity that directly meets the need of a customer. An example of a healthcare value add would be the action of a surgeon completing a surgery. The need to have a problem resolved through surgery is directly met.

Non-Value Added

Non-value added is, by default, the opposite of value added. It is more clearly defined as any activity that takes time, space, or resources, but does not change the form, fit, or function of the product. Another definition includes any activity taking time, space, or resources that the customer is not willing to pay for. Examples of industrial non-value added activities would include conveying a part from one machine to the next or counting inventory items to ensure accuracy of on-hand quantities. Within healthcare, an excellent example of a non-value added activity would be filling out insurance forms. No patient would "pay" to complete this activity. Filling out insurance paperwork doesn't directly meet a patient need to receive assessment, diagnosis, and treatment for a medical condition. In the IT space, a non-value added example would be redesigning an assessment screen because we failed to get all the requirements right the first time.

A third category of activities that organizations perform are activities required by law or business requirements (accreditation or third-party certification). These might include following Occupational Safety and Health Act standards (OSHA), or ISO standards, or Generally Accepted Accounting Principles (GAAP). While it can be tempting to classify these activities as a third category, non-value added but required, at the end of the day, each of these activities is usually non-value added to the end customer.

As stated previously, within healthcare, a value-added activity is any activity that *directly* meets the need of the customer. In order to determine if a step is value added, you need to be clear on two things: (1) who is the customer? And (2) what are their needs? Many times in healthcare the dialogue jumps from the customer being the patient and/or the caregiver to the customer being the provider, or administration, etc. It is helpful to remember that value is always specified by the *customer*. And there can be only one customer.

The easiest way to determine the true, single customer is by defining who is creating the *pull* for the services needed. So if we are trying to figure who the customer is in a surgical procedure, we try to understand where the pull (need) for the service comes from. Since we would not need a surgical center, sterile processing, materials and supplies, equipment, surgical staff, a surgeon, a billing department, etc., without a patient needing surgery, the patient is the customer. In this surgical procedure, value will be specified by the patient, so value added and non-value added activities are from the eyes of the patient.

The second decision we need to make is to define what the customer *needs*. Healthcare professionals often have expertise and knowledge, which can be very helpful in determining customer needs. However, it is not exclusively the role of the staff and provider to specify the customer's needs. Nor is it the insurance company's role. With information available at a click of a mouse, many customers (patients) are quite capable of specifying their needs. As I tell healthcare professionals, when I work with highly skilled engineers designing new products, they are quick to articulate that consumers do not know what they want/need. They have to make those decisions for the consumers since they have the technical expertise. I think everyone as a consumer can determine the features and benefits they are looking for in a new product or service. It would be quite expensive and impractical to drag an engineer around with us every time we shopped for a product. As a consumer, we have no problem specifying a value-added and non-value added activity within our purchases. This same theory holds true with patients when they seek medical services. Even though you may be the healthcare "engineer," the patient is generally quite capable of determining their needs. Your job as the service provider is to identify the activities that directly meet those needs, as those are the value-added activities. If you have any questions, the person who can best answer whether a process is adding value or not is the patient.

To further illustrate the differences between non-value added and nonvalue-added activities, let's discuss a clinic visit to see your doctor. Being an outdoor enthusiast, you fell during a recent snow skiing trip, and your knee is hurting. The physician provides an examination and gives a diagnosis of an ACL injury. To further refine this diagnosis, he or she orders you to get a CT scan. When you get a CT scan, you will likely need to schedule the exam date and time, register with someone when you arrive, and complete some paperwork. While all of these activities are common during a typical CT exam experience, none of them will directly meet your needs. So the collection of all of these activities, as described, would be considered non-value added activity.

To summarize, in order to determine the value added activity, we need to identify the customer, specify their needs, and determine which activities directly meet those needs. The customer of this process is you, the patient needing the CT exam. The "needs" you must have met include the examination and the corresponding results. The value-added activities would be the actual CT scan (which takes minutes) and the actual reading of the exam (which also takes minutes). But what about the cleaning of the table, the preparing for the exam, the transcribing of the results, the charting of the activities, the sending of an invoice, etc.? Since these activities do not directly meet your need, these are all classified as non-value added activities.

The understanding of a value added (VA) and non-value added activity (NVA) is the first lesson that must be learned in improvement, and it is not always an easy lesson to understand. As you can see in Figure 4.2, when we

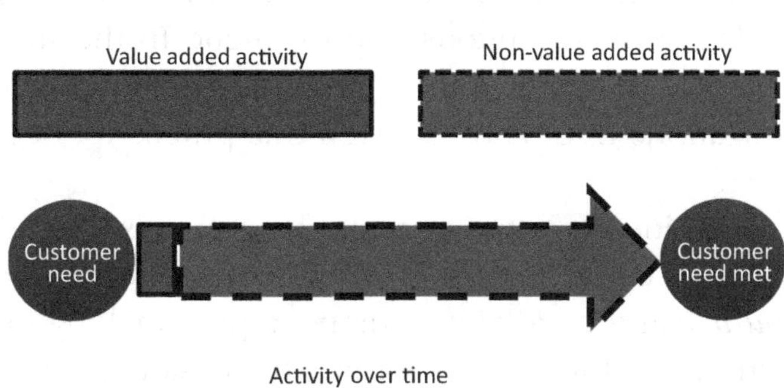

Figure 4.2 Value added/non-value added principle.

can understand both VA and NVA activity, we can compare the ratio between the two activities. *A typical process is 95% NVA to 5% VA!* World-class organizations understand this and take advantage of the insight this ratio provides.

Improvement using Lean fundamentals involves the identification and elimination of a non-value added activity. Another term for a non-value added activity is "waste." When 95% of the activity in a typical process is non-value added, that leaves a *lot* of room for improvement. Focusing on a non-value added activity provides two benefits. First, the improvement potential is much larger. Would you rather pay attention to the 95% opportunity or the 5% opportunity? This is why Lean organizations can, and do, routinely show 25% to 50+% improvements! They understand the value added/non-value added principle, and they choose to play in the 95% space. Second, the cost of the improvement is significantly less. When we focus on eliminating a non-value added activity, we are in essence "stopping" some kind of work. How much does it cost to stop doing something? The definition of a non-value added activity is any activity taking time, space, and resources, but not directly meeting a customer's needs. So if we eliminate a non-value added activity, then we free up time, space, and resources. The capacity found in these resources can be used to add even more value to our customers.

First Theme of Lean Improvement—Continuous Improvement

Earlier we discussed that Lean improvement is based on two themes: continuous improvement (the elimination of non-value added activity) and respect for all people. We just spent a fair amount of time discussing value added and non-value added activities. Understanding this concept is the foundation of continuous improvement. In the simplest terms, improvement consists of seeing and eliminating non-value added activities. Lean organizations frequently shorten this phrase to "seeing and eliminating waste."

The theme of continuous improvement, however, has two other tenets. Culturally, we want to create a work environment where we strive to meet targets using *courage* and *creativity*. Courage implies making individual and team decisions in the best interest of serving the customer. For example, clinic hours of operation may best serve their customers from 1 pm to 9 pm. We have been comfortable working from 8 am to 4 pm for years. A courageous decision would include altering work hours in the best interest of the customer. How many times have you given up your lunch hour to get something accomplished only to find out the organization is closed during lunch?

Creativity entails using new approaches and techniques in lieu of adding resources and capital cost. A term used by Lean practitioners is use "creativity before capital." This implies generating solutions that take minimal resources to implement before making a significant capital investment in equipment, IT, space, and facilities or hiring additional staff. Remember, if the solutions implemented involve eliminating a non-value added activity, then by design, additional time, space, and resources have been freed up. Even after becoming a giant among electronic companies, Hewlett-Packard still uses a phrase "let's go back to the garage," a phrase that elicits the process that the company started with no money, few materials, and just a garage to work in. This phrase was a "battle cry" to relook at the problem without immediately going to the "just add more resources" to the inefficient process or identified need. This is the essence of the concept of "creativity before capital."

Another tenet of continuous improvement is the concept of *Genchi Genbutsu*, loosely translated as "go to the source to find facts." When problems arise in the workplace, how would a manager traditionally respond? Many organizations would schedule a meeting, get a small group of knowledgeable experts together, and try and solve these problems. To illustrate my point, if you are a manager/leader in healthcare, I would be willing to bet the majority of time you spend each day is either attending a meeting or travelling from one meeting to the next. A Lean company views problems as treasures of information, telling a story of where the current process is not adequate. A Lean manager will always go to the area where the problem occurred and observe the process to see if the source of the problem can be identified. This is tremendously different than the traditional approach. Not going to the area where the problem occurred is the equivalent of a police investigator not going to the scene of the crime to uncover forensic evidence. How effective would investigations be if the standard approach to crime solving involved scheduling a meeting at the police office and bringing in some experts to try and solve the crime? The clinical healthcare example I like to use is this: let's assume we had an instance where a dose of medicine was missed. This resulted in an adverse event that, while not catastrophic, warranted further investigation. The question I'd like you to ponder is, how many missed doses occurred in the conference room? We need to go to the source to find facts.

In assigning resources to our EHR, we want to employ each of the cultural tenets of continuous improvement. We want to show courage in developing the organizational standards for our software implementation. We want to show courage in listening to the voice of the customer (system user) when developing workflows to maximize the value of the EHR, while minimizing screen clicks and data entry requirements. We want to employ creativity to use the EHR for its intended purpose. Many activities to start work, for example, can be signaled very inexpensively with flags and magnets that can replace more costly electronic triggers. Finally, we want to design the workflows in the area where work is done, not in a conference room. Go to *gemba* as an integral part of the requirements definition and design phases of the project. You will learn many important things that have nothing to do with the content of the EHR system or the documentation. Many workflow concerns are more about when to document, and with what tools, than the actual software. These subtleties are best picked up in the place where work is done.

Second Theme of Lean Improvement—Respect for All People

From a global perspective, respect for all people means having a purpose for improvement. How can improvement in healthcare benefit our patients, our staff, our physicians, our community agencies, and our service providers? How can we improve our local community, our country, and the world as a whole? From an individual and organizational perspective, showing respect for people comes in the form of understanding each other. What work do I do, and what work do you do? Together, how do we build a foundation of mutual trust? Respect is also demonstrated in taking individual and team responsibility. Are we doing the right thing, every time? Are we following the known best method? Are we putting forth our best effort? As an organization, we want to optimize both team and individual performance. Additionally, we must also ask ourselves if we are sharing opportunities for personal and team development.

A Lean organization is not excited by benchmark performance and peer comparisons; rather, a Lean organization gets excited about knowing they are making a difference in the world. Maybe they are not directly affecting the entire world but most certainly their community and customers (patients). This organization's staff knows that they are continually providing better and safer care, reducing lead times for services, thus increasing access, and continuously lowering the cost of services, increasing the value of the healthcare that is delivered. This relentless pursuit of perfection is how respect for all people is realized.

Our EHR can assist in the mission of healthcare delivery. Safer, more timely healthcare can be assisted by having the right information at the right time. Having information available can reduce the amount of resources needed to track information, request orders, and request consults. The data from the system can provide valuable information for further improvement and population health. Research can be accelerated and best practices shared by tracking not only the outcomes, but also the processes that lead to those outcomes. This is respect for all people in action.

Seven Wastes

The early founders of the Toyota Production System spent a lot of time observing waste. Waste is another term for non-value added activity. Because of the repetition of certain forms of waste, it proved helpful to put the wastes into common categories. The major forms of waste found in operations became known as the seven operational wastes shown in Figure 4.3. A discussion of the seven forms of waste follows.

Overproduction

Overproduction is producing too much stuff or producing stuff too early. Let's say we were unable to use a pre-mix IV and had to mix an IV solution in the pharmacy. Subsequently, we delivered 2 days worth of this mixture

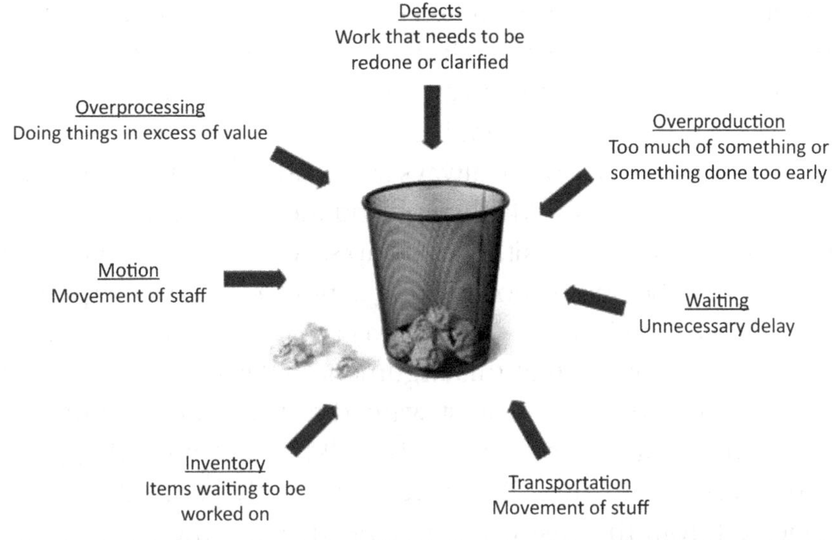

Figure 4.3 Seven Wastes.

to the unit where the patient was being treated. At the end of the first day following the delivery of this solution, the patient was discharged home. The remaining solution would need to be returned to the pharmacy and likely disposed of properly; we overproduced. When overproduction occurs, we have expended labor to mix IV solutions that can never be recovered. Additionally, the corresponding solution now has to be disposed of, another unnecessary and unrecoverable expense.

In our EHR deployment, overproduction might show up in the form of starting a design before the requirements are specified. In this case, the design work started too soon and, as the requirements change, the design will need to be redone. This is a common occurrence in the IT world. In order to meet timelines, downstream work begins before upstream work is finalized. This results in a lot of rework that on occasion can lead to an even longer timeline for design, as well as wasted resources. Organizations deploying the Lean EHR will use strategies to eliminate overproduction both in the design and in the day-to-day operations of using the system.

Waiting

Waiting causes a disruption of work flow. This disruption can result in idle resources, stopping and starting, and time delays to our customers (patients or staff). Within healthcare, we can experience waiting for service providers, diagnostics, information, equipment, and materials. I typically find waiting to be the largest single waste within healthcare. For service providers who work in the emergency department or in a clinic, I'm sure you can recall an occasion where a patient or family member verbally expressed disappointment with the amount of time they were spending in the waiting room.

Staff members, however, do not always see waiting as a waste. If a therapist walks to a patient room to provide therapy and the patient is not present, then the therapist likely would not wait. The therapist would simply go to their next patient. So since the therapist is not idle and is now adding value (providing therapy) to a different patient, the waiting was not considered wasteful.

I would like to point out that this argument is flawed on two fronts. First, waste was created when the therapist walked to the patient room only to find out the patient was not present. This walking to a missed appointment would be the waste of motion. But more importantly, remember that waste is always viewed from the customer's perspective. For the therapist to not see the missed therapy session as wasteful is looking at the waste from the wrong pair of eyes. The patient is the customer, and it is that customer that is *waiting* for their therapy.

Even though 95% of the activities going on around us are non-value added, it still takes time and practice to be able to see waste. Understanding the seven key wastes is a good start to being able to identify waste in your organization. It is a bit humorous that oftentimes in healthcare the waste of waiting is easy to spot; in fact, many times it is even labeled. Do any of your organizations have a *waiting* room?

Regarding the EHR, waiting is prevalent in IT services. Waiting for help desk services, waiting for a line of code to be written, waiting for funding to cover the expense of a change, and waiting for a report to be written are all common occurrences we experience. A Lean organization designs out waiting both as part of the deployment of the EHR and in the design of the workflows that will be using the functionality.

Overprocessing

Overprocessing is a waste generated by performing work in excess of value. While this may be hard to believe, it is quite possible to do *more* work than the customer values. For example, many of us use spreadsheet solutions daily. Software solutions are invaluable; they enable us to sort numerical data, determine averages, sum column totals, and quickly build charts and graphs. Have any of you ever considered the work that went into the engineering process of these solutions? You have the ability to do conditional formatting, data validation, pivot tables, and logical formulas in a matter of moments. It is my belief that you could spend years trying to learn all the functionality of this type of software, but 99.9% of us will never use greater than ~5% of this capability. As the customer, this product is over-engineered; the use of this product can easily create overprocessing. It is important to note, however, that other people may find these many features beneficial. Thus, from their perspective, the product does not appear to be overprocessed.

As an example of overprocessing within healthcare, we might consider interprofessional assessment. A complex patient might get assessed by multiple nurses, multiple physicians, and several members of the allied health team. While each team member is looking for different pieces of information to provide the best possible care, a patient might be asked the same question by two, three, or even more people. Many of you in the course of your work have heard from patients, "I've been asked this five times already. Do you people talk to one another?" Again, from the patient's perspective, as an organization, you have overprocessed. The redundancy in questioning and the corresponding documentation creates work in excess of value.

Another example of the waste of overprocessing within healthcare: are all the tests that were ordered medically necessary?

EHR overprocessing shows up when we gather information in multiple places, or report data in multiple reports. Gathering unnecessary information not needed for the care of a patient or the operation of a business is yet another form of overprocessing. The Lean EHR seeks to eliminate overprocessing by simplifying workflows and minimizing handoffs and information touches. It also seeks to ensure the correct information is gathered once and shared with many to eliminate redundancy.

Inventory

When we think of inventory, we think of supplies. Everyone, whether in a production environment or a service environment, can relate to the disruption in work when we run out of materials and supplies. Disruption also occurs when we have too many supplies. Excess supplies can lead to damaged product, obsolescence, and time wasted on inventory management. We all also have to insure these supplies and light them and heat/cool them within our facility. None of these activities meet the need of the customer.

In healthcare, however, there are other forms of inventory present. One inventory that we do not frequently think about is patients waiting for services. Patients could be waiting for an admission, waiting for an inpatient bed, waiting for test results, etc. The collection of these patients can be defined as inventory as they are queuing up and occupying space. A simple definition of inventory is "things" (people, items, information) waiting to be worked on. Another form of inventory is things waiting in your inbox. Within administration, there are lots of places where work queues up. Bills waiting to be paid, charts waiting to be coded, invoices waiting to be processed and mailed, e-mails waiting to be answered, performance appraisals waiting to be completed, payroll waiting to be processed, supplies waiting to be ordered, financial reports waiting to be generated. The backlog of these items is inventory.

A Lean EHR will be designed to minimize the backlog of work. We desire work to "flow" in a Lean environment with no waiting or inventory buildup between steps. Work that flows might not need a time stamp for reporting, or an electronic signal for someone to do something, or a work queue to manage. Lean organizations want to keep inventory to a minimum and ideally at zero. We don't want help tickets backing up or reports to be written queuing up.

Motion

When we speak of the waste of motion, we are talking about movement in excess of that required to create value; this movement is from the staff and providers. One form of motion is present when we walk from one area to the next looking for supplies and equipment. A simple example of wasted motion occurs when we must walk an extra 10 steps to get to the hand sanitizer because the dispenser is not located near the point of use. I often hear the argument that it is "healthy" for the staff to be active. We can all agree that it is healthy to have an active lifestyle, but unnecessary movement in the workplace is wasteful. The following example demonstrates how easily wasted motion accumulates in the workplace.

One organization, I'll call them "St. Gerard," did an extensive study of the waste of motion for their inpatient nursing staff. They used a stopwatch to record the percentage of time that a nurse spent walking during their 12-hour shift. The results of the study revealed that 53% of the time, a nurse was simply walking from one place to the next. That is more than half of their total time working. This organization had over 800 full-time nurses on their staff across the hospital. A simple mathematical calculation would imply that over 400 nurses were being paid throughout the week to walk from one point to the next. If this organization could reduce the nurse walking time across the organization by 25%, that would be the equivalent of getting an additional 200 nurses (25% of 800 nurses = 200 nurses). Could any of your organizations (or patients) use the equivalent of 200 nurses? For free?

In the IT world, wasted motion is frequently expressed as a number of clicks. Have you ever heard, "I had to click through three screens to get the information I was looking for"? Or, "I had to click through seven fields to enter the required data"? Having to click through multiple screens to find information is wasted motion. Information input, information viewing, and data extraction/reporting should be intuitive, and the screens should be designed to work within the flow of the users of the system. Any effort beyond that is the waste of motion in action.

Defects

Defects create waste because they result in work needing to be completely redone or corrected. Before we get too far into the waste of defects, we need to differentiate between a defect and an error. Work that is completed by humans is subject to errors; an error is a mistake in the execution of a task. An example of an error is a physician order for a medication that was inadvertently not signed. Regardless of how well trained people are, or how often they complete a given task, or how diligent/conscientious they are, errors will be made. This is part of being human.

However, an error need not turn into a defect. A defect is an error that makes its way to the customer and results in work needing to be redone, corrected, or clarified. In healthcare, defects frequently appear in the form of missing information, incorrect information, or information received in the wrong format. But defects can also be clinical in nature and appear in the following ways: the wrong test could be ordered; the wrong diagnosis could be made; patients can be harmed through infections acquired at the hospital; and recovery can be lengthened by not following evidence-based best practices. Regardless of whether the defect is related to the outcome of the service, the quality of the service provided, or the back office work required to run the business, a defect is wasteful because it leads to activities of rework, checking, and clarification. None of these activities support directly meeting a customer's need.

In the IT world, and in the development and deployment of our EHR, defects show up in the rework of previously designed work. There are many reasons for this, but some opportunities to reduce defects exist in improving our ability to define requirements, standardizing between clinicians before designing the work, agreeing on definitions, and agreeing on order sets as a small sample. Defects delay the timeline for testing, training, and deploying your EHR and add expense to your system cost. The cleanup of system defects is expensive, and you will likely spend a lot of emotional human capital in the process. Defects also occur when there is no plan to maintain the system. Order sets change when new evidence is introduced. New medications are added. Best practices evolve. Your EHR becomes a source of frustration when the system functionality and the practice of medicine are not in sync.

Transportation

Transportation is the conveyance of materials, equipment, information, and patients through an organization. From the patient's perspective, the movement of items or information doesn't create value; thus, transportation is considered a waste. Transportation consumes staff resources and also takes time, while failing to directly meet the needs of the customer. You might think "How is this any different from the waste of motion?" Motion differs from transportation in that motion involves the movement of staff, while transportation is the movement of items.

Consider a patient that shows up for a surgical preadmission visit. This patient must first be registered. Next, the patient has to go to the lab for a blood test, followed by walking to diagnostic imaging for a chest x-ray. Finally, the patient returns to the clinic for a nursing screen and pre- and postsurgical education, followed by a trip to a different office for a meeting with the anesthesiologist. While this workflow might have optimized the utilization of the staff and leveraged the footprint of the facility; we have created a lot of transportation for the patient and added time to their visit. Consequently, the customer might perceive the visit as a nuisance rather than as an efficient process engineered to benefit the customer.

While this transportation example focuses on the movement of a patient, wasted movement also applies to conveying cotton swabs, Band-Aids, and sutures as well. Conveyance of supplies, materials, and equipment does not deliver value to a customer.

In the IT world, transportation is not the movement of things, but rather the movement of information. One of the benefits of an integrated EHR is the ability to share information with many people. What we strive to eliminate is any transaction that does not add value to the patient, the care team, or the operation. Transactions take time and resources, and thus they fall under the category of waste.

Summarizing the waste discussion, great organizations work relentlessly to identify and eliminate waste. Operational waste presents itself in seven common forms to include overproduction, waiting, overprocessing, inventory, motion, defects, and transportation. The Lean EHR strives to eliminate waste in two ways. The first is by eliminating the wastes associated with the activities of requirements gathering, designing, testing, training, and rolling out of the EHR. This is done using a Lean approach to project management. The second is the Lean EHR will help reduce the seven wastes in the delivery of healthcare. Designing the EHR to enable flow and pull in our clinical work and reduce errors will improve the quality, timeliness, and cost of care delivery.

One Additional Waste: Unused (Wasted) Human Talent

There is another type of waste that shows up within organizations that is not operational in nature: the waste of unused human capital. From an improvement perspective, the focus to "see and eliminate" waste is generally on process and the seven wastes that will show up when we study a process in detail through direct observation. The waste of unused human capital does not generally present itself when studying a process, but can be present.

This waste presents itself when we fail to take into consideration and utilize all the talents that people have. I believe that every staff person, administrator, and physician wants to do magnificent work; the challenge is creating the structure and process to enable this great work to happen. Many organizations are top-down in their approach with a command and control management structure. With the heavy amounts of firefighting that occur each day, it is difficult to find the time to empower and engage staff and medical staff. Without daily formal and informal mechanisms to engage and empower, opportunities for process improvement and personal growth are missed. These missed opportunities are the unused human capital.

Principles of Improvement

Having a working definition of the seven common forms of waste (with the addition of the waste of human capital), we will discuss some concepts to help us both identify and eliminate this waste. The value added/non-value added principle holds that 95% to 99% of the work we complete is non-value added to the patient. After you practice identifying waste over a brief period and get comfortable with the concepts of value added and non-value added, waste will start to become obvious and abundant. Of the two tasks of seeing and eliminating waste, the harder of the two is eliminating the waste.

Before we discuss how to eliminate waste, we must first understand some improvement principles to help guide our thinking. Every time we want to eliminate waste, we should use these principles as the foundation. These principles are flow, pull, defect-free, visual management, and kaizen as shown in Figure 4.4. Let's review each of these in further detail.

Flow

The place we almost always want to begin when making improvement is by creating flow. People often think of flow as a means of lining up the activities to be completed one after another in a continuous manner. In healthcare, we want to "flow" patients though our healthcare system. Lining up all of the activities to occur one after another would be a great improvement, albeit very difficult to accomplish. However, the concept of flow is

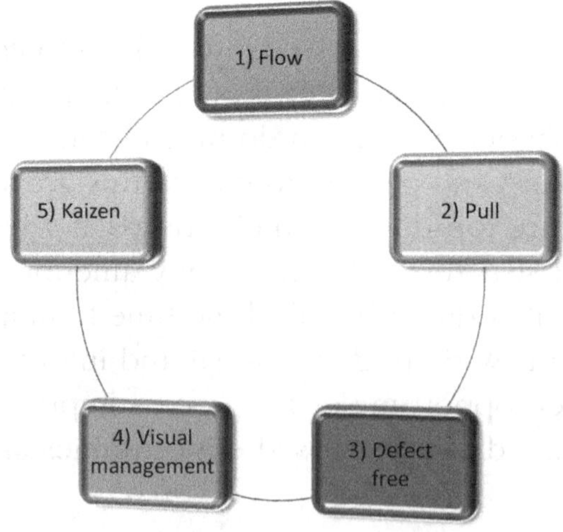

Figure 4.4 Lean principles.

more than just continuous processing of tasks. The Lean definition of flow is completing *value added* tasks in continuous flow, at the rate of customer demand, in a standardized way with no waiting or piling up of work between steps.

By linking only the value added steps together, this implies that we have eliminated the non-value added activities between the steps. It would not make sense to only link all the tasks together in continuous flow, as it is obvious that we want to avoid expending resources completing non-value added work.

Let's imagine that we have eliminated some waste, and now we have linked the value added tasks together. For an x-ray procedure, assume that the x-ray technologist can perform the exam and, immediately following, have the exam read by a radiologist. The result is now available for review by the ordering physician. The physician can now complete the diagnosis and discuss the treatment plan with the patient. The patient can then leave with a full understanding of what the next steps would be. This would be flow in practice. Now we need to ensure that this new process is capable of meeting customer demand. If this process can be repeated 28 times in an 8-hour shift, but we have patient demand of 36 per shift, we still have not satisfied the principle of flow. To meet the spirit of flow, a process has to be paced to the rate of the customer demand into the process.

Finally, let's assume we have now lined up the value added steps and have a process capable of meeting customer demand. However, due to variation in the process, we get varying outcomes. If we fail to perform the activities in a standard way, and continue to get inconsistent outcomes, we have not met the spirit of flow. A process is flowing when the value added activities are lined up one after another with no waiting or inventory between each step. The process will be capable of meeting the customer demand, and the work is being done in a standardized way with consistent outcomes.

The Lean EHR can help enable flow by capturing and delivering the right information at the right time. This enables the customer (patient) to flow through the system with minimal delays and redundancy. It also reduces time spent looking for information and minimizes data entry requirements, two favorable activities that both optimize healthcare resources and contain labor costs. The Lean EHR must work in concert with a Lean design to accomplish flow. A great Lean workflow design can simplify electronic needs and minimize transactions that can be managed using creativity before capital.

Pull

Sometimes it is not possible to create continuous flow across all of the steps. Constrained resources, or access to resources used intermittently, can make continuous flow very difficult. An example of this would be a patient arriving in the ER after being struck in the face by a baseball with considerable trauma. After an assessment and image studies, the patient is now in need of a dental plastic surgeon. How many ERs have one of these on staff? So the work will come to a halt while the referral is made and a response is received. The principle of pull enables areas of continuous flow to be linked together.

The concept and principle of pull comes from the supermarket, the same supermarket you buy your groceries from. How does the grocer know when to restock the shelf? The answer is when there is an empty space on the shelf. How did the empty space get there? A consumer put something in their grocery cart to take to the register for purchase. The signal to restock the shelf comes from the consumer removing an item. The item has been *pulled* from the shelf, creating a signal to replenish. This simple concept is the basis for pull. Without a signal to replenish, what could happen? We could run out of product, causing a loss of sales, or we could overstock the area, leading to spoilage or obsolescence (think about meats, dairy, and produce). Overstocking the area causes us to lose time, space, and resources while failing to meet the customers' need. This is the waste of overproduction, and pull was designed to prevent overproduction. Conversely, understocking creates wasted motion and unnecessary waiting or worse: a total failure to deliver the product to the customer.

Pull in its simplest form is a signal to do work. In the case of the grocery store example, consumption is the signal to replenish. In Lean terms, the principle of pull implies that we would only perform work when we have a true need from the customer. To satisfy the principle of pull, the signal should contain certain attributes in its design. First, we'd like to standardize the signal to one type. Although there are multiple ways to trigger any form of work, we would like to have a single trigger. Other attributes for a good pull system include words such as seamless, no gaps, no overproduction, no asking, no searching, no clarifying, and synchronized.

We will first discuss the standardization of a trigger signal. As an example, let's talk about referral workflow in healthcare. On an inpatient medical floor, let's assume we need to trigger a respiratory therapist (RT) to perform an assessment. To trigger the assessment, we could page the RT, call the RT, key an electronic referral, send an e-mail, do a face-to-face request, trigger the referral in medical rounds, etc. A great Lean organization has a *single*, authoritative way to trigger the referral. Pick the best one for your organization.

Once we have standardized the signal to perform work (trigger), then we want to find one single way to respond to the signal. How do you acknowledge the referral? Again we could acknowledge by calling, e-mailing, etc., but a great pull system employs a single method in response to a trigger.

In healthcare, an example of a good pull signal is placing a physician paper-based order in an "orders to be entered" basket for order entry into the system. There is one way to trigger the work: placing the order in the basket. There is one way to respond: pulling the order from the basket. Assuming the order entry resource has other responsibilities besides just order entry, the response time to get orders entered can be standardized to get us near continuous, but not full continuous, flow. Additional examples of where pull signals have been utilized in healthcare include

1. Using the supermarket concept to trigger supply replenishment of medicines, supplies, and equipment
2. Triggering of a physician to see the next patient in a clinic
3. Triggering that results are available so reassessment can occur
4. Triggering a consult for a specialty service not always in house
5. Triggering a service referral for home care
6. Using a visual queue to know when to porter the next patient for a procedure
7. Triggering a room clean following a discharge
8. Triggering the build of the next 2 hours of OR case carts

There are literally thousands of examples, and a great Lean organization utilizes the principle of pull to link steps together every single time that work cannot flow continuously.

The Lean EHR can automate two of the functions necessary to create pull. Electronic triggers can assist in standardizing the "one" way to signal. Electronic responses within the EHR can also be used to standardize the "one" way to respond. These two triggers can flow to anyone with system access. What the Lean EHR cannot do is standardize the response time. Response times need to be established organizationally based on customer demand, service levels required, or medical necessity. However, the Lean EHR can likely help track the response time and provide valuable data that can be used to measure performance and enable improvement to occur.

Defect-Free

Let's assume now that we have begun to design our work process, and we have been able to implement pockets of continuous flow, and where we couldn't create continuous flow, we have been able to implement pull systems that link our areas of continuous flow together. So far, so good! Will it matter that the work flows continuously and is closely linked with pull systems if the outcomes are wrong or inconsistent? Definitely not; and bad outcomes in healthcare can be very serious. In fact, our first mission in healthcare is to do no harm.

To prevent bad outcomes, we utilize the principle of defect-free. In Lean terms, defect-free means doing the work in a way that meets customer-specified quality requirements the first time. This implies that as the work moves from step to step, quality is designed into the process at each step with immediate feedback when problems do arise so the outcomes are consistent, meet customer requirements, and can be completed without rework and inspection. Some of the attributes of defect-free work would include no errors, no rework, standardized, quality at the source, nonpersonality-based, and no overprocessing or redundancy.

A Lean EHR can greatly assist in designing out defects from healthcare processes. Designed properly, standard order sets, pull-down menus in lieu of free text, and automation software that calculates drug quantities and checks for drug interactions all contribute to safer care and fewer errors. Automated coding, smart phrases, real-time referrals, physician order entry, and bar coding systems all simplify transactions, handling, transcription, and movement of information. The EHR has already made healthcare safer and even more can be done.

Visual Management

Once a process has been designed using the principles of flow, pull, and defect-free, we need a system to manage the process. A Lean system is one that is designed to be managed visually. Visual management allows everyone to "see normal from abnormal conditions." What kinds of things are we interested in managing visually? Anything you can imagine! Are we ahead or behind in the schedule? Is everyone following the standard work? How have our outcomes been? Are all the necessary equipment, materials, and supplies available? Do we have a home for everything? What are the top three problems we are working on? Who is responsible for the corrective actions? When will they be completed? What have the results been for the last month? Are we on budget? All of these types of scenarios can be managed visually.

There are a few attributes we like to see in a Lean visual management system. First, we need absolute transparency; this means that everyone can see normal from abnormal conditions in five seconds or less. We shouldn't need to run a report or open a drawer to see the status of normal from abnormal. A crucial point to remember in creating a Lean culture is that finding issues that need to be corrected is a good thing. Every effort must be put in place to have the organizational culture accept both good and bad information with a respect for both accuracy and appreciation.

Another attribute of visual management is that it must trigger action. Part of a visual management system is to see normal from abnormal; the other part is doing something about it. If we are behind, what is the intervention to catch up? If something is not in the correct place, who is going to find the missing item and return it to its home? Many Lean visual management systems operate exactly as designed: exposing opportunities, but the staff and management fail to act to address these opportunities. In concept, visual management systems should deliver visualization of issues at a stage in the process that allows "abnormal" to be seen at the earliest possible point. This allows corrective action sooner, minimizing risk of harm or delay to patients.

It will not matter how great the Lean design was, how great the flow and pull worked, and how many defects were eliminated if the system cannot be managed *visually*. The culture of your organization will always pull the new, improved system back to the previous status quo without a robust visual management system. A sound visual management is the first key step to sustaining improvement. Great organizations can see normal from abnormal conditions at a glance and take immediate action when abnormal conditions arise.

The Lean EHR can be designed to assist in visual management. Tracking tools displayed in a visual manner can show actual versus expected in real time. And with the EHR functionality, trends can be analyzed and reports can be generated to assist in problem solving. Many EHRs have status boards for the surgical department, the emergency department, and clinic operations. Electronic status boards also exist for pharmacy, lab, and diagnostic imaging. Keep in mind that visual management is more than status. Visual management systems need to show normal from abnormal conditions. Trackers need to show plan versus actual, and they need to trigger action.

Kaizen

The fifth principle of improvement is known as *kaizen*. Kaizen is two words: The first word "kai" means "change," and the second word "zen" means "for the better." In order to create a culture of improvement, we must build a system that is continuously improving. Great organizations get better every day; employees leave the workplace in better shape than when they arrived. Imagine what that could look like in healthcare!

To practice kaizen, we want to make small, incremental, continuous changes to our work in order to deliver more value to the customer. This usually shows up in eliminating small amounts of non-value added activity, for example, by creating better standard work, relocating items to eliminate wasted movement, or mistake-proofing something to avoid a defect being made.

In the spirit of practicing kaizen, Lean organizations frequently benchmark their performance, not necessarily against their peers or within their industry, but in the areas you might not yet have considered. Actually, two types of benchmarking occur simultaneously. The first is benchmarking against perfection: deliver all value-added activity in continuous flow with no defects. When you compare your current performance against perfection, you will see that you have much to improve upon. This comparison of current performance against perfection is designed to create a state of tension spurring further improvement.

The second benchmark is to compare your performance against the best in the world. Great organizations compare their processes against industries with world-class performance. How does your performance in infection prevention compare with safe drinking water? How does your quality in medicine administration compare with the safe practices of a nuclear power plant?

You can compare your organization to other healthcare organizations, but I am not aware of any place in the world that quotes healthcare performance for benchmarks as the best in the world. To achieve dramatic results, we need to do things dramatically differently. So stop comparing yourself with your peers, and look outside of healthcare.

Industry has many examples that healthcare should aspire to. This is not meant to put healthcare beneath other industries, but rather to give you a different vision for what is possible. Practice kaizen. Improve every day. You never get to a state of being "Lean." *Never* be satisfied with your current performance. Challenge the management, staff, and the medical staff to do better. When you create a mindset of continuous improvement, you are meeting the spirit of kaizen.

Optimizing the Lean EHR in the spirit of kaizen, can we continually make our systems better? Can we tweak functionality to improve our quality, delivery, and cost of healthcare? Can we use the data from our EHR to identify further opportunities for improvement? Can we leverage information to accelerate population health and research to create better evidence with better outcomes?

Lean Healthcare Defined

What is Lean healthcare? Envision a system where work is constantly scrutinized by everyone to eliminate waste and deliver more value to your patients. Envision a system where the entire workforce is engaged and inspired to improve. A workforce that continuously improves the quality and safe delivery of care. A workforce that reduces wasted time and activity, freeing up capacity for other work. A workforce that decreases lead times for services, while lowering the cost of the delivery of these services. Envision the delivery of healthcare with accurate and timely information shared seamlessly among the care team. A system where the clinical staff and administrative support staff collaborate to provide patient-focused, evidence-based care with seamless transitions between specialties and subspecialties and levels of care, where the staff constantly strives to ensure the majority of work content is value-added. Resources that are freed up when redundancy and non-value added activities are eliminated are redeployed so all talent can be maximized and additional services can be created with the same budget dollars. Envision a system where the patients, families, and communities participate in the design of the services leading to healthier communities with preventative strategies driving lower and lower costs. I'm not sure there is enough ink to describe all the attributes of Lean healthcare. Table 4.1 provides a brief glimpse into what Lean healthcare is and what it is not.

Lean healthcare is a management system for continuous improvement. This healthcare system is constructed based on the two Lean themes: elimination of waste and respect for all people. Work is designed for the patient in systems and subsystems that reflect continuous flow processes. Work is pulled through the system, not pushed. Activities are designed and delivered in a defect-free manner. The status of work, results, and process are monitored visually; any abnormalities to the work are identified

Table 4.1 Lean Healthcare

What Lean Healthcare Is	*What Lean Healthcare Is Not*
Patient/family/caregiver centered	Provider focused Staff focused College focused Organization focused Insurance focused
Creativity before capital	Technology, equipment, or adding resources lead the solution set
Systems thinking	Program focus
Problems solved in the workplace (gemba)	Problems solved in the conference room
Focus on the process	Focus on blaming individuals
A team of interprofessionals	Individual contributors and heroes
Seamless care	Care provided in silos
Collaborative and integrated care	Profession-centric care
Transparent information	Hidden and difficult to access information
Pursue quality and safety first	Pursue access and cost first
Inspired and engaged staff and medical staff	Leadership and management make most decisions
Continuously improving	Firefighting or spot, localized improvement

and fixed in real time. Every system is continuously being improved by an inspired and engaged staff and medical staff, working side by side with one focus: servicing the patient.

The Lean EHR is a critical component of providing Lean healthcare. In today's environment, the healthcare industry is completely dependent on IT systems. Virtually all healthcare organizations, systems, and private practices have or will have EHRs. Funding sources such as governments and insurance organizations already, or will soon, require data and submissions from these EHRs. The EHR, while extraordinarily valuable, is not a savior in and of itself. The system must be both designed and deployed using Lean principles and must be built to enable Lean operations. Failure to do so will result in a lot of frustration, wasted time, poor outcomes, a loss of meaningful resources, and a dysfunctional environment. The costs to acquire, implement, and deploy an EHR are steep. It is in the best interest of the patients, the organizations, and society to get this right the first time. This book was written to close the gap between the current state and the future state. If you have already deployed your system and find yourself wanting to optimize and enhance your current capabilities, this book will also share some valuable insights.

Chapter Summary

- Lean improvement is based on the fundamental concept of value added and non-value added. A value-added (5% of a typical process) activity directly meets the needs of the customer. A non-value added activity (95% of a typical process) takes time, space, and/or resources, but does not directly contribute to meeting the needs of the customer.
- The two themes of Lean improvement include continuous improvement and respect for all people.
- Non-value added activity is also known as waste; there are seven common forms of operational waste. These include overproduction, waiting, overprocessing, inventory, motion, defects, and transportation. One additional waste present within organizations is the waste of unused human capital.
- Waste is eliminated using the five principles of improvement: flow, pull, defect-free, visual management, and kaizen.
- Lean healthcare can be defined as a complete business system of continuous improvement. This system is operated by a team inspired and engaged to deliver more and more value to patients. A well-run Lean healthcare system will deliver year-over-year improvement in performance and culture.

Chapter 5

EHR Vendor Selection

Thus far in the book, we've defined the problem we're trying to solve in healthcare via the EHR and approaches to solving those problems using Lean thinking. In this chapter, we're going to focus on the processes and information needed to select an EHR vendor, whether you're moving a clinic from paper to computer or moving from one EHR vendor to another. According to the U.S. Centers for Disease Control and Prevention (CDC), by 2013 almost 80% of physician practices had some sort of EHR implemented. So more than likely most organizations today are not starting from square one but are aiming to optimize their existing system or, perhaps, migrate to a new system. If your goal is to migrate, you are essentially starting over, but with the lessons learned from your previous EHR implementation. In this chapter, we'll review the high-level requirements for selecting an EHR system. The cost of making the wrong decision is enormous, and sometimes catastrophic for an organization, so creating a standardized approach to your decision-making is very important.

We're also going to look at this from two distinct perspectives. Hospitals (and hospital systems) have a distinct set of needs with respect to EHR vendor selection. Primary care clinics, specialty provider offices, and others may have different needs. We'll call these out separately, where appropriate. For ease of reference, we'll simply refer to "hospital" or "clinic" when calling these differences out. While not exhaustive, it should give you a good starting point for internal discussion and decision-making.

Typically, we'd start by asking what problem we're trying to solve with this proposed plan. However, we're going to hold that question until the end of the chapter. Some problems are obvious, some less so. First, though, we're going to look at organizational requirements that need to be assessed in advance of an EHR selection. Then, we'll discuss selection criteria and walk through a Pugh analysis to wrap up this chapter.

Patient Perspective

Regardless of whether you're selecting an EHR for a hospital or clinic, you should begin here. Starting by discussing the patient perspective may strike you as unusual—and it is. It's a rare organization that begins by understanding how the patient will impact and be impacted by the EHR. However, if we go back to our fundamental Lean tenant that value can only be defined by the customer, we have to start with our patients. What will they find valuable? Clearly there are numerous elements of the EHR that they might not appreciate or understand—regulatory requirements, for example. However, in today's environment, there is a growing demand for consumer-facing technologies and solutions to meet rapidly evolving patient needs. Some of these have been mentioned already in Chapter 1. The consumerization of healthcare in today's environment currently includes these needs, though the list is ever-evolving.

1. *Ability to self-schedule*—whether it's for a primary care visit, an emergency department visit, an imaging appointment, or a surgery. Patients want to be able to electronically access scheduling systems, set up alerts or reminders, and more.
2. *Electronic access to patient data*—many EHR systems provide at least rudimentary ability for the patient to access their own patient data such as normal lab results, imaging results, primary care visit notes, diagnoses, prescriptions, and more.
3. *Online information, electronic forms, signatures*—patients often arrive for a clinic visit or planned hospital admission only to sit filling out paper forms (which are then scanned into the EHR and printed back out or faxed). An increasing number of patients want to be able to fill out electronic forms online in advance of the visit. They want to be able to access needed information and forms and register online securely and easily. Ideally, they'd like to know the cost of a service (especially with the increasing number of people with high deductible insurance plans), and patients also want the ability to pay copays or bills online.

4. *Near real-time electronic communication*—increasingly, patients want to be able to communicate securely (and privately) with care providers via email or text.
5. *Home or remote monitoring (and use of consumer devices)*—an increasing number of patients are looking for opportunities for home monitoring of conditions from cardiac events to diabetes management and beyond. The use of consumer technology, including fitness devices (step trackers, heart rate monitors), as well as home care (diabetes testing, for example), is growing each year, and the ability to incorporate these data for monitoring purposes is becoming more important.
6. *Relevant electronic content*—consumers are becoming more involved in their care and many do extensive online research regarding their symptoms, conditions, diagnoses, and treatment plans. A proliferation of inaccurate or unreliable information came with this online explosion. Providing a trusted source of health and wellness information for your target population is becoming a more prominent requirement.

This is just a partial list of the changes that patients are demanding of their healthcare providers. While some of these technologies may not yet be ready for primetime or for true clinical use, this move toward consumerization of healthcare cannot be ignored. Putting the patient experience at the top of your vendor selection requirements list will ensure that you examine vendor options in this regard to guide your selection.

At the end of this chapter are some helpful resources. Among them is a Request for Proposal issued by a New York state healthcare organization. This document provides a lot of detail that you may want to incorporate into your process. There are many online examples available if the one provided doesn't suit your needs.

Organizational Requirements

There are an increasing number of articles being written about the experiences of organizations moving from one EHR to another and the lessons learned. The key elements are always about conducting well-designed planning sessions and ensuring there is broad organizational engagement. That means having executive sponsorship and visible leadership driving the effort. It also means having people throughout the organization dedicated to the planning and decision-making tasks. If you don't have those elements in place, then that must be your starting place. For now, we're going to assume you have the right leaders engaged; we'll focus our discussion on the discrete tasks required for planning an EHR implementation.

Assessing Readiness

Assuming you have the leadership engagement needed to be successful, the next step is assessing organizational readiness. This is true for hospitals and clinics. If you don't have an EHR now, you'll have different considerations than an organization that is assessing their readiness to migrate from one system to another. However, there are common elements to all readiness assessments, which we'll cover here.

You should start by asking yourself and your organization a few key questions. Do you know if you are positioned to successfully select and implement an EHR? Based on a broad review of industry articles on EHR deployments, it's clear that the vast majority of failed deployments have nothing to do with the vendor or the software selected and everything to do with the organization's ability to successfully manage the planning, implementation, or deployment of an EHR (at the highest level, these can all be referred to under the heading *change management*). There are many resources available for anyone who would like to perform an in-depth readiness assessment. We've provided some of the basics here to get you started.

Who Are the Key Stakeholders and What Are Their Objectives?

Hospital: You have various clinical perspectives—from physicians to nurses, patient care techs to respiratory therapists, pharmacists, and more. You also have various business perspectives—supply chain, business office, revenue cycle management, medical records management, finance, and HR—to take into consideration when you implement or migrate an EHR. Everyone who will be using the EHR for any portion of their job is a stakeholder and should be represented in some manner.

Perform a gap analysis to make sure you're not missing anything. Take a moment to list all the departments in your organization that interact with the patient record (whether that's a paper record or a collection of electronic systems or a consolidated EHR program). Now compare that list to the list of all departments in the organization. What departments are not represented on your first list and why? If you think the department does not currently interact with patient data, you need to ask two questions. First, are you correct? Talk to the director or leader in that area and confirm (or refute) your assumptions. Second, how is that likely to change in the future? It's entirely possible that with a new EHR in place, new departments will be working with patient data in new ways. Hopefully that's the case where streamlining the patient experience can be done through automating workflows through an EHR.

Clinic: A clinic may have some of the same stakeholders as a hospital (especially if they are owned by a system), but clinics will have distinct needs to address. The stakeholders are often the owners (hospital, management company, providers, etc.) as well as the providers in the practice and the support staff (medical assistants, office staff, billing/coding/scheduling, etc.). What are their objectives for the EHR? For example, there are user needs, patient needs (see the previous section), business needs (the ability to bill and collect revenue), and regulatory needs. Of course, there may be more, but defining the stakeholders and their objectives prior to selecting an EHR is vital to selecting the correct solution.

Regardless of organizational type, the key is to question current assumptions and ensure you're asking enough questions about current and desired future state. One of the key mistakes organizations have made is assuming a group would not need to be involved with the EHR only to find out later that their input and perspective in the planning stages would have had a materially positive impact on the outcome.

Who Will Form the Implementation Team and What Are Their Roles and Responsibilities?

Hospital: You will need to create a cross-functional team to be involved with planning and implementing the EHR. During your readiness assessment, you should be forming your implementation team and ensuring it has the right people involved. Over the course of the project, implementation team members may change—either because people change jobs or because different roles are needed at different times. Be sure to map out (and document) your team needs then fill the roles with identified individuals. This will help reduce the tendency to plan based on who's available or the skills of the individual in a particular role at a given point in time.

One of the problems that often arises is that one person cannot effectively represent an entire line of work. For example, an OR nurse leader may not be an effective representative of the ED or the inpatient needs.

At the same time, you can't invite a cast of hundreds to every single meeting. Therefore, you'll need to look at your current organizational structure and determine if there are existing groups (and meetings) that could be utilized for your implementation planning. Rather than add meetings and reinvent structures, you might find that a quick assessment of existing arrangements provides a ready-made solution for planning and implementation.

Beyond that, ensure that there is a mechanism for representatives to bring key information back to their stakeholders for discussion and decision-making. If that's not possible, hold open forums and allow large groups to come hear a brief presentation (or create a video and share it) so that consistent information is shared across all stakeholder groups.

Clinic: Often this decision is less complex in a clinic setting unless the organization is a multiple-provider, multiple-location, and/or multiple specialty clinic. Regardless, you need to decide how you'll implement. Will you pull your office and support staff to work on this project? Will you fully hire this out to the EHR vendor? Will you hire a consulting company to run this from start to finish? Regardless of how you will staff this, you'll need to define roles and responsibilities.

For both hospital and clinic implementations, once you've determined the correct roles, responsibilities, and communication forums, document this and disseminate to stakeholders and your executive sponsor. As you move forward, it will be important to document key decisions and hold everyone accountable for moving forward based on those agreements.

How Will We Include the Patient Perspective?

Hospital and clinic: We touched on the patient perspective earlier in this chapter in terms of features and functions patients are likely looking for. However, those are all assumptions until you actually hear the voice of the customer. How will you get their input on the features/functions discussed earlier as well as other decisions that need to be made that are patient-facing?

Many organizations implemented EHRs a decade ago before there was a clear view of how this whole "electronic record thing" would work. As an industry, we've learned a lot since then. Most importantly, perhaps, is that our patients are our customers. As stakeholders, their input matters. From a Lean perspective, we know that value is defined by the customer. In healthcare, the customer is almost always the patient (though there are certainly intermediate customers we work with as well). If we do not seek to add value to the patient through this process, we're just spinning our wheels.

Thus, including the patient experience and perspective is vital to overall success. Each organization will need to engage with their particular patient populations in different ways, depending on the nature of the organization.

As you may be thinking, that can be challenging. Many patients don't really want to spend time helping to plan an implementation of an EHR, and rightfully so. However, if you ask patients to help you understand where their care could have been better and what things would be more valuable to them, you can ensure that your EHR planning incorporates those improvements. For example, perhaps you have a patient council that provides feedback. Perhaps through discussion you learn that your patient discharge instructions are confusing and not helpful to a majority of patients. When planning your EHR deployment, you'll want to look at your current practices and procedures regarding patient discharge instructions and find a better way to implement that as part of the work you're doing.

In a perfect world, you'll be incorporating Lean process improvement findings as part of your implementation planning. You'd be missing an enormous opportunity if you did not engage with your patients during your planning phase.

What Is the Overall State of Our Information Technology (IT) Infrastructure?

Hospital and clinic: In planning for an EHR deployment or migration, it's vital to assess the current state of the IT infrastructure as well. Though we're primarily concerned with how to effectively plan the elements of the EHR, it's a good time to mention that your IT leaders should be looking at things like the reliability and redundancy of the wired and wireless network, the age and specifications of the storage and server platforms, and the existence (and age) of end-user computing devices (desktops, laptops, label printers, paper printers, prescription printers, document scanners, bar code scanners, etc.). These will all be part of the assessment and planning process for the EHR, and this aspect can be done early in the cycle. Knowing the current state will help the team assess potential EHR providers (if you're selecting one), and it will be required for a gap analysis once an EHR vendor platform is selected.

Concepts such as business continuity (BC), high availability (HA), redundancy, reliability, virtualization, backups, disaster recovery (DR), and information security are all tied into your assessment of your infrastructure capabilities. Most EHR vendors address these elements in their solutions. However, questions such as whether or not you're willing to implement a cloud-only solution are important factors. Cloud-based solutions have improved dramatically in recent years, but there are still considerations for cloud-only, hybrid (cloud and on-premises), or on-premises only.

Clinics often prefer cloud-based solutions to minimize the need for IT infrastructure and ongoing support and staff costs. While this may be a valid approach, it should not be the default decision without understanding how the business of the clinic might be impacted.

The move toward mobility and mobile devices is a current driver of requirements. If your organization has not yet embraced mobile computing, this is the time to step back and assess how your workflows would change if mobility was introduced. As we discuss throughout this book, it's important to envision your desired end state before you start. If the desire is to incorporate mobility into the workflow, it should be discussed as part of your EHR requirements and should be planned for in revised workflows.

Cultural Climate

Hospital and clinic: Regardless of whether you're implementing an EHR for the first time, migrating to a different platform, or optimizing your EHR, every aspect of this involves cultural change. It requires leadership to explain and foster understanding to gain support for change. If it's a top-down "just do this" initiative, you will get compliance but you will not get sustainable results. If the process involves listening to stakeholders, gathering input, addressing legitimate concerns (or allaying false concerns), and aligning everyone's interests, you will have a better outcome. Therefore, the cultural climate is a very important aspect to assess when looking at readiness. Often cultural change can be effected when leaders in various business and clinical areas champion the potential benefits of the change—by being change agents themselves, they can influence their teams. Conversely, if you have leaders who are not on board, whether in word or action, you will have pockets of resistance that can substantially impact the outcome.

Clinical and IT Governance Structures

Hospital and clinic: Let's remember that deploying an EHR is *not* an IT project; it's an organizational project with deep IT roots. IT should not, but more importantly cannot, drive an EHR project; it will fail. Having engaged organizational leaders is a key element of success. Those organizational leaders should develop (or participate in the development of) functional governance structures. These structures will make decisions around how the EHR is initially built and then how it is maintained, upgraded, and optimized in the future. Once you identify the desired structures and how they will operate at a high level, you should consider creating policies and procedures to support the ongoing work of these groups so that as members come and go, the structures and processes remain intact.

These structures may be greatly simplified in a clinic setting, but a clear structure should still be defined. Without a governance plan (even if it's pretty basic), each request for change will be handled in an ad hoc manner. You lose any gains you may have made during a thoughtful EHR deployment.

Incorporating SAFER Guidelines

Hospital and clinic: The Office of the National Coordinator for Health Information Technology (ONC) has issued a number of guidelines, The Safety Assurance Factors for EHR Resilience, referred to as SAFER Guidelines, regarding the safe and effective use of the EHR. These can be found online at http://www.healthit.gov/SAFERGuide. According to the ONC, "The SAFER Guides are designed to help healthcare organizations conduct self-assessments to optimize the safety and safe use of electronic health records (EHRs) in the following areas:

1. High Priority Practices
2. Organizational Responsibilities
3. Contingency Planning
4. System Configuration
5. System Interfaces
6. Patient Identification
7. Computerized Provider Order Entry with Decision Support
8. Test Results Reporting and Follow-Up
9. Clinician Communication

Each of the nine SAFER Guidelines begins with a Checklist of 'recommended practices.' Following the Checklist, a Practice Worksheet gives a rationale for, and examples of, how to implement each recommended practice." (http://www.healthit.gov/SAFERGuide).

Regardless of where your organization is on the EHR deployment continuum, you would be well served to review these guidelines as you develop your requirements for your EHR as well as your requirements for your project once the EHR vendor is selected. By incorporating these best practices into your planning, you can optimize the safety and usefulness of your EHR at the beginning, which is the most efficient and effective place to insert those criteria.

Systems Integration

Part of the decision-making process for EHR selection includes which systems will be replaced by the EHR (especially in an environment where numerous discrete systems are currently in use), which modules in the EHR will be utilized, and which systems will subsequently need to share data.

Thought should be given to both internal and external data sharing. For example, will your lab system share data electronically through an interface? How will diagnostic imaging images be stored, shared, and resulted? How will data from one system get to another system? There are many ways electronic data can be shared, and it's important to understand at the outset what the options are. For example, some vendors may talk about "integration," but what they really mean is that they can export a .CSV flat file that can be imported into another system. So, yes, data get electronically from one system to another, but that's not exactly integration.

Interfaces

Another of the lessons learned from organizations moving from one EHR to another is that you must have a thorough inventory of your interfaces and the dependencies of those systems. If you are consolidating, you need to have a clear understanding of what contracts are in place, and the duration and terms of those contracts, in case these impact your EHR evaluation. For example, if you're locked into a 5-year multimillion-dollar contract for a system that provides a capability that is in your new EHR, you would have to assess whether you attempt to negotiate a buyout of the old system or use that system until the end of the contract term. In turn, that impacts what features and functions of your EHR you may require on day 1 versus 3 or 5 years down the line.

Interfaces to various systems all have different technical requirements. Some are simple (such as standardized HL7 message formats); some are complex and customized. (Please refer to Resources at the end of this chapter for more detailed information on HL7 and EHRs.) Understanding your inbound and outbound data needs by performing an assessment and creating a data flow map will get you organized. The first step is to know what you currently have. The second step is to determine if all of those are still in use and/or needed. In some cases, interfaces that are abandoned without proper termination leave loose ends (and security holes). Finally, once you have a view of all the required interfaces, you need to assess whether you are sending the minimum necessary. In one organization, a request to send data from the EHR to an external source was fulfilled by the IT staff without proper instructions. Three years later, an audit revealed that they had been sending all data fields rather than the four requested data fields. This was a security risk for the organization.

Installing a new EHR will require you do this assessment on future state systems and interfaces. Moving from one EHR to another will require a gap analysis of current existing to future required. In some cases, you'll get rid of interfaces; in other cases, you may need to revisit the interface source and destination and the associated data. For optimization, the same process is needed—an inventory of all current interfaces (in use or not) as well as the data requirements for each interface and an assessment of whether or not they are still needed, still bring value to the organization, and still send the least data required.

Of course, because we're discussing how to implement a Lean EHR, special attention should be paid to whether or not these interfaces are necessary. Just reproducing the current state without examination will lead not only to waste but also to bigger problems down the road.

With that in mind, the following four steps provide the broad stroke steps to take when evaluating interface options during your EHR vendor selection process:

1. Conduct a full inventory of interfaces (existing or future needs). Include source, destination, method, data format, and other pertinent details. Be sure to look at upstream and downstream systems as well as medical device system interfaces and cloud-based interfaces.
2. Assess future state needs and create a final list of all required interfaces. Where there are unknowns or questions, create placeholders so you can revisit these items once more information is known.

3. Document minimum necessary data for all required (or desired) interfaces so you reduce security and privacy risks and build security compliance into the front of your work (rather than remediating it later).
4. Create a checklist for interfaces you will no longer need that will need to be shut down later. You can build on this as you go, but if your assessment quickly yields a list of interfaces that will no longer be needed once you move to the new EHR, you should capture that information now and validate it after go live. Of course, if you discover unused interfaces at this point, you may want to eliminate those immediately. Undocumented interfaces should be investigated to ensure they are (1) legitimate, (2) still needed, and (3) sending the minimum data necessary.

Up and Downstream Systems Integration

We've discussed interfaces, which are electronic connections between two systems in order to move data from one place to another. This implies up- and downstream systems are sending and receiving data. Whether you're starting from scratch or moving from one EHR to another, you'll need to have a full inventory of up- and downstream systems, which we'll refer to here as ancillary systems. They may not be very "ancillary" in the scheme of things. Your supply chain management system or your enterprise resource planning system may be very major enterprise-wide systems, but from the perspective of the EHR, they are ancillary. Figure 5.1 shows a simple diagram of the types of systems and integration that occur; mapping out your systems at a high level may assist in ensuring all systems are considered in your planning. Figure 5.2 shows a simple example of how application data might need to flow into and out of your EHR. These will vary greatly depending on the extent that your EHR is an enterprise system providing full capabilities or whether it's a more focused system providing a more limited set of capabilities. (There is always a trade-off that should be reviewed to meet your organization's unique needs.)

Developing an understanding of your data flows (from the work we previously discussed related to interfaces) will give you a list of these ancillary systems. It's important to map out what data you need to flow between systems and in what direction, as well as what data you do not need to flow between systems. For example, you may have an integrated EHR that has

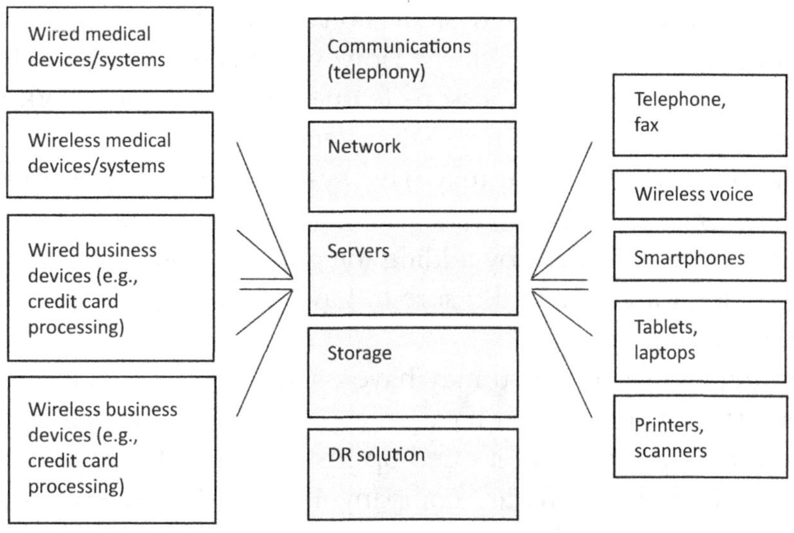

Figure 5.1 Infrastructure systems example.

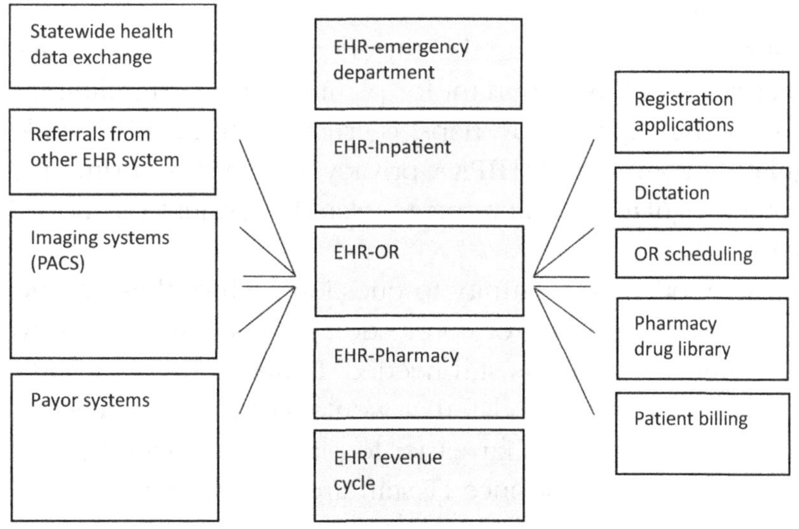

Figure 5.2 Applications data flow example.

the billing system included, in which case you may need your supply chain management system to have a bidirectional interface between these systems to share supply costs, inventory locations, inventory levels, etc. On the other hand, if you have a standalone billing system, you'll need to determine what data need to flow between the billing system, the supply chain system, and the EHR to ensure proper charges are generated and billed appropriately. Unless you're starting a new healthcare organization from scratch (rare these days), you'll already know what systems contain the data you need and where you need to focus your efforts. However, this is also the perfect time to improve data flow based on lessons learned from previous work or from identifying opportunities in your existing state.

One caution here is that you may have system dependencies about which you're not currently aware, if you are moving from one EHR to another, or if you are optimizing your EHR by adding integrated modules from your current EHR vendor, for example. Be sure to have a very detailed current state map as your starting point.

Another reminder is that you may have contract dependencies that are not on your radar. Suppose you have an interface from your billing software to your current EHR and it's tied up inside of a software maintenance contract from the billing software company. If you're legally bound to a 6-year contract and you're in the first year of that contract, you could find yourself paying unexpected costs for systems that will no longer be in use. While contracts like that are not the norm, it's always wise to find this out in advance, if possible.

The best practice of mapping the current state to the future state and creating that crosswalk is important for planning. Understanding the existing state, including gaps and overlaps, is crucial both for EHR work as well as for regulatory compliance (HIPAA privacy and security primarily, though there are other regulatory requirements related to patient records, billing charges, etc.).

This is also another opportunity to question each of these elements and ask what purpose the system (or connection between systems) serves, what value it adds, and whether it is still needed. In addition, it's important to ask what data you're *not* getting today that would streamline processes, improve workflow, or reduce costs. It's far easier to plot this all out on paper in advance than it is to revise it once IT staff are involved with building, connecting, and testing systems.

This is also your most optimal opportunity to define system dependencies and document why they exist, what purpose they serve, who the system owners are, who the IT owners are, and how these systems are managed going forward. This helps avoid the "orphan application" syndrome where no one really owns the application, the vendor sort of manages it, and some years later after everyone who knew about it has moved on, it sits there in the background without active management. This scenario has the potential to create all kinds of problems (including security, privacy, and hidden costs, to name three), so using this phase of review can be very useful on many fronts. Though not specifically related to a Lean EHR, these elements are also important parts of a business impact analysis (BIA) in a DR plan. We'll discuss more about DR later in this chapter in the section entitled "Business Continuity and Disaster Recovery Considerations."

Hardware and Infrastructure Considerations

Probably one of the first assessments your IT organization will need to undertake regarding hardware is whether you will host your EHR and related systems in your own data center or whether you will outsource that to a cloud-based provider, as mentioned earlier in this chapter. There are numerous things to consider when making this decision, and we'll discuss the key considerations in this section. Hardware includes systems, storage, and network, as well as end-user devices. Other considerations include organizational strategies, risk assessments, BC and DR considerations, the state of your current infrastructure systems, the state of the organization's finances, and staff capabilities. While this is primarily an internal IT-based discussion, it should include the right IT leaders (CIO, VPs, division directors, etc.) to ensure that the review and subsequent recommendations meet the entire organization's needs and not just those whose sway is strongest or voice is loudest.

Organizational Strategies

Reviewing organizational strategies might not seem like a logical starting point for reviewing hardware and infrastructure, but it is. If you start working on infrastructure planning without awareness of organizational strategies, you could build a solution that is out of alignment with the overall direction of the company. That would lead to waste and rework, at best. While a lengthy discussion about organizational strategies when trying to select an EHR vendor could certainly pull you down the rabbit hole, it should be reviewed so you don't end up out of step with longer range organizational initiatives.

Risk Assessment

You should conduct a hardware or infrastructure risk assessment. If you have vendor-provided hardware specifications, you can use those as part of your risk assessment, though that should not be the entire basis of your review. For example, if you are considering moving from vendor A to vendor B, you should review both vendors' hardware requirements and perform not only a gap analysis (what is different between them) but a risk assessment as well. Here are some questions to consider; you may come up with additional details to examine for your risk assessment.

1. What systems are in place today and what is their current state?
2. Are they state-of-the-art? Are they legacy? Do you have the skills and knowledge to support them? (Or do you have support contracts in place that supplement your in-house expertise?)
3. Are they still being sold and supported (i.e., have not reached "end-of-sales" or "end-of-support" dates)?
4. Are they functioning well? Are they constantly in need of repair?
5. Are those hardware vendors providing excellent products, services, and support, or are you struggling to get the vendor to address ongoing issues?
6. Are your hardware vendors (and value-added resellers) providing the products and services you need or the ones they have incentives to sell?
7. What is the state of your data center?
8. Do you currently outsource any hardware or software systems and, if so, how are those arrangements working?
9. Are you meeting service level agreements with the organization or are you falling short? If falling short, are the root causes related to hardware or software or both?
10. Do you have solid processes in place for managing your hardware infrastructure or is it rather "loose" in terms of process and procedure?

These are all risks related to your hardware decisions. While some of these elements also cross over into software risks, the two are clearly interrelated in some areas.

Once you've thought through these elements, you should document this in some way—most choose to create a risk assessment matrix. You can use any of a number of commonly used structures for this process. Table 5.1 shows an example of how you could map this out.

Table 5.1 Risk Assessment Matrix for Hardware

Equipment Description	*Age/State*	*End-of-Sales (End-of-Support) Dates*	*Reliability*	*Vendor Support/Cost of Contract*	*Ranking (5 Best, 1 Worst)*
Brand A storage area network (SAN)	5 years old; 1 release behind newest generation hardware.	12/2015 (12/2020)	Increasing hard drive failures; replacing with solid state drives	Average. Cost of contract is average.	3
Brand B server farm	2 years old; on current platform but unable to expand further.	None published	Very reliable	Unknown due to lack of need to use support. Very expensive contract.	4
Brand C servers	Various ages; on current platform.	None published	Very reliable	Excellent support, average price.	5
Brand D network core infrastructure	Core is 8 years old; 2 releases behind newest generation.	1/2012 (1/2018)	Very reliable, but concerns about age	Average. Cost of contract increasing due to age of equipment.	2
[Other]					

Based on the details in Table 5.1, we would propose addressing core network infrastructure first followed by the storage area network. If these are significant issues to be addressed, they must be discussed in tandem with your EHR considerations. For example, you may be considering an EHR platform that is hosted or cloud-based. If you have an aging server or storage infrastructure, this may point toward using that hosted solution. On the other hand, if you have relatively new (expensive) hardware and the expertise to properly manage it (internal staff or vendor support), this may point you away from a hosted solution. Of course, it's never that simple, and there are numerous interconnecting details to review. Using this type of assessment matrix to map out your infrastructure will help you organize your thinking around your hardware. In this way, you can create a prioritized list of infrastructure to review when assessing your EHR. Using this same example, you might determine that your Brand B server farm and your Brand C servers are in excellent shape and could be repurposed for some other use in your future state. Even though you can no longer expand your server farm, it might have significant useful life left if deployed in a different way. The key is to achieve the stated objectives for the EHR deployment while optimizing resources (capital, operational, hardware, software, staff, etc.).

Business Continuity and Disaster Recovery Considerations

In today's environment, most healthcare organizations have a DR solution in place. Of course, implementing a DR solution and keeping it current are two very different propositions. A discussion of the maintenance of a DR solution is outside the scope of this book. However, most organizations have defined what data they back up and how that backup is managed, as well as what they would do if the data center went dark or if their Internet connection went down. What is becoming of more concern to healthcare organizations these days, especially in light of increasing ransomware attacks on healthcare information systems, is BC. This is a set of activities and plans related to being able to run the business in the event of core system failures. In the past, we tended to plan for natural disasters such as earthquakes or hurricanes. While that's still an important part of BC planning, it's not the only aspect. Today, we need to plan for a fully functional hospital, clinic, or practice, but without some or all electronic systems. IT BC usually addresses things like high availability, redundancy, etc. through network and systems architecture.

For the purposes of this book, we'll assume you have a BC and DR plan from an IT perspective. So, if you're migrating to a new EHR, for example, how are BC and DR impacted? What IT changes will need to be made? What operational changes need to be made? These may not be part of your EHR vendor selection per se, but they need to be tightly integrated. For example, if your EHR vendor says "We do it all, you don't need BC or DR with us!" what they might be saying is that they will back up your data and will provide always-available systems via a cloud offering. Great, but what happens if that cloud-provider goes down (think Amazon Web Services, for example, going down and the impact that has on organizations reliant on that infrastructure).

If your current DR is in dismal shape, you may choose to simply identify required and desired future states and start working toward implementing that as part of the EHR migration. While it may not be worth the time or money to remediate what you currently have, you should absolutely take time to figure out why you ended up here and what measures you can put in place to avoid repeating this. Performing a root cause analysis via an A3 process may be enlightening and may help avoid repeating this in the future.

In assessing a vendor's DR solution, you may want to determine whether the vendor's offering does the following:

1. Meet business and operational needs
2. Be able to meet service level requirements (Restore Point Objectives, Restore Time Objectives, etc.)
3. Would be feasible from an IT perspective
4. Reduce capital and/or operational costs
5. Reduce need for specialized staff (see Current Staff Capabilities and Limitations section later in this chapter)

Gap Analysis—Current Infrastructure vs. Vendor Requirements

You started reviewing the state of your current infrastructure in the risk assessment section. In addition, you may also consider doing a hardware crosswalk, as shown in Table 5.2. In this case, you're comparing your current state with your potential future state. If you're considering multiple EHR vendors, you may want to perform a separate crosswalk for each vendor so you can clearly map out opportunities and risks.

You may have a far more formalized method of assessing these capabilities and that would certainly be appropriate in a complex IT environment. This table was presented to provide insight into how to approach this assessment. Essentially, you want to identify what you have and whether or not you can or should reuse it in your future state.

If your organization is considering expanding, replacing, or optimizing your EHR, these hardware elements must be part of the discussion early on. If not, there will be some very large (and negative) financial surprises for the organization. In fact, these cost considerations are vital to the overall assessment of the EHR strategy, so they must be included in the mix early on.

Table 5.2 Hardware Crosswalk Example

Equipment	*Current State*	*EHR Vendor A Requirements*	*Exceeds, Meets, Fails*	*Recommendation*
Brand A storage area network	5 years old; SATA drives; average reliability and cost	SSD drives with x, y, z (IOPS, capacity, etc.)	Fails; could replace SATA with SSD drives ($$) but would still be at low end of meets	Replace
Brand B server farm	2 years old; unable to expand further	[OS, processor, amount of cache, RAM, local storage, network IO, etc.]	Meets; depending on deployment, may need to purchase additional units	Assess
Brand C servers	Various	Could be used for application X, Y, Z	Meets; for specific uses only	Identify specific use case

The key decision elements with respect to the EHR strategy are not likely to be hardware based. EHR decisions should be workflow based (what will best serve the needs of our patients and their care providers), but these hardware elements most certainly inform the costs as well as some of the deployment decisions.

Current State of End-User Devices

End-user devices can be broadly defined as all the computer-related devices used by end users in the organization. This includes workstations, desktops, laptops, tablets, smartphones, and possibly other specialized electronic endpoints. It includes all types of printers: standard laser printers, label printers, wristband printers, prescription printers, and multifunction copier/scanner/printers. It also includes other devices such as bar code scanners and document scanners. These types of end-user devices are relatively inexpensive on a one-by-one basis, but if you were to have to replace all computers (workstations, desktops, laptops, and tablets) in an organization at once, you'll quickly have a multimillion-dollar project on your hands. Therefore, when reviewing EHR options, it's vital to review these four key elements:

1. Current state of end-user devices
2. Clinical and operational end-user device strategies
3. Requirements of EHR
4. Licensing requirements

You can use an assessment matrix similar to that shown in Table 5.2 earlier. It's relatively easy to map out the current state of end-user devices. Some organizations purchase 25% of their fleet each year so that no computer is older than 4 years old. Some organizations fall behind and replace only 10% of their fleet each year and find that they end up running 8- to 10-year-old computers. If you're using thin-client, zero-client, or virtual desktop technologies, this may be just fine. If you're still running traditional computers, these older devices will be causing productivity loss (slowness, frequent repairs, etc.), which is an often hidden form of waste.

Regardless of the state of your systems, you need to assess this against your future state EHR requirements. While it's easy to push these costs off as "noncritical," you will do your EHR deployment a major disservice if you don't provide end users with a fast, seamless, and reliable computing experience. End-user devices are a key link in that chain. This also directly impacts the patient—slow devices cause the patient to wait. That delay in care (however slight that may be) is multiplied by the number of patients cared for per hour or day, as well as provider complaints and dissatisfaction.

In addition, you need to understand how operations plan on using computers in patient care in the future. This is where Lean thinking is crucial. We'll discuss more about this aspect later in the book (see Chapters 6, 11, and 13). Are you going to move to personally assigned mobile devices, shared mobile devices, in-room computers, laptops on carts, etc.? What is the desired future state and what do your optimized workflows look like? How will those inform your hardware purchasing requirements now and in the near term? How will that impact your software licensing such as Microsoft™ operating systems, client access licenses (CALs), etc.? What about software that requires concurrent connection licenses such as Citrix™? Will you allow all users remote access or just some users? (There are both security and licensing considerations for remote access.) Figure 5.3 shows an example of a licensing challenge many healthcare organizations face with

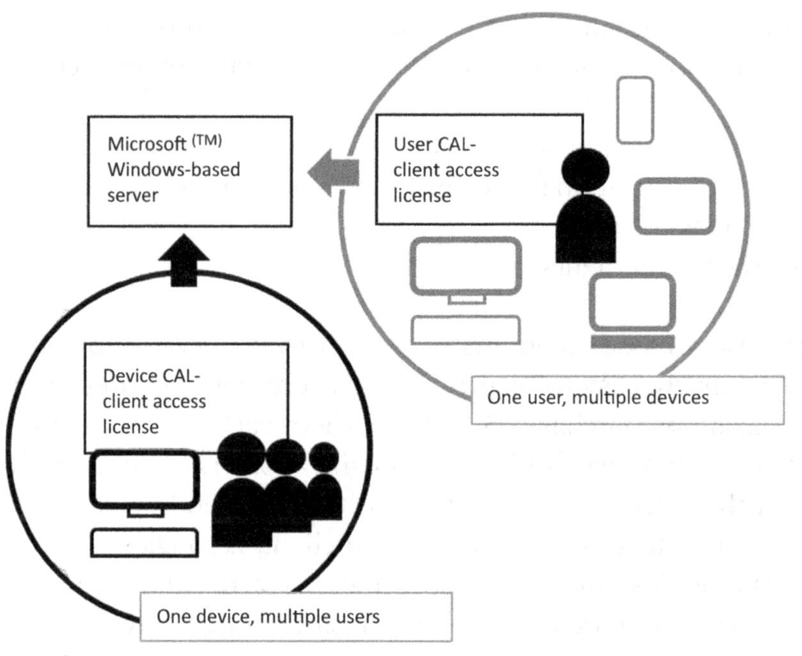

Figure 5.3 Licensing example.

respect to server access licensing. Will you have many users sharing a device or a user with multiple devices?

You'll need to assess the net impact to your hardware and software licensing environment and prepare estimated budgets to reflect changes that will be needed to meet future state EHR requirements and organizational workflow needs. Talk with your respective hardware and software vendors about license requirements for expansion—including costs for DR. Each vendor has different requirements for licensing (DR, test, development, backup, production), and it's wise to understand the entire licensing landscape before finalizing your budget because there can be some big surprises in store if you overlook this aspect.

State of Organizational Finances

Every healthcare organization today has an operating method related to capital expenditures, operational budgets, IT as a percent of revenue, IT as a percent of total FTEs, etc. Sometimes these are limitations for IT departments, especially when considering an EHR deployment, which creates an enormous demand for a defined period of time. Meeting that demand, whether financial or operational, can be challenging. Reviewing these aspects during EHR system evaluation can help you identify optimal strategies to address these needs as the overall solution is being discussed and developed.

Some companies routinely allocate sufficient capital for ongoing IT infrastructure investments. They understand the cost of doing business and the costs associated with not remaining current in this area. They understand, for example, there is a soft cost to productivity when servers, storage, network systems, or endpoint devices are slow or unreliable. They understand that these soft costs add up and that, rather than spending time on quantifying those soft costs, there is value in ensuring all infrastructure systems remain current (i.e., latest vendor platform or release level) or are replaced within 6 years of original deployment, for example.

Other organizations, for many legitimate reasons, want (or need) to eek every bit of useful life out of infrastructure systems, and they will keep systems installed and in service for up to 12 or 15 years, if they can maintain support (often third-party support at that point). They may be strapped for capital funding, or they may have other strategic initiatives that are using the majority of that funding. In addition, each company has its own unique approach to capital management that will drive high-level decisions. While you may not be in a position to influence your organization's approach, you certainly need to articulate the current state of infrastructure as compared to the required future state so the organization can determine the best path forward. In some cases, this may require special board approval for higher capital costs, or it might drive decisions that push some of these costs to the operational budget. Further, it might involve decisions regarding vendor-provided solutions versus in-house solutions or even, ultimately, the vendor selected.

One of the current trends in software and hardware is the rental of these capabilities through "*something*-as-a-service" such as software-as-a-service (SaaS) or infrastructure-as-a-service (IaaS), etc. When these services are used on a rental or subscription basis, they often move from capital to operational expenditures. In some cases, this may be beneficial to the organization, but in other cases, it might be problematic. Knowing how your future state hardware and software will be delivered will drive certain financial decisions because in many cases, you do not have a choice. For example, for software vendor X, it's possible that today you can choose to install the application or use the SaaS and pay an annual subscription fee. If it's likely that in the next few years that may no longer be an option, you know you'll have to pay the yearly subscription or find an alternative.

The takeaway here is that you need to understand how your hardware and software environment is changing now and in the near future in terms of delivery model (installed, hosted, etc.) as well as how those costs impact your budget. Moving from capital costs to operational costs might solve one problem, but it creates numerous others, including an increase in the overall IT operational budget as a percentage of revenue. Unless this is clearly understood, discussed, agreed upon, and documented in advance, there will be some large financial disconnects that will cause even bigger problems down the road.

Finally, if your organization is considering acquiring (or being acquired), you need to do an even broader assessment of your current and future states in this combined environment. Though that is, and should be, part of an acquisition due diligence process, it can be very complex if you're also looking at standardizing on a single EHR.

We'll discuss funding your EHR project briefly later in this chapter.

Operational Considerations

There are a number of IT operational considerations associated with assessing EHR requirements. In the preceding section, we discussed developing hardware and infrastructure requirements. However, there are also associated requirements such as staff capabilities, network infrastructure, telephony, and service desk capabilities that should be noted during an EHR assessment. While there may be slight overlap between some of these items and the previous discussion, we'll review the items here in terms of operational considerations to provide a thorough end-to-end view.

Current Staff Capabilities and Limitations

This is an area of review that is often missed so it's the one we'll discuss first. Most IT leaders don't want to say "we can't" or "we don't know how" when it comes to providing a service. Perhaps the more relevant question is not "can we?" but "should we?" Just because you can do something does not mean you should. And the reverse is also true. Just because you cannot do something today doesn't mean you shouldn't. For example, you may be able to provide support for some strange, one-off system requirement from a vendor, but should you accommodate such a nonstandard requirement or request? If it's truly a requirement, it may make sense to sign a contract and have the vendor, who has specific expertise, handle support of that item. On the other hand, just because you don't currently have staff today who can support some technology doesn't mean you should pay the vendor for support. It may mean training existing staff or hiring new staff to provide internal support.

A full assessment of strengths, weaknesses, and capabilities gaps needs to be completed. Be sure to include an assessment of your leaders—whether they are executives, directors, managers, supervisors, project leaders, or even super users. Figure 5.4 depicts teams that have weak leaders, weak team members (or weak skills), and team gaps. Weak leadership skills are often more detrimental to an organization than weak technical skills, which typically can be shored up through training or hiring temporary contractors.

When looking at an EHR deployment, you need to understand what the future state hardware, software, and support requirements will be. From there, you can map that to your current staff capabilities. It's not only about knowledge; it's also about staffing levels. You may have one experienced engineer who can support 14 different technologies, but that is a problem for two reasons. First, that engineer will be asked to carry a disproportionate workload, and second, you will be injecting significant risk into your organization by having just one person with a particular skill set. This scenario may mean you need to reassign work to redistribute workload and free up another one or two engineers to take on this work. It may mean you need to train existing staff in new technologies or to learn new skills. It may

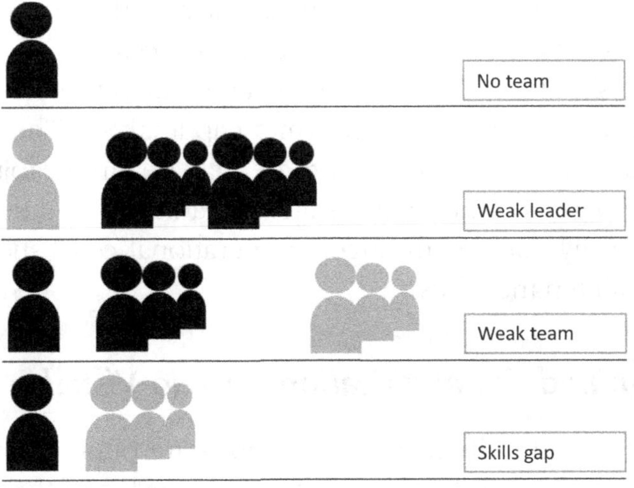

Figure 5.4 Staffing assessment example.

mean you need to add to your staff because the future state will demand far more than your current team can deliver.

It's important to differentiate between capabilities and actual staffing (usually referred to as full-time equivalents or FTEs). Being short on skills is different than being short on staff, though they often are closely related. Be sure to identify gaps in both areas so that you can address them as part of the overall EHR plan. If you don't know what the exact impact of the future state will be, you can at least identify current skills, capabilities, and constraints so that can be used as the basis of discussion as EHR future state details unfold.

Network Infrastructure (Core, Wired, Wireless)

The network infrastructure assessment is a necessary part of every EHR deployment. The network is composed of core and edge connectivity. Core connectivity refers to the hardware components that manage the entire network. This refers to how the network is designed, how it is segmented, and how it is configured for reliability and redundancy. While this is outside the direct scope of the EHR project, IT leadership should be reviewing network architecture to ensure it is prepared to deliver connectivity in the future state.

In addition, every EHR depends on network-connected devices. These are wired computers at workstations and desks or wireless devices such as laptops, tablets, and smartphones used for mobile work. It also includes additional types of devices such as printers, document scanners, or wireless bar code scanners that need to communicate across the network to the EHR system as well as network-connected medical devices.

IT leadership should assess the current state and develop a set of requirements for a future state and then perform a gap analysis. The organization should understand and recognize that there may be large capital investments required to get to a necessary state of readiness, and that those capital investments typically come with ongoing operational costs such as hardware and software maintenance fees.

Telephony, Unified Communications, Audio Visual

Though telephony and unified communications are often outside the scope of an EHR project, it's useful to keep these on your list of things to consider. With continuously evolving communications capabilities, forward-looking organizations can plan on leveraging these innovative new capabilities as part of workflow enhancement and EHR deployment. For example, nurse call systems can interface with wireless communication systems to reduce noise and more seamlessly alert nurses to patient needs. Nurse call systems can also send data into the EHR for better data on response times to patient nurse calls. Radio frequency identification systems (RFIDs) can interface with the EHR to provide detailed information on which devices were used on a patient in an OR or which care providers used proper hand hygiene methods. These types of integrations often rely on forms of telephony and other communications methods. While they may not immediately be on your roadmap, understanding your potential future state will help you assess these technologies during this process.

For some organizations, adding this element to the mix can be overwhelming and/or distracting. If that's the case, consciously choose to omit these elements from the initial discussion, but do keep them on your list so you can come back to them for Phase 2 enhancement opportunities.

Service Desk

Service desk (or help desk) considerations are often last on the list or left out completely. Make sure you include your service desk leadership in early discussions. There may be opportunities to leverage their expertise in planning activities by more clearly understanding current state (number of calls on topic A, average resolution time to issue B, etc.). In addition, you may find that you need to revamp or revise your service desk capabilities to better support a new EHR system.

When developing planning, implementation, training, and post–go live support activities, be sure to include your service desk leadership. Not only will they be able to more effectively plan for staffing and issue management but also they may provide key input on plans to avoid future problems. They are the IT staff who interact directly with all customers so they are in the best position to provide input and suggestions on many aspects of operationalizing your plan.

Data, Analytics, and Measurement Considerations

Earlier in this chapter, we discussed defining desired outcomes for your EHR system. The concept of data, analytics, and measurement may or may not have come up during your discussions. If it hasn't, you might want to pause and consider why that is. Is it because the organization is not yet data driven? Is it because everyone made some assumptions about data that would be automatically (and magically) available? Is it because no one in your organization is actually in charge of data management? There are a myriad of reasons why data, analytics, and measurement may not have been specifically discussed, but it's worth thinking this through.

In this section, we'll go over some very high level elements worth discussing. You may want or need to do further research on this topic to ensure you are architecting a solution that will lead your organization forward in this new, data-driven world of healthcare.

Data Needs

One of the key decisions you'll need to make regarding your EHR is what type of data you need to collect and when, as well as how those data will be used. What is the official source of data, how and when are they collected, and how and when are they validated? The elements that your organization deems appropriate or required for the legal medical record are not the only data elements you'll be capturing. What other data you capture, and how and why you capture them, will be part of your EHR planning sessions. However, beyond those elements, you should assess your data needs in advance (when possible) so you can avoid collecting data you'll never use or miss collecting data you need.

Remember, not all data should be part of the legal medical record. Some data may be collected and then discarded later. There may be a tendency to preserve every data point about a patient that could be collected, but that's usually not the best approach. Collecting unneeded data is a form of electronic waste and runs counter to Lean principles. Most organizations are swimming in data and the results have been mixed. Most healthcare organizations are now embarking on business intelligence (BI) path in order to more intelligently leverage the data that are being collected. The ultimate goals, of course, are to improve quality, improve patient outcomes, and reduce costs.

As you evaluate your EHR vendor's capabilities, be sure to discuss data management. Ask them how other organizations have looked at and managed the massive amount of data collected by the system.

Though you don't want to get bogged down in defining and implementing BI at the outset of your EHR project, keeping these elements in sight can help inform decisions as you go forward and enable better data management in the long term.

Reports

Reports are often overlooked by software vendors or included as an afterthought. Reporting, however, is how data collected by the system is extracted, correlated, and presented to become actionable. Reporting comes in many forms and, in more advanced organizations, it has evolved into a BI function. The EHR needs to be able to provide "out-of-the-box" reports as well as a method for customizing reports, but the organization needs to understand what types of reports it needs. There should be mechanisms for providing self-service reports (a nursing unit manager may want a real-time report of available beds, a census report, or a discharge report, for example), as well as scheduled reports such as average daily census on the unit for the month prior, supplies costs for the month prior, agency staffing costs for the prior week, etc.

Analytics and Measurement

Data are only useful when they become actionable, which is the underlying intent of BI, data analytics, and the like. Healthcare as an industry is a bit behind other industries in terms of managing and leveraging data, but it's evolving quickly. If you have adopted an EHR and are working now on either migrating to a new vendor or are working on optimization with your existing platform, you are also likely looking at data management, data warehouses, and analytics. In the coming years, IT will need to participate in the transformation to value-based care, and much of those efforts will hinge upon having quality data from the EHR and supporting systems. Figure 5.5 represents a data dashboard, which is often part of the analytics package from major EHR vendors or which can be purchased as an independent software solution.

This image of a dashboard is intended to evoke a bit of thought around how data need to be presented. Many executives want data-at-a-glance, and a dashboard is the most convenient method for providing that. How will the data elements in the dashboard be selected? What is the source of those data? How often will it be refreshed? Do all executives get the same dashboard? Can executives select data elements to customize their own dashboard?

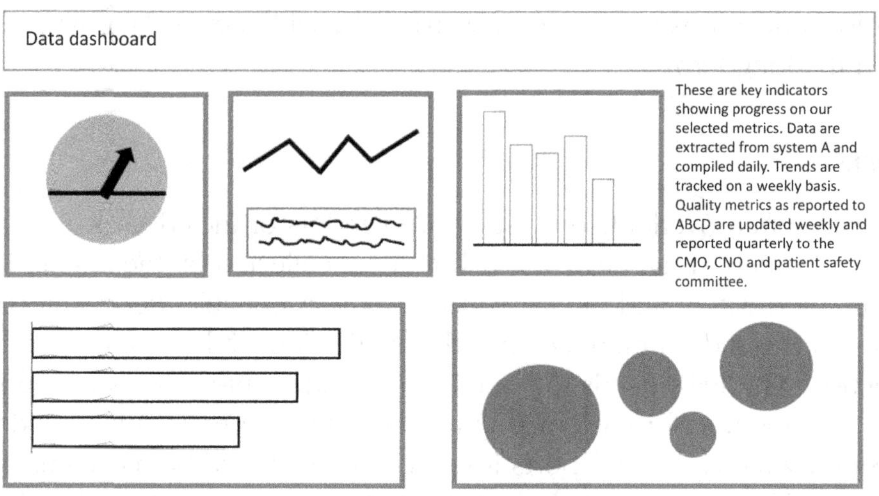

Figure 5.5 Data dashboard example.

As a healthcare organization, you should understand that developing a BI function goes far beyond a module or capability in your EHR. It is not just "another IT project" but an enterprise-wide initiative to derive actionable intelligence from business data. It's also important not to underestimate the total effort it will take to spin up this capability. While you can engage outside vendors to assist or do most of the heavy lifting, you will need to have organizational leaders engaged in defining the key questions that need to be answered, the sources of data, and the agreed upon measurements. Without a clearly defined plan, the BI efforts will fail. According to IT consulting firm Gartner, Inc., it typically takes healthcare organizations about 3 years to find out their BI efforts have failed. That's a tremendous amount of time and cost for organizations that cannot afford these kinds of missteps. Plan on spending time developing a governance structure and a plan before committing time and resources to a BI program, but do include these considerations in your EHR planning process as well (https://www.gartner.com/doc/2664433/top-actions-healthcare-delivery-organization).

BI is a broad and deep topic that we've only just touched upon. However, as you plan your EHR deployment, you should be thinking about the kinds of data your organization will need. This typically ties directly into the organization's strategic initiatives around care delivery (clinical, patient, and population) as well as business operations (financial, operational). Developing a BI capability within an organization is a large, complex undertaking; it should not be allowed to detract from your overall EHR planning.

However, to the extent you can weave in data needs as you develop your requirements, you will be better situated when you're ready to fire up your BI function.

Population Health Management and Meaningful Use

No discussion of an EHR would be complete without at least a nod toward evolving regulatory requirements. In the United States, meaningful use (MU) along with changing reimbursement models (MIPS, MACRA, etc.) need to be considered in your selection process. Each EHR vendor provides methods of addressing these requirements; not all do them equally. Understanding how your organization needs to address MU requirements as well as how your organization is (and will be) expected to interact with your community and population health initiatives is important in selecting the vendor that will meet your needs. If your organization is fairly mature in these areas, you'll have a lot of experience you can leverage in your decision-making. If, on the other hand, you are relatively new to these requirements, your first step is to improve the organizational understanding of requirements, benefits, and penalties before developing your requirements. Again, all certified EHR vendors can address these needs, so it's a matter of understanding who can best meet the specific needs of your organization. These requirements will vary country by country, and state by state. The approach toward meeting these requirements remains the same.

EHR Funding

Throughout this chapter, we've discussed various methods of gathering and analyzing data related to selecting an EHR vendor. As you can see, we have stayed away from talking about specific attributes of any EHR vendor for obvious reasons. Your best opportunity for success is to evaluate your organization before reviewing EHR solutions. If you listen to the sales pitches for EHR vendors and then decide to do internal evaluation, you're likely to be swayed by the vendor pitches. You want to determine what you need and then compare that to vendor offerings.

Regardless, you will finally come to a place where you have to talk about funding. We discussed the potential ROI (and related pitfalls) in Chapter 3, but we didn't talk about how you go about funding your EHR project.

This section will not magically solve your funding problems. The intent is simply to remind you that this is a topic that requires serious discussion. The cost of the EHR software is just one of many costs related to implementing an EHR. In this chapter, we've pointed out numerous sources of cost—hardware, software, staffing, etc. It's likely that this project is will be one of the most expensive IT-related projects the organization has ever undertaken.

As you saw in Chapter 3, some organizations have spent hundreds of millions of dollars on these implementations. Most were probably not sitting on a pile of cash that size and needed to go acquire funding. The financial vehicles companies use can be varied and complex, and a discussion of these is outside the scope of this book. However, you should be deciding how you will pay these costs as you're discussing this massive undertaking. Ensure you have developed at least an order of magnitude estimate of all costs and that the financial arm of your organization is closely involved in understanding cost and developing an adequate (and timely) source of funding.

EHR Selection—Requirements and Selection Criteria

As we mentioned at the outset of this chapter, we waited to discuss requirements and selection criteria for the EHR until after we had gone through the information presented thus far. As you begin to narrow the field of potential EHR vendors, you will need to develop high-level objectives (what problem are you trying to solve, or what outcomes do you expect to achieve), which will turn into requirements for selection criteria. For most organizations, the list includes items like

- Improved patient care
- Improved care coordination
- Practice efficiencies and cost savings
- Improved patient participation
- Improved diagnostics and patient outcomes
- Improved provider efficiency or utilization
- Reduced length of stay, reduced readmissions
- Reduced costs
- Improved revenue cycle (fewer AR days, for example)

Because you've worked on your assessment, engaged stakeholders, and developed requirements for project outcomes, you should be pretty well set to develop your project requirements (if not already complete) and your EHR selection criteria.

Selection criteria become much easier to develop when you've done all the preliminary planning steps. Selection criteria line up with project elements. You can create a matrix that lists criteria in the left column and the various vendors along the top row. Each of the selection criteria is fully or partially met by the vendor, or it is absent. Therefore, you could use fully, partial, and no and score each of those. For example, an attribute that is fully present gets a score of 5. Each attribute that is partially present gets a score of 3. Each attribute that is not present gets a score of 0. Potentially, if it's a key attribute, you could use a negative score that would reduce the overall score accordingly.

Typical core functionality (which become requirements) is often defined by these eight categories:

1. Health information and data
2. Order entry
3. Medication management
4. Results management
5. Decision support
6. Patient support/engagement
7. Reporting
8. Population health

While you may define additional categories, this list will get you started. Whatever method you use, you should define your selection criteria and evaluate each vendor's offerings against those criteria. Most organizations are able to make informed and ultimately successful selection decisions after working through this type of process. For more guidance on selecting an EHR vendor, you can refer to the HIMSS article "EHR Vendor Selection: The 5-Step Guide" (http://www.himss.org/news/ehr-vendor-selection-5-step-guide, May 2011). There are numerous online resources available to assist in developing selection criteria for various types of organizations (hospitals, physician office, etc.).

Most organizations will select some, or all, of the following as criteria in their selection process:

1. Software module capabilities (does everything we need it to do).
2. Software vendor reputation (quality of product, service, support).
3. Software vendor interoperability (interfaces or integrates with other systems).
4. Software vendor solution cost (software, ongoing maintenance, and support costs).
5. Licensing model (per user, per location, enterprise).
6. Scalability (can grow as we grow).
7. Hardware and infrastructure requirements and compatibility (implementation model, cost to implement, and impact on existing capital investments).
8. End-user needs are met (patient, provider, business, partners).
9. Future state capabilities (software roadmap has future features of interest).
10. Likelihood of solution to advance patient care, improve outcomes, and lower costs.
11. Feedback and recommendations from current customers.

Pugh Selection Method

A framework that is commonly used in Lean organizations to determine (select) the best option against a large set of deliverables is known as the Pugh method. "The decision-matrix method, also Pugh method or Pugh Concept Selection, invented by Stuart Pugh, is a qualitative technique used to rank the multi-dimensional options of an option set. It is frequently used in engineering for making design decisions but can also be used to rank investment options, vendor options, product options or any other set of multidimensional entities" (https://en.wikipedia.org/wiki/Decision-matrix-method). In our case, we will be using the Pugh method to rank vendor options in the selection of our electronic health record. This is shown in Table 5.3 and we'll discuss the elements next.

We begin by adding the evaluation criteria on the left-hand side of our matrix. Keep in mind that these criteria can and should be tailored to your organization's needs. Next, we add the vendors we would like to evaluate in our EHR selection process. These are added across the top of the matrix from left to right. Our matrix is now almost ready for evaluation as shown in Table 5.3.

Table 5.3 Pugh Matrix with Evaluation Criteria and Vendors

Evaluation Criteria	*Weight*	*Vendor A*	*Vendor B*	*Vendor C*	*Vendor D*	*Vendor E*
1. Software module capability						
2. Software vendor reputation						
3. Software vendor interoperability						
4. Software vendor solution cost						
5. Licensing model						
6. Scalability						
7. Hardware/ infrastructure compatibility						
8. End-user needs met						
9. Future state capabilities						
10. Likelihood to deliver outcomes						
11. References from other users/ organizations						
Total						

One of the common mistakes organizations make when completing evaluations with decision matrixes is they give equal weighting to all the criteria. Of these 11 criteria, it is likely some of these are more important than the others. The Pugh method allows you to weight your criteria prior to scoring. The weighting allows for the criteria you deem to be the most important to have a bigger impact than those that are less important.

A common approach is to spread 100 points across the various criteria. For the purposes of our evaluation, let's assume criteria 10, 3, and 4 are the most important. We will assign 15 points to each of these criteria. Criteria

1, 8, and 7 are the next most important criteria to our organization. We will assign 10 points to each of these. And the remaining criteria are equally important, so they will be assigned 5 points each. Using this approach, some criteria are now weighted three times heavier than others. Our matrix now looks like the one shown in Table 5.4.

The next step in making our selection is to rank how well each of the individual criteria is met on a vendor-by-vendor basis. This process is known as coming up with the contribution. Contribution is calculated by ranking how well the vendor meets the specific criteria. Let's proceed with an example. First we will evaluate the software module capability of vendor A. We rank the ability of the vendor to meet our specifications on a score of 0 to 5,

Table 5.4 Pugh Matrix with Weighted Evaluation Criteria

Evaluation Criteria	*Weight*	*Vendor A*	*Vendor B*	*Vendor C*	*Vendor D*	*Vendor E*
1. Software module capability	10					
2. Software vendor reputation	5					
3. Software vendor interoperability	15					
4. Software vendor solution cost	15					
5. Licensing model	5					
6. Scalability	5					
7. Hardware/ infrastructure compatibility	10					
8. End-user needs met	10					
9. Future state capabilities	5					
10. Likelihood to deliver outcomes	15					
11. References from other users/ organizations	5					
Total	100					

0 points being assigned if the vendor meets none of the requirements and 5 points being assigned if the vendor has maximum ability to meet all the specifications.

After evaluating our vendor, we find that they can meet a few more than half of the capabilities we desire, so we will assign them a ranking of 3. To get the contribution, simply multiply the ranking times the weighting. In this case, 3(ranking) × 10(weighting) yields a contribution of 30. It is recommended that you do the evaluation one vendor at a time, and rank the evaluation criteria by going down the matrix from criterion 1 to criterion 11. Table 5.5 shows our ranking and contribution for vendor A.

Table 5.5 Ranking the Criteria for Vendor A and Determining Contribution

Evaluation Criteria	*Weight*	*Vendor A*	*Vendor B*	*Vendor C*	*Vendor D*	*Vendor E*
1. Software module capability	10	3/10				
2. Software vendor reputation	5	4 /20				
3. Software vendor interoperability	15	5 /75				
4. Software vendor solution cost	15	1 /15				
5. Licensing model	5	2 /10				
6. Scalability	5	4 /20				
7. Hardware/ infrastructure compatibility	10	4 /40				
8. End-user needs met	10	3 /30				
9. Future state capabilities	5	0 /0				
10. Likelihood to deliver outcomes	15	3 /45				
11. References from other users/ organizations	5	3 /15				
Total	100					

Ranking from 0 to 5

Contribution = Ranking × Weighting

The evaluation will continue until all of the vendors are ranked against all of the criteria, and the contribution calculations are completed.

The final piece of the evaluation is to calculate the total score for each vendor. This is done by summing the contribution for each vendor. For vendor A, the sum of the contribution is 280. Table 5.6 shows what the matrix looks like when the ranking and scoring are completed.

Once the scoring in our example is completed, we find that vendor E has a total of 240 points on the low end, while vendor C scores the highest at 330 points. Using our Pugh analysis, vendors D and E should be eliminated from further analysis and vendors A, B, and C be reevaluated. After negations, I would reevaluate the vendors and select the vendor with

Table 5.6 Pugh Matrix with Scoring Completed

Evaluation Criteria	*Weight*	*Vendor A*	*Vendor B*	*Vendor C*	*Vendor D*	*Vendor E*
1. Software module capability	10	3 / 10	1//10	5 / 50	2 / 20	4 / 40
2. Software vendor reputation	5	4 /20	5 /25	1 / 5	4 / 20	2 / 10
3. Software vendor interoperability	15	5 /75	2 / 30	3 / 45	3 / 45	0 / 0
4. Software vendor solution cost	15	1 /15	4 / 60	4 / 60	1 / 15	1 / 15
5. Licensing model	5	2 /10	3 / 15	2 / 10	0 / 0	3 / 15
6. Scalability	5	4 /20	1 / 5	5 / 25	2 /10	4 / 20
7. Hardware/ infrastructure compatibility	10	4 /40	5 / 50	0 / 0	4 / 40	2 / 20
8. End-user needs met	10	3 /30	2 /30	3 / 30	3 / 30	5 / 50
9. Future state capabilities	5	0 /0	4 / 20	4 / 20	1 / 5	1 / 5
10. Likelihood to deliver outcomes	15	3 /45	3 / 45	4 / 60	5 / 75	3 / 45
11. References from other users/ organizations	5	3 /15	1 / 5	5 / 25	2 / 10	4 / 20
Total	100	280	295	330	270	240

the highest overall score. The Pugh analysis makes the evaluation process completely objective. It removes emotions, relationships, and prior history from the evaluation allowing for your organization to select the best solution.

Chapter Summary

- We focused this chapter on the concepts and activities involved in selecting an EHR vendor, whether you're lighting up a new system or migrating from one to another.
- Hospital and clinic decision processes are sometimes different, and we highlighted key differences.
- We started with the patient perspective to ensure that we drive value through the selection process.
- Organizational and operational requirements must be fully understood and documented in order to make an informed EHR decision.
- Evaluating interfaces and system integration needs during your selection process will help ensure you design the solution with the critical interconnections in mind.
- Hardware and infrastructure considerations include types of systems and infrastructure in place compared to what your potential EHR vendors may require. The impact of these decisions may be the type of software solution you select as well as the overall cost of the project.
- Organizational strategies will inform the future state of the company and therefore must be included in your EHR selection as much as possible to avoid dead-end solutions.
- Data needs must also be defined during the EHR selection process. Understanding the data you expect to have in your system, how they will be presented and reported, and how you want to use those data for things like analytics and population health initiatives is important in the EHR selection phase.
- The total cost of the EHR implement can run in the tens of millions to hundreds of millions of dollars. Understanding how the organization will obtain funding for this project should be part of your planning process.
- We covered EHR requirements and selection criteria to wrap up your EHR selection process. While every organization will have different criteria, having a defined selection process will standardize the work and

ensure you've done everything possible to select the right solution for your organization.

- The Pugh method can be used as a very systematic way to select your EHR vendor.

Further Reading

Busch R, M S. *Leveraging Data in Healthcare: Best Practices for Controlling, Analyzing, and Using Data.* CRC Press, Boca Raton, FL, 2015.

Gensinger R, Melton G, Ott K, Smaltz H, Garets D, Van Norman S, Wells N, Adams J, Simon G. *Analytics in Healthcare: An Introduction.* HIMSS Publishing, Chicago, IL, 2014.

Health Level 7 International (HL7), "EHR product matrix," http://www.hl7.org/implement/standards/product_matrix.cfm?Family=EHR, May 2016 (accessed July 11, 2017).

Health Level 7 International (HL7), "EHR definitional model," prepared by HIMSS Electronic Health Record Committee, Thomas Handler, MD, Research Director, Gartner, https://www.hl7.org/documentcenter/public/wg/ehr/archives/030616-EHR%20Definitional%20Model%20Version%201.doc, 2010 (accessed July 11, 2017).

HIMSS, "Business intelligence," http://www.himss.org/library/clinical-business-intelligence/ (accessed July 12, 2017).

HIMSS, "EHR vendor selection: The 5-step guide," http://www.himss.org/news/ehr-vendor-selection-5-step-guide, May 2011.

HIMSS, "RFP sample documents," http://www.himss.org/rfp-sample-documents-0, 2010, (accessed July 12, 2017).

McKinney C, Hess R, Whitecar M. *Implementing Business Intelligence in Your Healthcare Organization.* HIMSS Publishing, Chicago, IL, 2012.

New York State Office of Mental Health, Request for Proposal (RFP)/C009999, For the Procurement of Electronic Medical Record (EMR), https://www.omh.ny.gov/omhweb/rfp/2011/emr/EMRRFP.pdf, 2011 (accessed July 11, 2017).

Shaffer V, Beyer MA. "Top Actions for Healthcare Delivery Organization CIOs, 2014: Avoid 25 Years of Mistakes in Enterprise Data Warehousing," February 10, 2014, Article ID G00261429, https://www.gartner.com/doc/2664433/top-actions-healthcare-delivery-organization (accessed July 11, 2017).

Snedaker S, Rima C. *Business Continuity and Disaster Recovery Planning for IT Professionals, Second Edition.* Elsevier Press, Waltham, MA, 2014.

Chapter 6

Lean Project Management

Deploying the Electronic Health Record as a Project

Now that you have selected your vendor, it is time to begin the work to develop and deploy your electronic health record. The tried and true phases of deploying IT functionality and hardware will apply to this project. A project begins with requirements definition. To deliver an EHR in the least waste way, we should know what to build before we build it.

Great designs, delivered on time and on budget, come from having well-scoped requirements. Once the requirements are defined, the project will move into the design-and-build phase. It is here where the detailed functionality is configured, interfaces are designed, and electronic and physical workflows are created.

Following the design-and-build phase, great projects undergo a rigorous testing and user acceptance process. Technical testing, unit testing, and integrated testing are performed to ensure that the requirements are all met. When the system functionality and hardware requirements are met, go live activities can occur.

Go live activities can be planned concurrently with user testing and acceptance. Key elements of go live planning include readiness planning to ensure resources, training, and trouble-shooting resources are on hand. A command center needs to be established with standard work to route, triage, and resolve issues found at the time of go live. Transition implementation practices need to be established to migrate from a paper-based system to an electronic system. Criteria need to be established to determine objectively when to decommission the implementation support and training resources.

And there needs to be a formal requirements validation process to ensure the high-level requirements of the EHR system have all been satisfactorily met.

The art of developing and deploying your Lean EHR is not in completing these tasks, as many organizations deliver IT solutions through these phases every day. We are tasked, rather, with two goals in deploying our Lean EHR: delivering a value-added product that works well *and* delivering this product in the least waste way. Project and product speed, cost, and efficiency are irrelevant if the system fails to deliver safer care, improved organizational efficiencies, better security of information, less handling, etc. Conversely, if we deliver a wonderful solution, but it goes way over budget and takes years to deliver, the project will also be deemed less than successful.

Deploying a Lean EHR is a project. The great news for all of us is that a Lean tool exists that allows project work to be done in a Lean way, delivering both compelling value and minimizing wasted time and activity within the project. If we look at any project through a Lean lens, can we identify waste? Let's review the seven wastes and determine if they exist in the activities of an IT project. Examples are provided in Table 6.1.

The difference in applying Lean to a project and applying Lean to a process is the waste doesn't yet exist, we can't see the waste in a project until it shows up. So, the approach used in Lean project management is to anticipate the waste and design it out of the project. Lean organizations use a tool

Table 6.1 Waste Found in IT Projects

Waste	*Project Examples*
Waiting	• Waiting on people, information, decisions, approvals, resources, equipment, vendors, etc
Motion	• Staff movement traveling to meetings, work areas, and training sessions • Looking for resource documents, files, and folders
Inventory	• Tasks waiting to be worked on, modules waiting to be deployed • Decisions and approvals waiting to be made
Transportation	• Movement of information • Movement of equipment
Overprocessing	• Designing and building functionality beyond customer value
Overproduction	• Designing and building something prior to the requirements being defined
Defects	• Items defined, built, and tested that do not meet customer requirements

Phase 1										
	Customers		Project team					Suppliers		Standard work
Time	X	Y	MD	RN	PM	IT	IPAC	D	E	
5 days					Task	1	1	1		Not in place
			Task		2		2	2		In place
			Task		3					In place
			4		Task					In place
3 days					Task	5	5	5		In place
1 day			6		6	Task	6			N/A
3 weeks			7	7	7	Task	7	7		Not in place
3 weeks	8				8	Task		8		Draft
	9			9			Tollgate review	9		
						Inputs		Outputs		

Figure 6.1 Lean project management—vertical Gantt chart.

that operates like a vertical Gantt chart to manage projects. Using such a system, the project moves through several distinct phases and passes clearly defined "tollgates" before moving to the next phase. A simple example of the Lean project management approach is shown in Figure 6.1.

Key Steps in Lean Project Management

Listed below is a simple overview of the key steps in applying Lean project management.

1. Identify a representative sample of the key stakeholders who will define requirements, design, build, test, deploy, and use the EHR.
2. Assign the end date for the project.
3. Define the key phases the project will go through. A project phase is a key body of work in which we answer key questions about the project.

Answers to these questions become specifications that move through the project. Each phase will end with a tollgate in which we validate if the questions have been satisfactorily answered.

4. Develop the criteria for passing each milestone (tollgate). Criteria are questions that must be answered before moving to the next phase of the project. Tollgate examples are shown in Table 6.2.

Table 6.2 Example of Project Tollgates and Criteria

Tollgate	*Input Criteria*
Requirements definition tollgate	• Patient information needs have been identified • EHR modules are selected • Technical interfaces have been defined • Hardware platforms have been selected • Pilot areas to be used in design and build are defined • Super users have been identified
Design and build tollgate	• Gaps between current process and new EHR functionality are known • Physical workflows are defined • Standard work is in place to support physical and electronic workflows • Electronic workflows have been configured • Interfaces are defined • Information is accurate • Information is secure
Testing and user acceptance	• Technical testing meets requirements • User training plan is in place • Unit testing meets requirements • Integrated testing meets requirements • Users have been trained • Go live readiness has been planned • Transition planning is complete • Standard work to support transition is written • Command center staffing is defined • Command center standard work practices are defined • Go live support resources are identified • Decommission plan for go live resources is documented

Go live tollgate	• Safety issues have been mitigated
	• Critical requirements have been met
	  • System reliability
	  • System response time
	  • Data integrity

5. Determine the tasks needed to pass the tollgate.
6. Assign accountability for the tasks to meet tollgate criteria. (A great benefit from Lean project management is the visual map that clearly details exactly who needs to be involved with each key step and when.)
7. Execute the tasks needed to meet the tollgate.
8. Hold a formal review to confirm that the tollgate criteria have been met before beginning to work on the next phase of the project plan.
9. Capture lessons learned from the tollgate reviews to improve the organizational knowledge.
10. Repeat steps 7, 8, and 9 for each phase of the project until the project is completed.

Now that you have a high-level understanding of the Lean project management approach, let's expand the key steps. The Lean project management process is applied using highly sophisticated tools: butcher paper, sticky notes, and markers. The process starts by putting butcher paper on a wall and assembling the team that will be doing the work.

Identify a Representative Sample of the Key Stakeholders Who Will Design, Build, Test, Deploy, and Use the EHR

What we are assembling first is the team of resources needed to complete the project. The team will be composed of three sets of stakeholders; each stakeholder will have a role to play in developing and deploying the EHR. The first stakeholder group is the project team. This group will consist of IT resources, clinicians, administrative personnel, and management. This group will coordinate and complete the activities necessary to deploy the functionality and hardware.

The second group of stakeholders is the customer group. These are the stakeholders that will be receiving the outputs of the new EHR. At the highest level, there are three main customer groups. The first customer group consists of patients and care givers. The second customer group consists of organizations that receive either patients and/or their information like community agencies, nursing homes and rehab centers, and primary care physicians. The third customer group consists of the users of the system. This group includes allied professionals, doctors, nurses, and administrative personnel such as registration, bed placement, and billers and coders that will be using the system.

The third group of stakeholders consists of suppliers. The supplier stakeholder group, at a minimum, includes your vendor base necessary to make the EHR deployment a success. There will be many vendors engaged in the project, including hardware vendors, outsourced IT resources (if used), the EHR vendor, and third-party systems vendors such as bolt on scheduling software. Another commonly used supplier is a system integrator and their consultants used to configure, test, and deploy your EHR. Suppliers can also include third-party trainers and training module writers. What is important is to anticipate which suppliers will be needed to operationalize your new system so they can be available and included in discussions in a timely manner to allow your project to flow without interruption.

Assign the End Date for the Project

Lean project management uses a backward planning process. So, all activities, resources, and plans will be scheduled backward from the culmination of the go live phase.

Define the Key Phases the Project Will Go Through

For an EHR deployment, like most IT projects, the phases will generally be a Requirements Definition phase, a Design and Build phase, a Testing and User Acceptance phase, and a go live phase. Your project might have some variation to these themes, but a key point here is that you will want to ensure your project has no more than five phases in total. Each phase will end with a tollgate (also called a milestone). While the four elements of a Lean IT project are listed above as the core phases of a project, it is not uncommon to have a Vendor Selection phase as a fifth phase if you are acquiring a new system. In our vertical Gantt chart, the phases would be documented like the one shown in Figure 6.2. The project is mapped from top to bottom as opposed to left to right. Therefore, it is called a vertical Gantt chart. We map from top to bottom because there is finality when we get to the floor; we can't extend the map out onto the tile. We are out of time when our plan meets the floor and this is the date we have set for completing the EHR deployment.

When we map left to right, we are building a traditional Gantt chart. In a normal project, we extend the date by moving the project timeliness to the right. The vertical planning is designed to change our paradigm. It is *never* okay in a Lean organization to miss a due date.

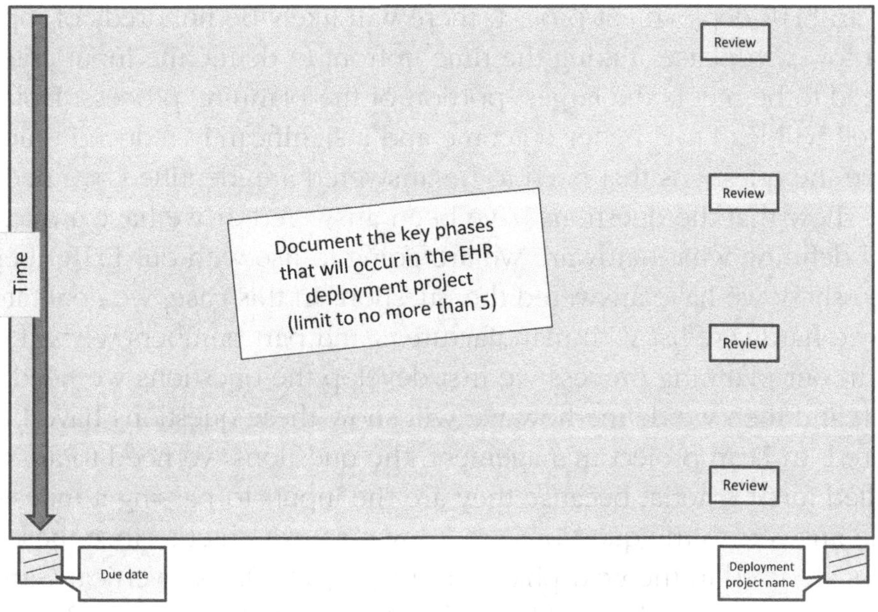

Figure 6.2 Project phases shown as reviews.

Develop the Criteria for Passing Each Tollgate and Define the Evidence Needed to Verify the Criteria Has Been Met

Criteria are questions that must be answered, and/or measurable outcomes of process/results that must be met before moving to the next phase of the project. Think of these criteria as go/no go criteria. If we do not have an answer to these questions, we do not proceed with the next body of work.

Why is this important? A large cause of project cost, rework, and timeline delays in any project is doing work on unclear requirements. If we start on designing and building functionality before we have confirmed the requirements, we run an inherent risk of rework because what we are designing and building can change as the requirements get defined. Regrettably this happens every day in IT projects. And we know why this occurs! Generally, to make the project schedule.

Another benefit of having clearly identified questions answered is that we only resource and schedule activity to answer these questions specifically. This ensures the majority of the project is value-added because tasks will *not* appear in the plan unless they are directly tied to answering a question. Think today about your IT projects; how many unnecessary tasks are built into your current planning process?

For an EHR deployment project, there will likely be hundreds of input criteria for each phase. Taking the time upfront to define the input criteria that need to be met is the largest portion of the planning process. Doing this step well will lead to a better outcome and a significantly reduced timeline.

Once the questions that need to be answered are identified, we need a way to show that the questions have been answered. If we have a question around defining what hardware we are going to use with our EHR, then we need to show we have answered the question. In this case, we generate an approved hardware list with manufacturer's and part numbers we will be using. In our planning process we first develop the questions we need to answer, and then we define how we will show these questions have been answered. In Lean project management, the questions we need to answer are called input criteria, because they are the inputs to passing a milestone, and the answers to the questions are known as exit criteria since these answers are used in the next phase of our project. On our vertical Gantt chart, the tollgate criteria would look like those listed in Figure 6.3.

Another consideration at this point of your planning process is to define if you will have any freeze points. Freeze points lock in specifications and requirements that will not be changed later in the project. For example, if hardware will be frozen after the question of which hardware we will be using is answered, then this decision cannot be changed later.

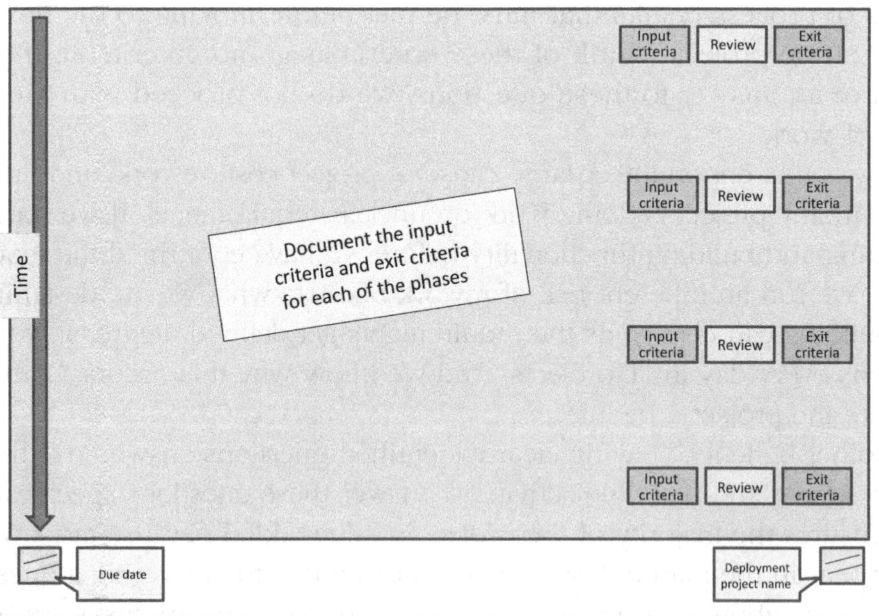

Figure 6.3 Tollgate criteria.

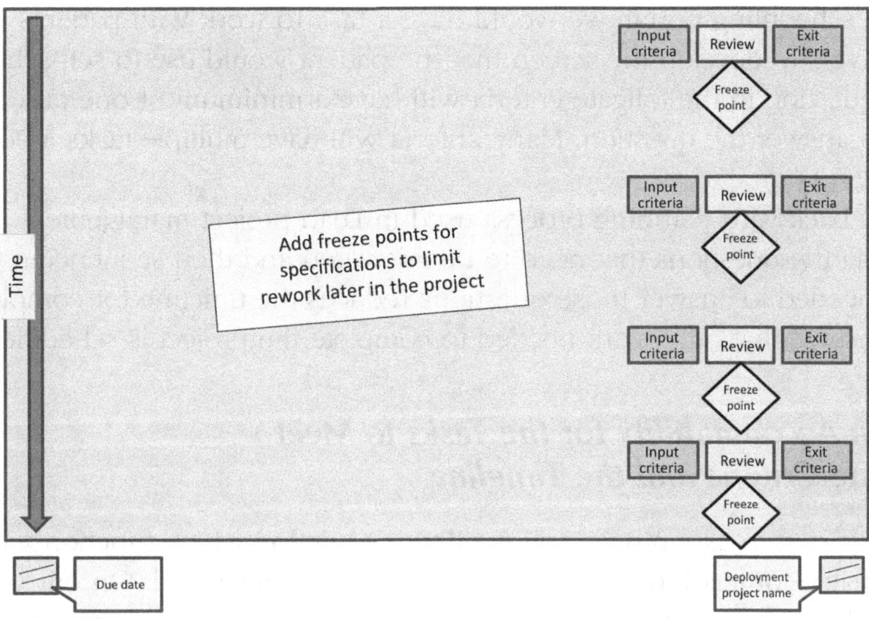

Figure 6.4 Freeze points.

Let's assume the team agrees that documentation will occur in the clinical exam room. From this decision, the team agrees that they will be using tablets to complete the documentation. If this is the case, the design team will begin to design, configure, and build the software to operate on a tablet. Later in the process, while in testing, a physician says he would like to document on his cell phone. If the hardware specification is frozen, the option of documenting on a cell phone is out of scope. We would not go back to design and build to enable this capability. This would slow down the project considerably.

Another example of a freeze point in an EHR deployment might include clinical documentation standards. Once the team agrees to these standards in the design phase, it becomes difficult and expensive to change them in the test or go live phases. On our vertical Gantt chart, freeze points would be documented as shown in Figure 6.4.

Determine the Tasks Needed to Pass the Tollgate

Once the questions that need to be answered are defined, the next task is to determine the work it will take to answer those questions. In Lean project management, we call this body of work *project tasks*. If we have a question that needs to be answered, such as define what the customer wants to see on the scheduling portal, we would have a task to work with patients and care givers to develop the screen that the patient would use to self-schedule. Each question in the tollgate criteria will have a minimum of one task necessary to answer the question. Many criteria will have multiple tasks associated with it.

The backward planning process used in Lean project management of defining the questions that need to be answered and then sequencing the tasks needed to answer those questions reduces the timeline for completion and ensures that only work needed to complete the project is scheduled.

Assign Accountability for the Tasks to Meet Tollgate Criteria and the Timeline

The first step in assigning accountability is to define which function will be responsible for leading the team to get a question answered. On our vertical Gantt chart, this activity would be documented as shown in Figure 6.5.

Different tasks require different expertise, so we want to ensure that the different tasks have different leads. A common mistake is to give the lead responsibility for all the tasks to a project manager. This process will ensure

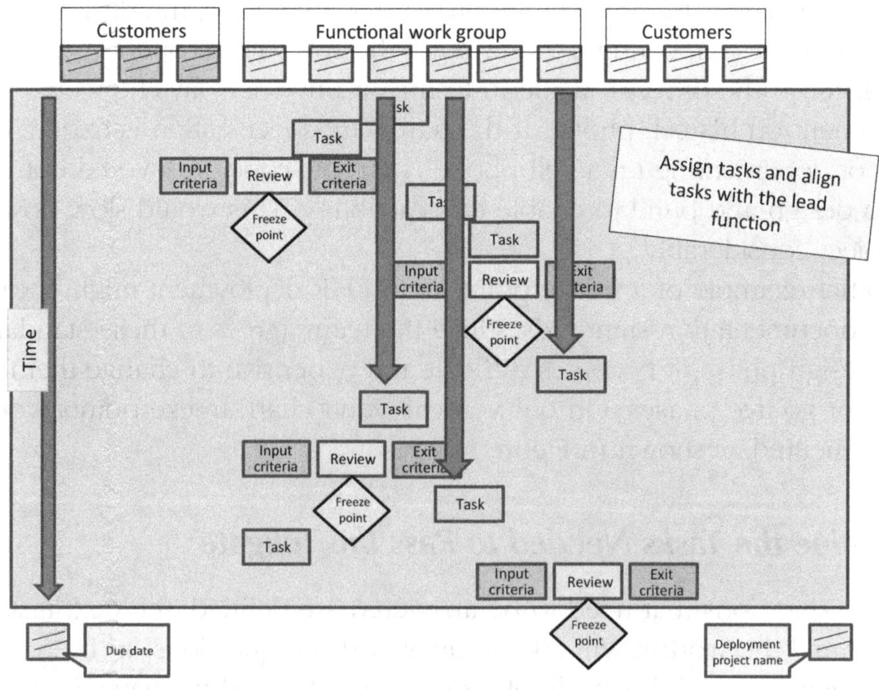

Figure 6.5 Assigning the lead for the tasks.

less accountability for getting tasks done and a slower project, funneling all the work through a single resource.

Once the tasks have been defined, the next critical step is to identify the functions that are needed to collaborate on the tasks. Very few tasks can be completed in a vacuum. For each task, look across the customer, the design team, and the supplier functions and identify who is needed to successfully answer the question.

Using Lean management techniques, we want to complete the work in the least wasteful way. Knowing who we need and when is critical to keeping the project on time and not wasting critical resources. Common mistakes found in Lean IT projects include both not having the right people in the room and having too many unnecessary people in the room. This approach assures the exact people requirements are identified up-front.

When the task leads are assigned and the team members needed to collaborate on answering the issues to advance the project are identified, you are now ready to schedule the project. Using the thinking in Lean project management, we want to deploy concurrent engineering principles in the scheduling of the work. Said differently, we want to schedule tasks to run concurrently instead of in series. This shortens the timeline for our project.

The other consideration when putting the timeline together is making sure the schedule will hit the target end date. When you backward-plan, you will soon find a task or series of tasks that will not be capable of hitting their timeline. In a Lean organization, if we are doing this work over and over, we would perform process improvement on this task and reduce the timeline by eliminating some waste in the process. In an EHR deployment, you will likely only get one opportunity to do this task, so running a kaizen event might not be possible. One possible approach is to schedule the cross-functional team meeting and hold a session to ask for ideas on what can be done to hit the timeline. Add these ideas into the standard work for completing the task.

We need to be careful not to extend the timeline based on *personal preference*. To keep the project on time, the correct resources need to be made available to make decisions and answer questions. Attendance at scheduled tasks is mandatory. Individual preference for attendance must be secondary to the project. Great Lean organizations prioritize the EHR task completion activity over all others. Look at this problem through a different lens. An EHR deployment is going to run in the tens of thousands of dollars for a physician practice to millions of dollars for a healthcare organization. If it were your business, would it be acceptable to allow one person to delay a multimillion-dollar project? On our vertical Gantt chart, the timeline is shown in Figure 6.6.

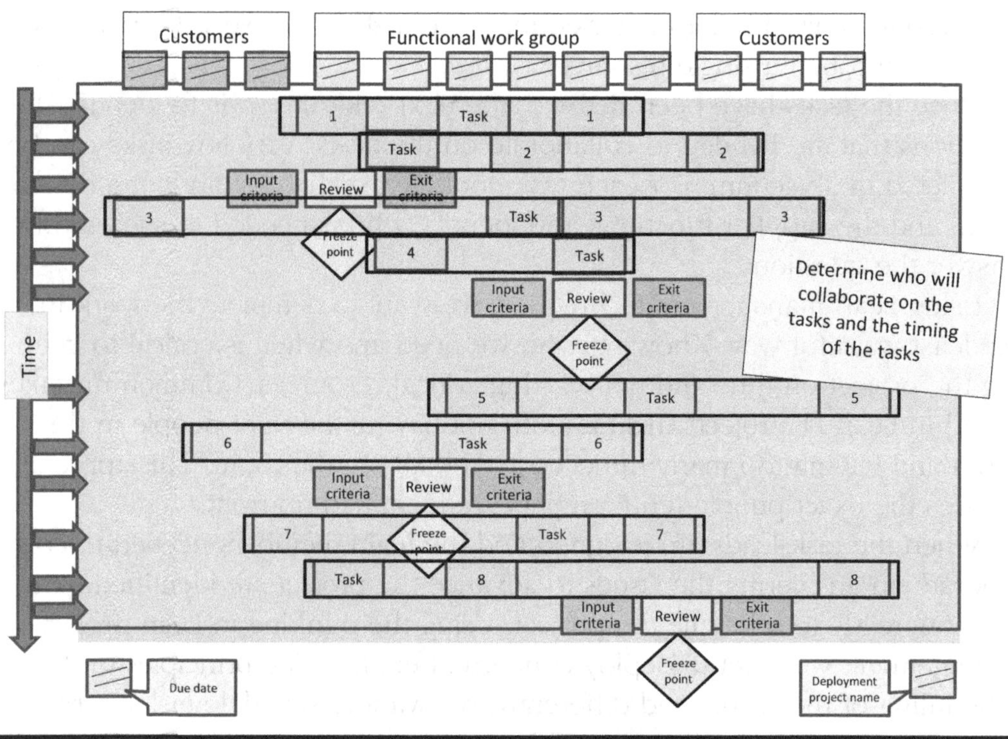

Figure 6.6 Timelines and collaborators on tasks are defined.

Execute the Tasks Needed to Meet the Tollgate

Now that we have built the plan, it's time to execute the plan. Lean organizations establish a meeting room, or rooms, for the team to meet to complete their tasks. This room in Lean organizations is known as *Obeya*. This loosely translates in Japanese to "big room." The room is designed in a way to allow the team members assigned to tasks to do their work on the project.

The team, led by the assigned functional leader, arrives at Obeya on the date scheduled in the planning session and completes their task or tasks. From the planning session, it should be crystal clear who is needed to complete the task in flow. Having the right people there should eliminate the waste of e-mailing people and waiting for feedback and responses.

The question that needs to be answered by the team to correctly complete the task is also known, as is the documented evidence that the task has been completed. When the task is completed (the question is answered), and the documented evidence is in place of what the answer is, the team disassembles and the next team comes to the room to complete their task.

In a world-class organization, the project plan is managed using another highly sophisticated tool—two pieces of string. One piece of string hung across the vertical Gantt chart identifies where the project is relative to the completion of tasks, and the other piece of string identifies where the project should be according to the planned date. An example of project tracking performed on the vertical Gantt chart is shown in Figure 6.7.

All significant IT projects have an IT project manager. In a large EHR deployment, many organizations also have an EHR project manager. Sometimes this role is the same person; however, sometimes it is not. The role of the EHR project manager in this process is to manage the vertical Gantt chart (schedule) and resources to ensure the project stays on time and the tasks are being completed correctly.

Another key responsibility of the project manager is to ensure a knowledge management system is in place to capture notes and decisions. For many EHR installations, the EHR vendor will have templates and tools to capture the decisions and requirements. If these don't exist, this responsibility will fall on the project manager to ensure information and decisions are retained and accessible when needed.

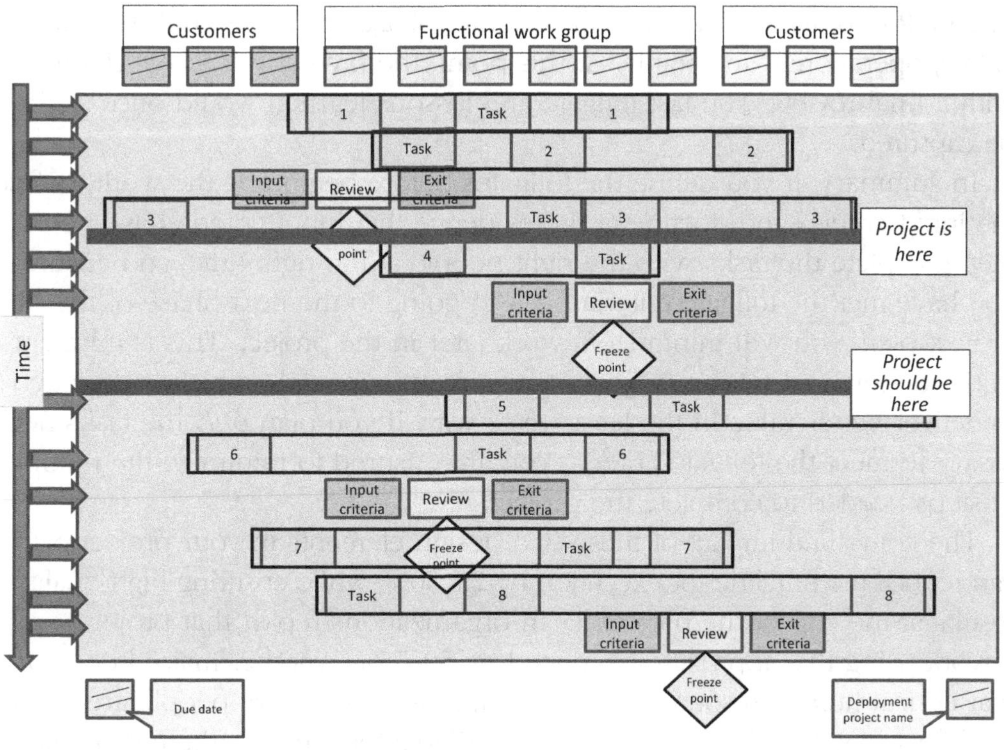

Figure 6.7 Managing the project.

Hold a Formal Review to Confirm That the Tollgate Criteria Have Been Met

Once all the tasks have been completed for a phase, the next step in our Lean project management planning process is to hold the tollgate review. It is at this point that the project team validates that all the questions have been answered and the project is ready to move to the next stage. If you followed the process, you should know the questions have been answered as there should be documented evidence. What you are covering in the review is a final validation that the tasks have been completed and an assessment of any risks you need to mitigate as you move to the next phase of the project.

This review should end with a compilation of lessons learned. Many IT projects are iterative in nature, and you should capture important organizational knowledge that will ensure better outcomes, or less waiting or rework, on future projects.

Repeat Steps 7, 8, and 9 for Each Phase of the Project Until the Project is Completed

The EHR deployment project will continue phase by phase until the system is live, operational, and stable. At this point, the project would conclude with a final review. The last tollgate and lessons learned would once again be captured.

In summary, if you define the tollgates before beginning the work, define the input criteria and document the evidence that input criteria have been met, complete the tasks with the right people at the right time, and ensure you have met the tollgate criteria prior to going to the next phase of the project plan, you will minimize rework later in the project. This is inherent in the design of the Lean project management approach, which is designed to deliver better value in the least waste way. If you plan *only* the tasks necessary to meet the tollgate criteria, you are ensured to minimize the number of steps needed to complete the project.

The combined impact of these two design elements in your project plan can reduce the timeline for execution by 25–50%, while ensuring high-quality results at the end of the project. Lean organizations report that project rework using this approach is reduced by 50–75%. Another major benefit is that critical human resources are freed up. Only necessary people are scheduled for tasks. People not needed are available for other work, and simultaneously the team is not held waiting on an individual.

There is a reason that world-class Lean organizations deliver products and services to the marketplace in half the time of their competitors. They know, understand, and have mastered the skills of Lean project management and utilize the vertical Gantt chart to plan and manage their project.

EHR Deployment Governance

Thus far, we have discussed managing the EHR as a project, and little of this book has been devoted to governance of the project. Lean organizations govern the project through strict adherence to meeting milestones and capturing lessons learned. The tollgate reviews are generally attended by IT, operational, administrative, and EHR vendor leadership. In the spirit of following the Lean principle of managing visually, everyone should be able to see the exact status of the project in real time by looking at the vertical Gantt chart.

Project management should be empowered to call a meeting with leadership if the timelines for the task completion get too far off track. Additional meetings are non-value added and Lean organizations strive to minimize this activity.

If you are deploying your EHR in a clinic environment, the same principles apply, but your vertical Gantt chart is going to have fewer tasks. As a physician practice owner, you should likewise be able to see the status of the project at a glance.

There is another layer of governance that sits on top of governance of an EHR deployment, that being the organizational governance of IT and data. This is critical in managing the technology roadmap that should be in place for your organization. Candidly, there could be a book written just on this topic alone, and corporate IT and data governance is outside of the scope of this book.

Chapter Summary

- EHR deployments are planned and implemented using a Lean project management approach and incorporate a Lean thinking philosophy toward planning the work and are managed visually using a vertical Gantt chart.

- This Lean management approach is a phased tollgate planning process that is designed to do two things: deliver a product with compelling value and complete the project work in the least waste way.
- For an EHR install, there are typically five major phases to a project: Vendor Selection, Requirements Gathering, Design and Build, Testing and User Acceptance, and go live.
- Using our Lean management approach, there is a recipe to follow that begins with assembling a team and ends with completing the final tollgate review.
- Lean project management begins with defining the inputs and outputs to each milestone and then determines the tasks needed to complete the milestones. Once the tasks are defined, stakeholders needed to complete the tasks are identified and then scheduled to ensure the right people are available at the right time to keep the project flowing.
- Tollgate reviews are held to ensure all questions have been answered so that work can move from one phase to the next without rework and to capture lessons learned for organizational learning.
- The project is managed visually using the vertical Gantt chart and the work is performed in the "big room" (Obeya).
- Using the Lean project management approach can reduce the timeline for execution by 25–50% and reduce project rework by 50–75%.

Chapter 7

Requirements Gathering—A New Approach

We're going to take a somewhat unorthodox approach to discussing requirements for your new or replacement EHR. In most cases, you've developed a list of functional requirements that led you to make your EHR selection, per our discussion in Chapter 5. That's a great starting point because you need to have defined what you need the EHR to do before you select your vendor and begin the planning phases. So, you know what you need the EHR to do at a high level. Now you need to define in more detail the requirements of the workflows to be built into the system.

You could take your requirements developed from your selection process and simply add more detail to develop your requirements. That's the pretty standard way of approaching these elements, and it works sufficiently well.

However, if you want to also improve your processes as you deploy, you can't just do the same thing you've always done. In this chapter, we'll look at a different approach to developing your requirements—by looking at what adds value to your customer (your patient) and by improving your processes through your planning. We'll describe the best case scenario with the understanding that reality almost always falls short of best case, but if you have a clear target set, you're going to drive a better outcome.

The approach for requirements in this case is going to be based on patient flows. Some organizations may call these tracers, after processes used in regulatory surveys and audits. We'll call them patient flows to differentiate them from provider workflows or electronic EHR workflows.

Let's start with a clinic. There are a finite number of patient flows in a clinic, despite the almost infinite variations that occur when caring for the individual patient. For example, the process of making an appointment is universal. The process of ensuring lab work or imaging is completed prior to a follow-up visit is universal. So, if you start with defining the number of standard patient flows you have (and it's okay to note where variation or customization occurs), you can begin to develop requirements based on these patient flows. If you take the time to map out your existing patient flows, you can do the work needed to reduce waste in those flows and then build your EHR requirements. Let's use a typical patient appointment with a primary care provider as an example of how this might work.

Map Existing State

First, map the existing workflow the patient experiences. Use caution here—you might *think* you know what that is, but your assumptions could lead you astray. You might start with signing up as a new patient to see the process yourself, or you might talk with existing patients. The key is to truly understand the current state, not document what you believe it to be. This is why we always suggest going and seeing for yourself how things actually work ("going to gemba")—to see what *really* is. So be sure to start here.

Let's say you try out setting an appointment as an existing patient, and you map the process, then you validate it with several existing patients. So you're confident this is the reality of your process. The steps are shown as a flow diagram in Figure 7.1 and are listed afterward. By the way, this is *not* intended to call anyone out or to be critical of any clinics, provider offices, hospitals, etc. This is just describing what is often seen as a typical process.

Patient Appointment Task List

1. Patient goes online and sees that they must call for an appointment.
2. Patient calls during business hours and enters a phone tree.
   a. Press 1 to make an appointment for provider A, B, or C.
   b. Press 2 to make an appointment for lab work.
   c. Press 3 to make an appointment for imaging (x-ray, ultrasound, CT, MRI, mammography, etc.).
   d. Press 4 to discuss prescriptions and medications.
   e. Press 5 for billing and insurance questions.
   f. Press 6 if you're a new patient.
   g. Press 7 if you want to leave a message for callback.
   h. Press 8 if you are a provider.
   i. Press 9 if you are an insurance company or payor representative.
   j. Press 0 to talk to the receptionist.
3. Patient presses 1 and gets hold music.
4. Patient waits on hold for 6 minutes.
5. Patient gets a message saying all agents are busy, please stay on the line or leave a message for callback.
6. Patient leaves message for callback.
7. Patient does not receive callback after 4 hours, so calls again.
8. Patient presses 1 and gets hold music.
9. Patient waits on hold for 4 minutes then gets receptionist.
10. Patient asks for appointment with provider A.
11. Receptionist says provider A is booking appointments 4 weeks out, would Tuesday at 1:15 pm work?
12. Patient asks for another time/date. Discussion for several minutes, and they settle on a time/date for appointment.
13. Reception asks patient if they would like reminder phone call and enters patient phone number in call list for reminder.

Patient visits website.
Obtains clinic phone number.
Patient calls during business hours and reaches phone tree.
Patient navigates phone tree, presses option 1.
Patient waits on hold 6 minutes and leaves message.
Patient does not get callback in 4 hours.
Patient calls clinic back, presses option 1, and waits on hold for 4 minutes.
Patient call is answered by receptionist.
Patient is offered first available timeslot with preferred provider 4 weeks out.
Time and date do not work for patient.
Patient and receptionist review additional times/dates available and find one that works after 5 minutes on the phone.
Patient is asked if they want a reminder phone call and phone number is written down and entered in call system for later reminder call.

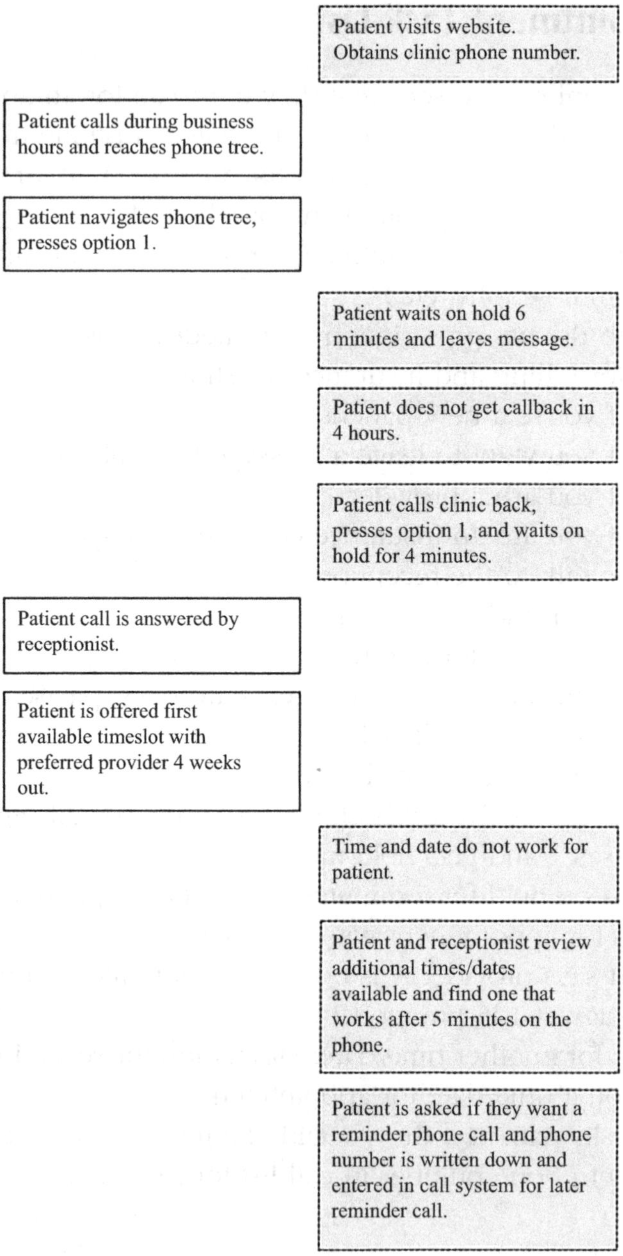

Figure 7.1 Example patient appointment flow.

As you can see in Figure 7.1, the tasks or actions listed in the gray boxes (on the right side of the diagram) represent potential waste from the patient's point of view, though these are clearly required steps in the process of making the appointment. The good news is, you've been able to confirm this is exactly how it works today. Now, is that how you want it to work tomorrow? Can this patient-facing workflow be improved from a patient perspective and a business perspective to reduce waste, improve efficiency, and drive a better outcome?

Let's look at one potential scenario that is more patient-centric. The tasks are listed and the revised workflow is shown in Figure 7.2.

Reengineered Patient Appointment Task List

1. Patient goes online and logs into the secure patient portal.
2. Patient views schedule for preferred provider and sees the first available appointment is 4 weeks out.
3. Patient determines that time/day won't work and reviews their personal schedule to determine the first slot that matches up with the provider's availability.
4. Patient determines that an appointment 5 weeks out at 10:30 am is perfect and clicks to book that appointment. The web page provides a few questions about the reason for the visit and notes that new lab work is recommended and that an order will be placed with the lab and the patient will be notified with details via selected method (text, email, phone call).
5. Patient adds the appointment to their calendar by clicking the "Add My Appointment to My Calendar" button.
6. Patient selects "Please Remind Me of This Appointment" and selects "text message" as the method and "24 hours in advance" as the timeframe.
7. The patient then logs off.

As you can see in Figure 7.2, the steps shown greatly simplify the process.

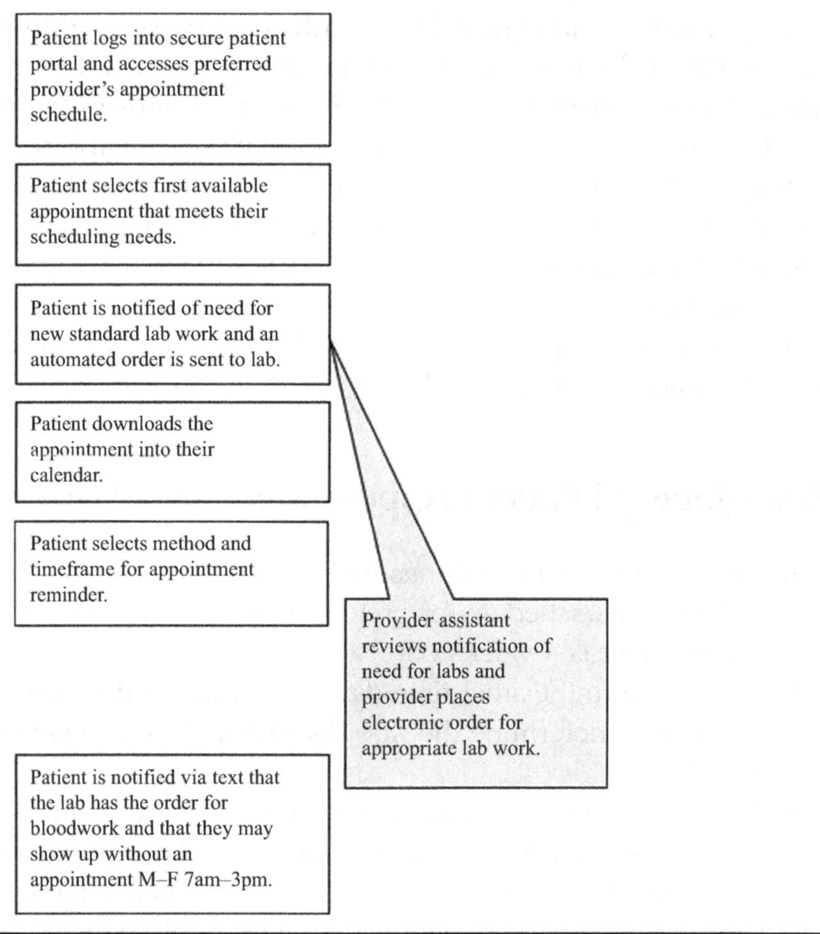

Figure 7.2 Reengineered patient appointment tasks.

In this revised scenario, all the steps add value to the patient; there is no waiting and the provider is notified electronically of the recommendation for lab work. The order for labs can be reviewed and placed electronically, or the patient can be notified that lab work was reviewed and is not needed at this time. In either case, the patient's time is not wasted, but neither is the clinic office staff time taken up with this basic function.

Of course, the workflow shows a potential ideal state and does not reflect situations where patients might not have Internet access, may not be comfortable with or capable of self-scheduling, or may not have a routine need. However, if you were to look at the number of phone calls related to setting, changing, and cancelling routine patient appointments, you might find that you can eliminate 50% of your daily phone call volume. How might that impact your patients, your staff, and your providers?

So, with that review of just one patient workflow, you can see how mapping out current state and potential future state could certainly drive functional and technical requirements for your EHR build. It is from this new view of patient flow that requirements and specifications for the software build should be developed.

We would imagine that you had "electronic patient scheduling" or "self-service scheduling," Rx information and renewals, and lab notifications as requirements for your EHR when you were selecting the vendor (most have some sort of patient portal or patient self-service functions built in these days), but this is where you pull together your process optimization work before you build your configuration so you can improve upon what exists today. You may not be able to get to the perfect state, but what if you could improve just 25% of this process? You're still better off, and you're creating an environment upon which to build.

Identifying Existing Workflows

Now that we've identified a single workflow and how you might work through improving before building, you can easily see how you can identify a finite set of standard workflows for each of your care scenarios. Here are some examples:

1. Routine patient appointment scheduling (shown earlier)
2. Routine follow-up appointment
3. Routine lab work
4. Routine imaging appointment
5. [Add your own here]

For a hospital emergency department, these may be a few of the most common patient flows:

1. Emergency department (ED) visit with discharge from ED
   a. Registration
   b. Triage
   c. Labs/imaging
   d. Results
   e. Diagnosis
   f. Treatment

    g. Discharge instructions
    h. Discharge
2. ED visit with admission to hospital inpatient room
3. ED visit with emergency Cath Lab procedure
4. ED visit with emergency OR procedure
5. ED visit with emergency stroke protocol

For a hospital inpatient unit, these may be a few of the most common patient flows:

1. Registration and admission
2. Labs/imaging
3. Results
4. Diagnosis
5. Treatment
6. Assessment
7. Discharge instructions
8. Discharge
9. After visit follow-up (notification to primary care provider or case worker)

Granted, this is extremely simplified to show that there are a finite number of patient flows in each area, and if the staff and management in those areas identify all patient flows and categorize them, they will be able to determine the 5, 10, or 20 types of flows that exist.

Even if no improvement activities are planned (we'd recommend against that, of course), having documentation showing how patients flow through your service areas is a valuable set of data to begin with for building out your EHR. However, if you have the time and the capability, you can really make significant improvements by modifying your patient workflows before building your system.

There is a human tendency, of course, to fall back into old patterns and old behaviors. By reworking these flows to be more patient friendly and patient-centric, a few positive drivers come into play. First, if they benefit your patients, it is possible that patients and staff will be more satisfied with the results and will want to keep the new workflows. Second, if the new workflows are tested, tweaked, and finalized into standard work before being configured into the EHR, the improvements can be solidified in the EHR making it more difficult to revert to old, inefficient practices. Of course, where there's a will, there's a way, and humans do like to go back to what is most comfortable—which is why both countermeasures to prevent relapse and positive results to encourage continued conformance with the new workflows are helpful in maintaining improvements.

Developing Requirements from Workflows

Most EHR vendors have a proven methodology for implementing their system and that includes developing requirements (in some form or another). We'll always recommend listening to your vendor's subject matter experts during the planning, configuration, and implementation of your EHR system, but keep this in mind: those experts may not know Lean. They do know their EHR system—what it can do, how it is best configured, in what order things should be done, etc. What they are often completely lacking in is specific knowledge of *your* organization and specific expertise in Lean, process improvement, or optimization. That's not to criticize these experts, but rather to reiterate that if you want to use Lean to deploy your EHR, you need to have a Lean way of approaching the deployment, not just subject matter expertise. Your vendor is very unlikely to bring that perspective to the table.

In addition, developing requirements from workflows helps you keep focus on standardization and reduces the opportunities for "random" or non-approved changes to sneak in. It's very common for scope to creep during the requirements gathering and definition phases. By documenting standards, you can minimize these tempting variations.

We'll use our patient appointment scheduling example from earlier in the chapter to discuss the next steps in developing requirements.

Functional Requirements for Patient Appointment

1. Ability for secure online access anytime, anywhere
2. Self-service functionality including appointment, labs, imaging, follow-up, referral, prescription list, prescription renewal, over-the-counter medication list, new address, new phone, new insurance
3. Easy-to-use functionality (intuitive web interface and simple navigation)
4. Easy to modify once scheduled (move, cancel, add appointments)
5. Multiple methods of contact (email, text, phone call) for each type of activity and ability of the patient to select the most suitable method as

default or modify for one specific type of activity (for standard appointments, always remind patient 4 days in advance but for lab work, remind patient 24 hours in advance, for example)
6. Self-pay options for copays, high deductible plans, and optional items, if applicable
7. Consumer cost data (what does a basic appointment cost, what does an intermediate or extensive appointment cost, and what does it include)
8. Related health education materials (automatically tied to diagnoses and/or medications prescribed)
9. Related health resources (free community resources)

While your team may drill down into each of these and get much more specific (define "simple navigation"—does that mean fewer, large buttons per page or does that mean the user may scroll down through several "pages" of data without having to click to move to another page?), these form the beginnings of your requirements. If you were to hand these to your staff or your consultant or your EHR expert builders, they may come back with questions about options for meeting these requirements, but they'd be pretty clear what the outcome needs to look like.

Patient Engagement Requirements

We covered these briefly in Chapter 5, and we specified that organizational strategies (patient engagement is typically one organizational strategic initiative) drive EHR requirements and vendor selection, so we'll only touch on them here. Your requirements should reflect that which provides value to your patients and that which allows you to run your business in the most efficient manner possible.

Functional requirements for patient engagement may include:

1. Secure online portal
2. Online bill pay
3. Online self-scheduling
4. Online patient data access (normal labs, imaging results, etc.)
5. Prescription data and renewals
6. Patient-entered data (vitamins, fitness trackers, etc.)
7. Private, secure chat or text with provider office (physician, NP, MA, etc.)
8. [Other]

Module Selection

Based on what you have as options in the EHR you selected, you will need to decide which modules you will implement. These requirements often align with these three high-level all-inclusive categories: *patient*, *provider*, and *business*.

Again, we go back to functional requirements for providers and come up with a list that includes:

1. Patient data and health status/conditions
2. Patient vitals and measurements
3. Patient history (diagnoses, diseases, surgeries, etc.)
4. New or outstanding lab or imaging results
5. Diagnoses
6. Care plans
7. [Other]

Of course, charting data into the EHR is the primary function everyone looks for and these requirements include:

1. Patient demographic data
2. Patient history
3. Assessments
4. Plans and notes
5. Provider documentation
6. Electronic order entry (computerized provider order entry, or CPOE)
7. Prescriptions
8. Alerts, warnings, verifications
9. Chart search
10. Organization of data in the chart
11. Electronic workflows (how the screen is laid out and how it is used)
12. After visit summaries, discharge instructions
13. Aftercare plans and follow-ups
14. Patient appointment reminders
15. [Other]

Business-specific requirements may include:

1. Revenue cycle management
2. Medical record management

3. Supply chain management
4. Financial management
5. [Other]

Alerts and Reminders

One of the key benefits that comes with the use of an EHR, of course, is automated alerts and reminders that can drastically reduce risk and improve patient outcomes. Examples are as follows:

1. Allergy assessments, results, and warnings
2. Drug interaction alerts, warnings, and guidelines
3. Lab results, abnormal lab results
4. Imaging results, abnormal imaging results
5. Procedural alerts (don't provide food or liquid prior to surgery scheduled for tomorrow morning, for example)
6. Notices and alerts (insurance preauthorization, insurance validation and verification, notice unpaid bills, etc.)
7. Electronic prescriptions (success, failure, hold, etc.)
8. [Other]

Of course, you can automate the system to provide alerts, but you need to be mindful that you don't overuse these features and cause alert fatigue or major roadblocks in providing care.

On the business side, you may choose to get alerts of things like:

1. Insurance claim acceptance (or rejection)
2. Coding issues
3. Electronic remittance advice
4. Billing issues
5. Collection issues
6. [Other]

Reports

We've discussed reporting needs in Chapter 5, so we'll just recap here. Providers (physician, nurses, respiratory therapists, pharmacists, etc.) and the business need data in various ways, so reports requirements might include the following.

1. Real-time, ad hoc reports available to end users on demand
2. Custom reports (scheduled or on demand)
3. CPOE reports
4. E-prescription reports
5. Medical record reports
6. Revenue cycle reports
7. Privacy and security reports (medical record access, frequency of access, access by noncare-team providers, excessive access, etc.)
8. [Other]

Technical Interfaces

Technical interfaces are those connections between systems that need to share data in some form or another. There are numerous technical specifications for the sharing of those data, but in healthcare IT, most often those interfaces use one of these standards:

1. Health Level 7 (HL7)
2. Digital Imaging and Communications in Medicine (DICOM)
3. Logical Observation Identifiers, Names and Codes (LOINC)
4. Extensible Markup Language (XML)
5. Simple Object Access Protocol (SOAP)
6. Fast Healthcare Interoperable Resource (FHIR)

Table 7.1 Data Exchange Matrix Example

Interface	*Source System*	*Receiving System*	*Data Format*	*Version*	*Frequency*
1	EHR patient demographics	Patient monitoring system	HL7	V3	Admits, discharges, transfers
2	Imaging system (vendor neutral archiver or other)	EHR	DICOM	V1.2	Link from VNA to EHR upon results
3	EHR	Coding system	HL7	V3	Upon chart review and completion

Understanding which systems use which types of data interfaces can help you create a requirements matrix for system-to-system data exchange, which might look something like that shown in Table 7.1. This is a greatly simplified view, but it gives you an idea of how to map this out. From here, you can have your technical builders work with specifications to define exactly what the technical interfaces require on a data element basis. This ensures that the right interface method, the right version, and the right data elements are selected and built to meet the defined requirements.

In the next chapter, we'll look at how to take these requirements and begin your design work. This is where all the preparation, planning, and analysis begin to form the design documents that will ultimately drive what you build and then how you test that build.

Population Health Management and Health Information Exchanges (HIEs)

Another set of requirements to discuss are those that relate to using your data outside of the normal patient care workflows. Many healthcare organizations today are involved with population health management initiatives and health information exchanges that typically aim to share data across systems (often on a state-by-state basis).

For these types of external-facing initiatives, you may wish to include the following types of outcome-based statements as requirements:

1. Improve population health results (by category or as defined in your organization)
2. Improve clinical results and patient care (by category or as defined in your organization)
3. More robust and actionable population health data
4. More efficient healthcare practices
5. More cost-effective healthcare practices
6. More empowered patients
7. More effective sharing of needed patient data
8. Improve patient treatment through timely data sharing (across systems or regions)

Data Migration Requirements

Finally, if you are on an existing EHR, you're going to need to specify what data need to be migrated over and how that will be accomplished. Though this certainly may pertain in large measure to your go live planning, you need to define your requirements for data migration. Your data migration requirements should answer some of these common questions:

1. Does your new EHR vendor have an automated process?
2. Do you have to migrate data manually?
3. Are there automated tools available?
4. What data will you pull in, and what will you leave behind?
5. How will you reconcile partial, missing, or duplicate data?
6. Will you leave some data behind and keep them in an archival manner for historical searches? If so, how will you support this system, how will you maintain it, and at what point will you decommission it?
7. Does your new EHR vendor support data migration from your old EHR vendor?
8. Does your old EHR vendor easily enable data migrations?

Data migration can be more complex if you have several systems you're leaving behind in favor of an integrated, enterprise-level system. Be sure to understand what data are coming forward, what are being left behind, and what you'll do with older systems when the time comes.

Chapter Summary

- We discussed the value of "going to Gemba" to see for yourself what the existing workflows look like, where there are inefficiencies or pain points, and how you might improve your process before you configure a single element in your new EHR.
- Mapping your existing state will enable you to see on paper what your workflows look like and how you might reduce waste (and add value) to each workflow.
- Identifying a standard set of workflows and noting exceptions will enable you to standardize to a large degree and reduce variation.

- Developing requirements from workflows helps keep focus on standardization and reduces the opportunities for "random" or non-approved changes to sneak in.
- We walked through developing functional requirements for patient engagement, module selection, alerts and reminders, reports, and technical interfaces. This is not an exhaustive list of requirements but a starter set that you can build upon.
- We looked at technical interfaces and how you can map out requirements, both for system-to-system data exchanges, as well as for the methods, versions, and frequency of these messages. While the work must be far more detailed than that shown, starting with this matrix and having your technical team build on these requirements will ensure you document every data interchange needed for go live and beyond.
- The need to manage population health and participate in health information exchanges creates another set of specifications that should be incorporated into your requirements.
- Understanding your data migration needs as you move from one or more systems to a new EHR system is another element with respect to migrating your system that can sometimes be overlooked. Making decisions about what data to migrate and what data to leave behind should be clearly documented.

Further Reading

Health Level 7 International (HL7), "EHR definitional model," prepared by HIMSS Electronic Health Record Committee, Thomas Handler, MD, Research Director, Gartner, https://www.hl7.org/documentcenter/public/wg/ehr/archives/030616-EHR%20Definitional%20Model%20Version%201.doc, 2010 (accessed July 11, 2017).

Outlook Associates. "Defining EHR System Requirements," http://www.schoolhealthcenters.org/wp-content/uploads/2011/06/4-Defining-EHR-System-Requirements-Tips-for-Success.pdf (accessed July 12, 2017).

Public Health Informatics Institute. "Collaborative Requirements Development Methodology (CRDM)." http://phii.org/crdm (accessed July 12, 2017). (This resource focuses on public health, but many of the resources, including this article, are widely applicable to other healthcare models.)

Chapter 8

Design and Build Phase

Standardize, Standardize, Standardize…

At some point during any EHR implementation, the following question will be asked: "Should we optimize (Lean) our workflows *before* or *after* we go live?" Obviously, something as large and impactful as a new EHR system seems like the perfect time to reimagine how care is delivered. Also, why would you want to take an old, wasteful process and put it into a brand new system? The preferred way is to vigorously apply Lean techniques to your existing workflows before you go live. A word of caution is that most organizations underestimate the effort involved and the time that it takes to truly "Lean out" any workflow, let alone *all* of your workflows. This path also required leadership all the way up to the CEO that is fully committed to a Lean transformation and the personal commitment required to pull it off. This scenario in the healthcare community is still a bit like finding a unicorn. If your leadership isn't quite ready for the unicorn option, a compromise is to take as many of the workflows "out of the box" as possible and keep customization to a minimum and focus on a model line. The leading EHR suppliers have implemented thousands of systems and have learned over the years what the best practices should be. When you think about it, how many ways *are* there to get a patient from the emergency department admitted to a floor? How many *should* there be?

At this point in the project, it's helpful to establish some guiding principles deployed from the senior leadership team. Recently, a health system, I'll call them Acme Health, implemented a new EHR and the following guiding principles were deployed at the beginning of the project:

1. A single process owner with a defined connection to an executive will be identified for every care flow.
   - All care flows, policies and procedures, and standard work will have an identified single owner across the health delivery system.
2. Assume minimal investment. Creativity used before capital.
   - All standard work should be developed assuming minimal investment.
3. Care flows—95% standardization.
   - Care flows endorsed during adoption sessions will serve as the model system for each application; 95% of care flows will be consistent across the delivery system.
4. Standard work—representation by all impacted departments/entities.
   - Standard work established in support of the care flows will be developed collectively with representation from all impacted hospitals and clinics.
5. Informed by best practices.
   - All standard work developed should investigate best practices for adoption.

As you can see, this particular organization is very focused on delivering a finished product that is as "out of the box" as possible and as standardized as possible. We've talked about standardization a few times in this book, and there is a good reason that this is a reoccurring theme. This particular health system learned a hard lesson in the recent past about the perils of variability. This EHR project was to bring the entire system (12 hospitals, 180 ambulatory locations, 26,000 employees, and 1,800 employed providers) onto one EHR system from the current state of five EHR systems. This health system grew very quickly through acquisition, and the customary rule of thumb was that the newly acquired entities (both hospitals and employed physician medical groups) were basically promised that they could have the "Burger King®" model, meaning they could have it *their* way. If the hospitals were happy with their homegrown or nonstandard EHR, they could keep it. The clinics were a little different in that the corporate medical group had standardized on an Epic® EHR, and newly integrated members were expected to adopt Epic®. The only problem was that when the new practices were integrated, they were allowed to customize the EHR pretty much any way they wanted. You can imagine how the discussion must have gone when the EHR programmer showed up at the neurology clinic:

Neurologist: "My practice is different. I need special templates that are custom to my practice style."
Programmer: "The system is infinitely configurable, and we can make it do anything you want!"

During the subsequent years, efforts were made to "optimize" the current EHR. During a rapid cycle Lean improvement event, while mapping the current state condition, it was revealed that Acme had 843 different visit types... just for primary care! You can only imagine the effort (and cost) associated with such variability. The organization was large, so a centralized call center handled the majority of the patient scheduling request calls. The variability that was caused by each physician's preferences manifested into a monster within the call center. The customer service representatives that answered the phones each had a special book that helped them decipher this massive amount of variation. The books were literally 6 inches thick. When a patient needed to book an appointment, the representative would consult the book and find the practice that the patient was interested in. This was only the first level of variation. Then, they would have to find the page for the specific doctor and find out things like, Were they accepting new patients? Did they accept the patient's insurance? Were they male or female? Older than 60? Depending on the answers to these questions, the "standard" visit time might be 40 minutes...or 15 minutes...or 20 minutes. It was madness! And this extremely complex process was thrust upon some of the lowest paid and newest employees in the organization, a recipe for disaster for the patients involved.

The breaking point for this particular situation was when system leadership deployed a goal to have online scheduling available for patients within the next 12 months. As you can imagine, this was impossible with the current level of variation. You can now understand the reasoning behind the corporate principles to deliver a standardized EHR.

When applying Lean thinking to a project as large as an EHR implementation, it's important to remember the Lean concepts that were covered earlier in the book. Key among them is the idea of *kaizen*. Continuous, incremental change for the better that should be hardwired into the culture. Some attributes of a kaizen culture are as follows: continual learning, problems are viewed as jewels, and respecting the people closest to the work. As shown in Figure 8.1, as we get ever closer to go live, the Plan, Do, Check, Act cycle will help refine the workflows, standard work, and software configurations that will allow your organization to deliver care in the least waste way, ultimately delighting your patients.

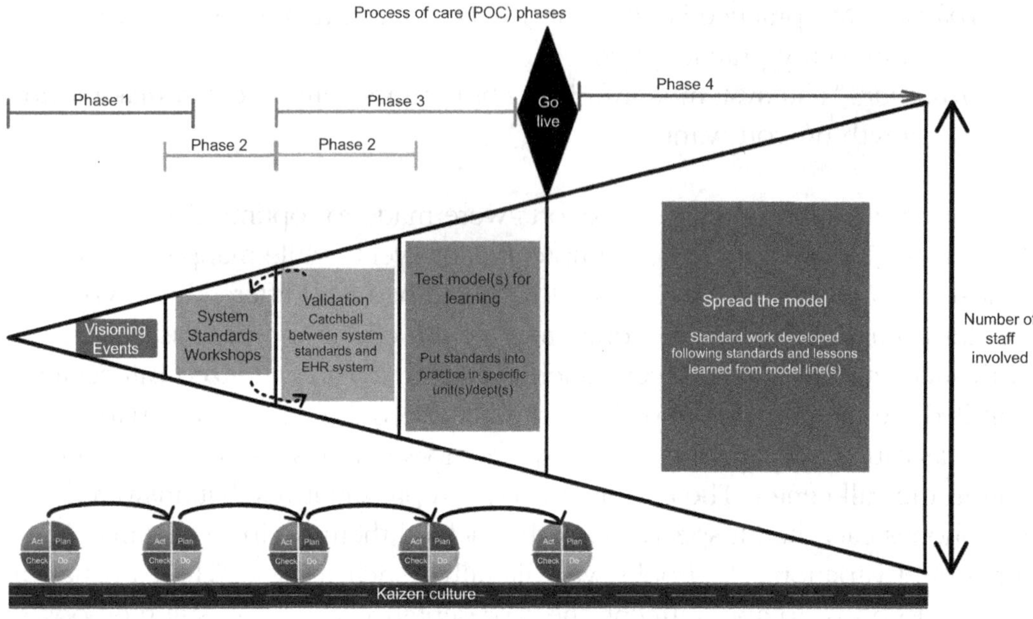

Figure 8.1 Kaizen culture process.

Visioning

Once there is a clear set of guiding principles, the real work can begin. As mentioned earlier, it's sometimes helpful to benchmark other companies and other industries, but it's also helpful to understand how you stack up to perfection. One way to do this is by conducting a series of "visioning" sessions.

Depending on the size and scope of your EHR implementation, this may be a one-time session with a small group or a handful of sessions centered on a particular "process of care" or POC. A POC is a particular process or department that may be replicated multiple times throughout a large integrated system. Examples of a POC include emergency medicine, surgery, primary care, pharmacy, and acute care. A visioning session is a chance for representatives from all of the stakeholders to get together and develop a vision for what a "perfect" EHR process would look like. The stakeholders should include clinical and operational leaders, nursing, physicians, and representatives from your patient experience councils. Figure 8.2 highlights the major steps that a visioning session will go through.

This provides a 30,000-foot view of the POC, and it's intended to find common ground that can be applied across all "like" POCs. The process will force the team to look at the process through the lens of the patient, the staff, and the organization. A visual map of the process will be created,

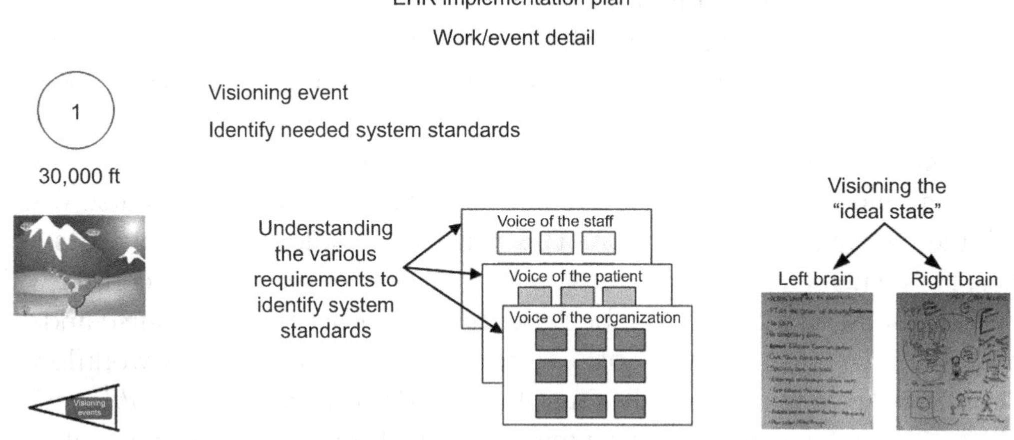

Figure 8.2 Sample visioning session diagram.

which uses the right side of the brain and the left side of the brain to create workflows that will accomplish the desired value-added steps in the least waste way.

This is a time to dream what is possible and describe what the ideal state would look like. Toward the end of the session, the teams will pull it all together and produce aspirational statements like

- "Patients will have a seamless journey across all aspects of our health system."
- "We will provide patients and families an 'itinerary' of their hospital visit, so that family members know when to expect physicians and other specialties on rounds."
- "Our patients will be able to read progress notes within *their* medical record where and when they choose."

Statements like these should describe things that are impossible with your current system, so that it creates a tension whereby the status quo is no longer acceptable, thus encouraging true transformative work.

Let's return to the discussion of standardization. At what level do we standardize? At the 30,000-foot level, there are certain things that will have to be mandated ("You shall do") into policies. At a lower level, certain groups of tasks will form standardized workflows that will be completed in a certain order ("You shall do"). These are procedures that are governed by policies. At the frontline level, standard work documents ("I will do") will spell out the "who," "what," and "how long" a certain procedure or step should take, in the least waste way.

For example, the organization has made the decision that all patients entering the emergency department will be asked if they have a durable power of attorney (DPOA). This becomes the policy for the entire system. The procedure might state that the patient must be asked about their DPOA at the earliest possible contact point in the emergency department. The standard work for a flagship hospital's Level I trauma center stated that the triage nurse will ask the patient about their DPOA. The standard work for the critical access hospital's emergency department stipulated that whoever had first contact with the patient asked the question, because they didn't have a triage nurse and their staffing was variable. In this example, the design of the EHR workflow is *standardized*, but the locally controlled standard work has *allowable* variability. This nuance has confused many people, because they do not make the distinction between high-level policies and the standard work that governs day-to-day work activities. Figure 8.3 describes this concept in further detail.

Another simple example would be when you visit the doctor for your annual checkup and he tells you that you need to lose weight and eat healthier ("You shall do"). Furthermore, he tells you that you need to eat more fruits and vegetables and that you need more exercise ("You shall do").

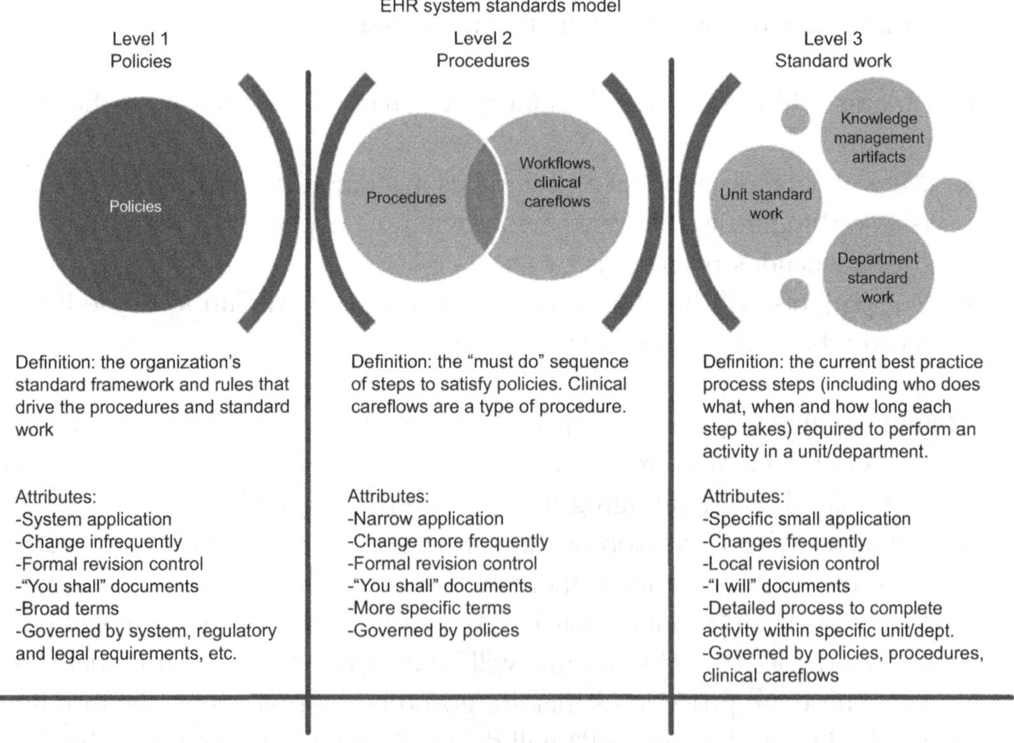

Figure 8.3 Standardization and variability.

Upon returning home, you resolve to create a daily checklist to monitor your diet, and you use a mobile app to monitor your steps ("I will do").

Returning to our 30,000-foot vision statements and ideal state workflows, we now will begin descending to 5,000 feet to see if what is being proposed is even possible and, if so, what gaps currently exist within our existing workflows and the EHR system that we've purchased. As shown in Figure 8.4, this task can be accomplished with a 1-day workshop or "sprint" session for *each* workflow. There may be dozens of identified workflows, so allow enough time to do this step properly.

There are many different tools that could be used at this stage, but a trusty pad of sticky notes, some flip charts, and a good Lean facilitator are really all that you need. In terms of the team members, it should be a smaller cross section of the visioning team as well as a representative from the EHR supplier. There will be two workflows that must be analyzed: the physical workflow and the electronic workflow. For the physical workflows, the goal will be to analyze the current state processes and compare them to the proposed vision and note where gaps exist. It's helpful for the team to go to the gemba and observe what is actually happening, not just what is *supposed* to happen. At the same time, the team will compare both the current state workflow as well as the ideal state workflow to the "out-of-the-box" workflow provided by the EHR supplier. High-level steps are as follows:

1. Review workflow (future state)
2. Capture gaps from each area for meeting workflow (current state)

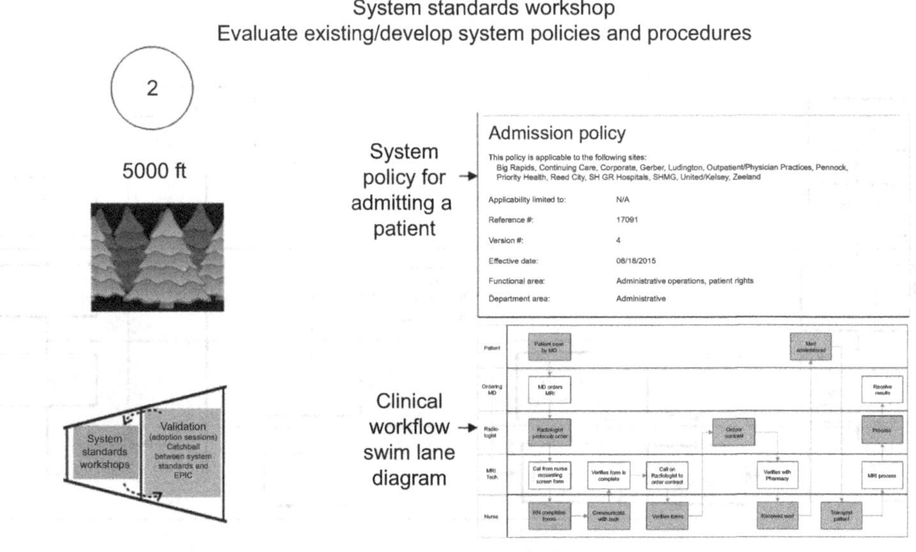

Figure 8.4 System standards workshop example.

3. Write agreed upon standard work with variation where only absolutely necessary
4. Capture action plans for each area to close the gaps

Deliverables: Gaps identified, standard work created, and action plan created.

The first step will be to conduct a simple gap analysis by mapping the current state workflow (after the team has walked the gemba) and comparing it to the proposed ideal state workflow. The team should note where the differences are, including changes to existing standard work, missing steps, and other gaps that the team has observed. At this time, it is helpful to get a demonstration of the electronic workflows in the EHR, as they exist at this point in the build. After viewing the demo, the team should answer the following questions:

- Are there any role changes in future state?
- How does the EHR help us close the gaps?
- What gaps remain?
- What can we do to close the gaps?
- Brainstorm ways for additional future state standardization.

From this exercise, the team will create a standard workflow diagram, as shown in Figure 8.5, that will address people responsibilities, process flows, and technology flows. This will help inform the EHR programmers as they work to finish the next phase of the build.

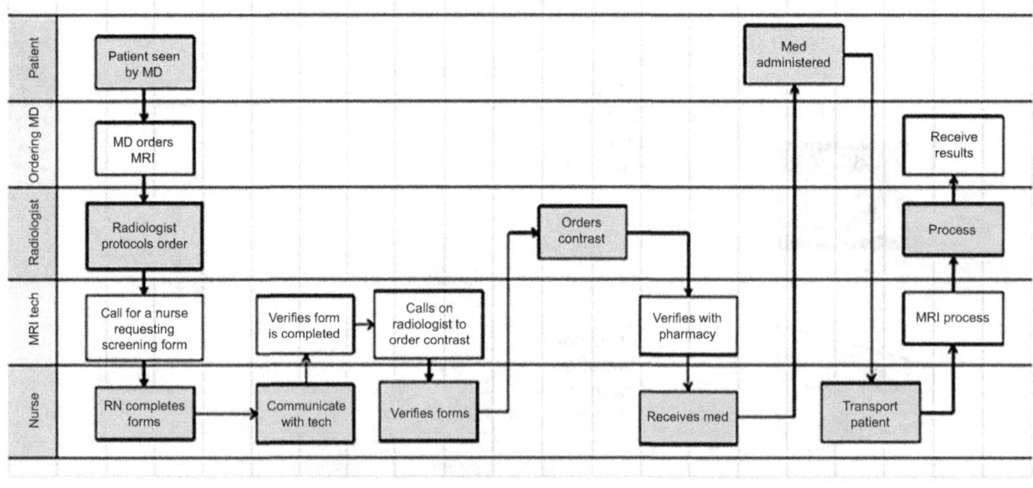

Figure 8.5 Workflow diagram example.

Once the updated workflow diagram is complete, it's time to determine what can be standardized across all POC teams. Obviously, if you only have one or two emergency departments in your health system, or you only have a few "like" specialty clinics, this could be fairly straightforward. But if you have multiple POCs across a high degree of variable physical locations, this conversation can be a little more spirited. Again, this is where your Lean facilitator can pull one of their tricks out to help drive the conversation to one of standardization, using the 80/20 rule. Sometimes a matrix, such as the one shown in Figure 8.6, can be helpful to drive the conversation.

If the team cannot reach consensus within 15 minutes, the process owner should be called in to make a decision. This may seem quick, but it's by design. If you give the team too much time, they will find more and more things that they can or can't live with or without. The details will be worked out in the model line and testing phase, so don't be afraid to press forward. At this point, it's also good practice to review the policies and procedures that govern this POC and determine if there are any edits required.

	Vivian Memorial	Grand Hospital	Haven Memorial	Parker Community Hospital	Paige Hospital	DeVries Regional Hospital	Eugene Edward Hospital	Wendell Memorial Hospital	Result
E.R. Registration	✓	X	✓	X	✓	X	X	X	X
Triage	✓	✓	✓	X	✓	X	✓	✓	O
Admission	✓	X	X	✓	✓	X	✓	✓	O
Trauma Surgery	✓	✓	✓	✓	✓	✓	✓	✓	✓
OBS.	✓	✓	✓	✓	✓	✓	✓	✓	✓
Discharge	X	✓	✓	✓	X	✓	✓	✓	O
Lab	X	✓	✓	X	✓	X	X	✓	X
Rad.	✓	X	X	X	✓	X	X	X	X

Figure 8.6 Care setting matrix example.

Once the team has come to consensus, it's time to draft the standard work, an example of which is shown in Figure 8.7. Remember that standard work is owned by the local work areas and should be governed by policies and procedures, and it should describe not only tasks and the order of the tasks but also the time required to accomplish the tasks.

Standard Work Activity Sheet		***Owner:*** Addy K. ***Author:*** Benjamin K.	***Rev. Date:*** 10/24/17
Step: Sprint	***Purpose:*** Sprint Session Event Facilitation Standard Work	***EHR – scope of standard work***	

Seq. No	Task Description:	Key Point / Image / Measure (what good looks like)	Who	Cycle Time mm:ss
1.	Executive kick off	• Drive Consistency • Executive Help Chain	Project Lead	5 Min
2.	Introductions		Group	5 Min
3.	Safety Story/Patient Facing Story		Project Lead	5 Min
4.	Agenda Review and Logistics	• Meals • Bathroom • Breaks	Lean Specialist	2 Min
5.	Training and Education PowerPoint https://community.lunahealth.org/docs	• Guiding principals • Pulse Checks w/ Concurrent Engineers • Approach Methodology • Team rules • Post Sprint follow up	Lean Specialist	15 Min
6.	Coach on writing the standard work • Pre-Populated with EHR case flow process • Other procedural elements will need to be added in • Reference applicable policies and adhere to policy and procedural elements • Patient Facing Scripting / Consensus for excellent patient experience and outcomes	Use form 301	Lean Specialist	10 Min
7.	Planning Summary Review	High level review of planning sessions decisions/ targets	Project Lead	10 Min
Concurrent Engineering				

Standard Work Activity Sheet/Ref Material/K Card	Page 1 of 1

Lean Form # 301 rev 12022016

Figure 8.7 Standard work example.

Some helpful hints to keep in mind: Don't include too much detailed information at the granular level. It's a delicate balancing act, but we are still at the 5,000-foot level, not the 15-foot level. Once the teams begin experimenting with the model line, the lower-level details will be fleshed out. Also, be sure to include those things that help you provide a safe and highly reliable workflow. One of the great things about a modern EHR system is the ability to error-proof processes and remove variability from patient care. Don't miss this opportunity to provide a safer, more reliable experience for your patients. Finally, the designated owners of the workflow have veto power and can make the final call on approval. While important to get everyone's input and concerns, the goal should be a process that is mostly standardized. As mentioned earlier in this chapter, do not allow personality-driven variability to be introduced into your new EHR. It is a slippery slope, and it could delay your project or, worse yet, recreate the very problems you are trying to eliminate.

Any Lean expert will tell you the importance of a "model line" or "model cell" when introducing process improvements. An example is shown in Figure 8.8.

It's the old adage "a mile deep and an inch wide" rather than "a mile wide and an inch deep." Most healthcare organizations are much more inclined to try to spread changes everywhere before testing everything out in a controlled environment, thereby dooming the improvement before it even has a chance. The model line will give the people closest to the work the opportunity to try out their ideas in real time and work through the inevitable problems that will come up. Along the way, the standard work can be updated with the new learnings and the software configuration can be updated, since we are still in the build phase. It's nearly impossible to anticipate every possible scenario that can happen in a clinical environment,

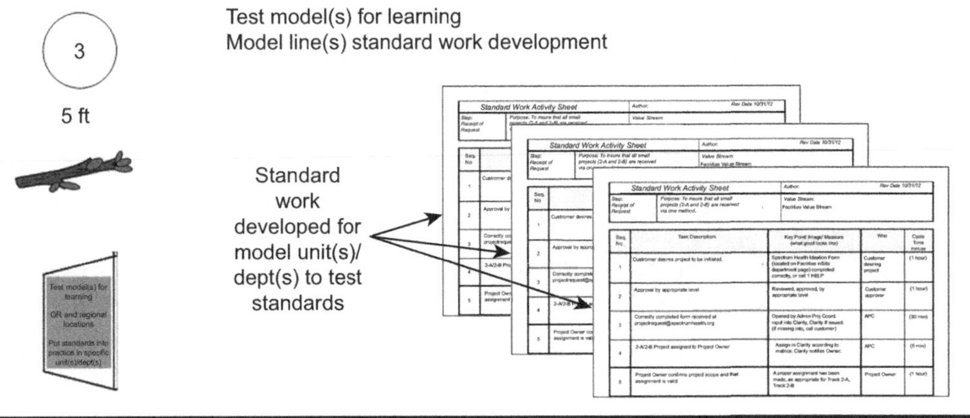

Figure 8.8 Model line example.

which makes this part of the process so valuable. Since the model line will still be in the current state with regard to the EHR, the full benefits of the future state model will not be realized until go live. A deeper dive on the model cell concept is covered in Chapter 13.

Chapter Summary

- If you plan to Lean out your workflows before implementing a new EHR, do not underestimate the time required to properly do this. A compromise is to implement the EHR system as "out of the box" as possible and optimize it after go live.
- Always engage those closest to the work to help define the vision of "what good looks like" in terms of functionality and requirements. Don't underestimate user involvement in the design of your system.
- Clearly define the policies that will govern the procedures, supporting the standard work at the frontline. Variability should be held to a minimum at the policy level, while allowing locally controlled, required variation to occur at the point of care.
- Follow the model line concept and go a mile deep and an inch wide. This will become your laboratory for situations that could not have been anticipated in a conference room. Always experiment with your model line in the gemba.
- Standardize process flows as much as possible, and rely on your EHR vendor for guidance, as they've implemented thousands of systems and should have a good idea of where to standardize and use the out-of-the-box functionality.

Chapter 9

Testing, User Acceptance, and Training

Overview

The testing and user acceptance phase of any software development/deployment projects is a critical phase that often has a disproportionate impact on the eventual success (or failure) of the overall project.

As with any other software deployment, the testing phase should be driven by the requirements developed early in the project lifecycle. The functional and technical requirements defined at the beginning are used as requirements for testing and user acceptance. This is also the point at which you can solidify your training and/or use of "super users" and your overall approach toward product and process testing. We'll begin with discussing testing and user acceptance and follow that by looking at Lean processes for product and process testing and acceptance.

Testing Considerations

Traditional software testing tasks include unit and functional testing, system testing, integration testing (sometimes called "end-to-end" or "go live" testing), and performance (load, stress, etc.) testing. We'll discuss the fundamental aspects of each as it relates to your EHR testing plan.

Be sure to define, in advance, what defects are and how you will prioritize them. If you haven't done this already in your EHR project, doing so before testing is important. Even if you've built a great system, you are bound to find errors early in the testing phase. Define how you'll prioritize and handle defects and errors. For example, a defect may be anything that is not built according to the specifications. An error may be something that is built according to specifications but does not work as designed. In either case, you should define what a critical, high, medium, and low priority defect (and/or error) is and how you will address these. For example, you may determine that all critical and high defects and errors cause testing to stop until resolved. For medium and low, you may batch them into a development cycle at the end of a test phase, such as at the end of unit testing.

In general, you should have test plans that define what is to be tested, at what stage it will be tested (unit or integrated, for example), who will test it, how results will be documented, and how issues will be addressed. Testing is an iterative process, but issues should become far less numerous the further into the testing process you get. Figure 9.1 shows the conceptual steps for testing and functional requirement validation (sometimes used interchangeably with user acceptance testing). For more on software testing in general, see the Resources section at the end of this chapter.

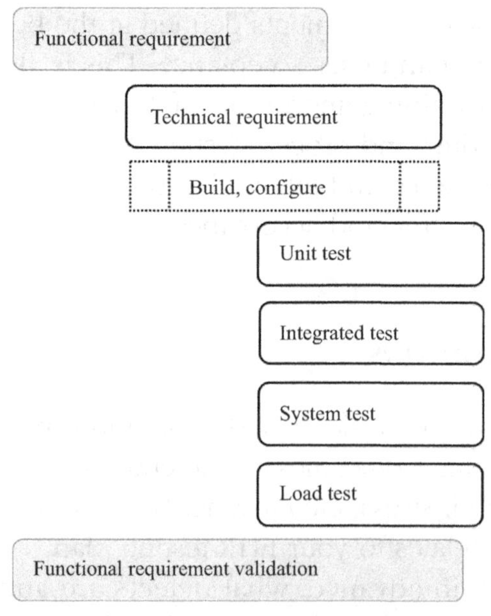

Figure 9.1 Testing phases.

Unit and Functional Testing

Your functional and technical requirements form the foundation of unit and functional testing. For the purposes of the EHR, a unit might be a specific module such as an ED module or your revenue management module. Functional testing, of course, tests the function of that portion of the software. This is the initial phase of testing that makes sure the build is accurate and complete. Some elements that should be tested during this phase are listed here along with questions you should be asking and answering.

1. Are all major functions present? This is a very basic question and should easily be answered. A project plan should have a list of all major functions required and their status, so this should really be just a final check to make sure no defined work has been accidentally missed.
2. Does each major function perform as specified? Specifications may be your organizational specifications or they may be vendor documentation.
3. Are the agreed upon changes or customizations present, and do they work as required? Though customization should be avoided at the early stages of an EHR deployment, there are some modifications that make sense. For example, if you have a unique patient or physician population, you may need to modify functionality to meet the fundamental needs of the organization. This is different from optimization that includes features that are simply deemed "nice to have."
4. Do screens appear as expected? This includes the order and placement of screens and elements on the screens. Do the drop-downs work, and do they have the right data elements? Do checkboxes or radio buttons work? Do pop-ups or alerts appear as expected? Does the screen fit on the computer monitor, are elements hidden, overlapping, or are there gaps?
5. Are all icons readable and logical (i.e., they represent something similar to the action)? If icons are links, do the links work?
6. Is navigation working properly? Can you go back, forward, scroll up/down, scroll side/side (try to avoid that if possible)? Can you click tabs or open other windows as expected?
7. Are color schemes consistently applied? Is text readable in all areas of the screen?
8. Is there consistency in functional behavior as well as look-feel in all areas of the module (and across the entire EHR)?

9. Is content presented effectively? Can it be easily located, read, printed, forwarded, or shared (as appropriate)? Is content accurate and in the right place? Is content edited (grammar, punctuation, spelling, pagination) correctly?
10. Are corrections handled appropriately (original data and associated correction shown)?
11. Are fields correct? Do they contain valid values and options, are the defaults correct, can they be modified, are they mandatory or optional, do they prevent the user from moving to another area if incorrect data are entered?
12. Do clinical decision support information screens and/or alerts appear as expected and when needed? Are there required responses? Are there accepted workarounds? Do they work as expected?
13. If you have set up scripting to consistently test certain functions, have you tested the scripts to ensure they generate the correct results (i.e., are your scripts correct?) before using them to validate EHR build?

While this list is not exhaustive (nor are the ones that follow), these give you a good starting point for developing your testing plans. Though we'll discuss super users later in this chapter, it bears noting at this critical juncture that, ideally, your super users are involved with some of this unit testing. Though many organizations may balk at subsidizing the use of clinical staff's time in this early phase of testing, there is a tremendous upside to doing so. Namely, clinical super users become familiar with the system early on (be sure they understand the stages of testing so they have correct expectations), and clinical eyes on the soon-to-be-final product may help correct errors and omissions earlier in the cycle. Fixing errors at this juncture is always more efficient and less expensive than fixing them after the product is released to the organization. Of course, avoiding errors prior to this point is even better, but that's why there are numerous opportunities to check work quality along the way.

If your unit testing is successful, you can move into systems testing. If your unit testing has exposed many issues, you have a problem with the quality of the work or a disconnect between requirements and testing efforts. It's time to step back and figure out the root cause before you move on to the next step in testing.

System Testing

System testing moves from individual functionality (drop-downs, check boxes, etc.) to test whether the overall system is functioning as expected. In this phase, you'll need to check that systems are processing information correctly, that data move as expected in the timeframe expected, and that all data are present, accounted for, and accurate. Some questions to ask during this phase are as follows:

1. Do data flow (send/receive, update, replace) between systems as expected? This includes (but is not limited to) the EHR and systems such as Laboratory Information Systems (LISs), Radiology Information Systems (RISs), pharmacy, billing systems, etc. Develop scripts to standardize this testing and update scripts when either the sending or receiving side changes. Create checklists to define what the expected results should be so that there is no question about whether or not test results meet requirements.
2. Are automated messages sent and received correctly? Are the data accurate; do they flow to the right location?
3. Do interfaces move data between systems in a complete, timely, and accurate manner? Test both the send and receive function.
4. Do you have interconnections with external organizations? Do data need to flow between your organization and another? Is this a new connection that needs to be established or an existing connection that needs to be validated? Examples of these types of systems might be health exchanges, payer portals, disease management portals, or registries, etc.
5. Is system access correct? This is a key security element for every organization. The principle of "least access" should be used to ensure (or audit) end-user permissions are the most restrictive while still allowing end users to perform their roles. Testing should include purposely trying to perform tasks outside of a defined role as well as the ability to gain unauthorized access to secure resources.
6. Does data from various systems flow into reports, summaries, or tables, as expected? Again, checklists of data sources and expected results can assist in consistently testing these parts of the system that may only be used "on demand."

System testing may surface interface or programming errors that can be easily corrected at this stage. Once system testing is complete and system functionality has been validated, you can move on to integrated testing.

Integrated Testing

Integrated testing typically mimics the live environment. During this phase, you'll cover these elements:

1. Do all system components that share data work together as expected?
2. Do the defined workflows in the system mirror the actual workflows as defined prior to the start of build/configuration?
3. Does the EHR works with all interconnected devices such as tables, bar code scanners, document scanners, rapid login devices (tap-in, biometric, etc.)? Checklists with specific device requirements and results will also assist when deployment of hardware begins or when final testing of hardware devices occurs before go live.
4. Do alerts and other warnings fire as expected and are they visible and actionable? Do they create hard stops (and is that the desired result)? Can they be circumvented or "accepted" or "closed" and is that the desired behavior?
5. Do any automated assistance systems work as expected (issue logging, etc.)?
6. Can you or your super users break the system? Often systems are used by end users in unexpected ways. Getting users and super users involved in testing before go live can surface these odd or unusual behaviors that sometimes are overlooked when testing is conducted by sophisticated users or IS staff. This provides an opportunity to better understand how users are likely to use the system and then error-proof your build.
7. Are overrides (medication, orders, etc.) handled correctly?
8. Are tasks in the system that may occur over time handled and documented correctly? For example, if assessments are done every 12 hours, do the data get collected and displayed correctly?
9. Are existing policies and procedures still aligned with the new workflows defined by the EHR? Do policies, procedures, or other documentation need to be updated?

An example of a master test plan is shown in Table 9.1. It defines stages of testing, elements to be tested, and outcomes. This example shows a simple "Pass/Fail" for testing. Your organization may choose to create a more detailed outcome column indicating next steps if the result is "Fail." However, this is a good starting point for developing your test plan.

For example, the first item, "Functionality is present and works according to vendor specifications," should be accompanied in the test plan with a list of functionality the vendor has indicated would be present and upon which the organization is depending. This list of functional elements, per module, is the baseline for the scope of the project, the system build or configuration, and testing. Thus, each of these items represents a longer list of tasks that must be defined by the team. The good news is that these data are built from prior work (scope documents, requirements documents, etc.) and results from this can be fed back into documents (build, configuration, test plans, training plans), so this work is productive and not duplicative.

In addition, each of the items should have detailed plans underlying them, as shown in Table 9.2. The sample shown in Table 9.2 is specific to downtime report testing so you can work with a very concrete example.

You would create these plans for all aspects of your EHR. Typically, your vendor is going to give you a starter set of test plans that covers all modules and all aspects of the software you are deploying. Your job will be to customize those test plans or templates to match the implementation decisions your organization makes. If your EHR vendor does not supply these types of starter test plans, push them to create them going forward and develop your own detailed plans. This is crucial to a successful go live, as well as to process improvement efforts after go live.

Performance Testing

Performance testing is conducted to ensure that the infrastructure upon which your EHR (and other systems) rely can handle the load. This is sometimes called load testing or stress testing. Whether your EHR is creating new demands upon your infrastructure or not, it is vital to test the systems, such as storage, servers, and network, under real loads in order to observe response times. A slow EHR will create dissatisfied users in short order, so be sure to test the performance before go live. Remediation can be as simple as modifying a configuration or as complex as reconfiguring servers, clusters, or storage.

Table 9.1 Sample Test Plan

Phase	*Tasks*	*Result*	*Owner*	*Pass/ Fail*
Unit and Functional Testing	Functionality is present and works according to vendor specifications.			
	Specified system changes have been made and work as defined.			
	Screens display data as expected and in order required. All fields, boxes, menus, lists, dropdown, text boxes, and other elements appear as expected.			
	Spelling and punctuation are correct. Color schemes as specified.			
	Appropriate representation of content can be printed if necessary for legal purposes.			
	Alerts and reminders (all clinical decision support actions) are present and work as specified.			
System Testing	Workflows for each specified area work as expected.			
	Data flow between areas of the EHR as expected.			
	Interfaces are working as specified (data elements are correct and sending least data necessary) and are sending/receiving data as expected.			
	Communication with external entities works as expected (interface, fax, email, etc.).			
	Security is in place and is tested (users have been assigned correct level of access and that level of access enables them to perform their jobs without undue restriction).			
	Reports and other data are presented accurately, completely, and appropriately according to specifications.			

(*Continued*)

Table 9.1 (Continued) Sample Test Plan

Phase	*Tasks*	*Result*	*Owner*	*Pass/ Fail*
	Data required for regulatory compliance (whether a report, a data set, an export, an interface or other) is fully populated and able to be sent.			
Integrated Testing	Ensure system is working as a whole and as expected. Data are flowing between modules and/or systems as expected (completeness of data and in a timely manner).			
	Electronic workflows are as expected and documented. (This will form foundation of training, so this is critical.)			
	Ensure all end-user devices (PCs, laptops, tablets, printers, scanners, speech recognition hardware/software) work as specified in all areas of the EHR.			
	Test high-risk functions (alerts, overrides, etc.) to ensure these work flawlessly.			
Performance Testing	Put the system under maximum test load and document key performance metrics (response time, screen refresh time, report generation time, etc.). If any are not within tolerance, investigate/ remediate. If within tolerance, document as baseline.			
	Simulate maximum load and take baseline measurements.			
User Acceptance	All planned functionality has been implemented according to specifications and is working as expected.			
	All outstanding issues have been resolved (remediated, accepted, or work around accepted) and there are no critical issues preventing go live.			

Source: Derived from test plan from Stratis Health, https://www.stratishealth.org/documents/HITToolkitclinic/2.Utilize/2.1Implement/2.1Testing_Plan.doc.

Table 9.2 Sample of Detailed Test Item—Downtime Reports

Description of Item	*Tasks*	*Owner*	*Time/Date/Result*
Verify that downtime reports are being generated by the system.	1. Examine location of downtime reports, verify all reports are present per requirements documentation. 2. Select specific downtime report. Open report, validate all content per documentation.	Rachel Medina, EHR Downtime Lead (ext. 366921)	05/15/19—all reports present (see "Downtime Report Inventory" checklist), selected report (see "Cardiac Inpatient Unit Downtime Report" checklist, file date 05/14/19) opened and contained all required content per documentation.
Verify that downtime reports are correct.	Inspect each downtime report (by functional or clinical area) and validate all data fields are present, all content is present, and all formatting is as expected.	Rachel Medina and each IS clinical Lead	05/15/19—see Downtime Report Inventory checklist. All reports tested and validated. All fields present, all content present, formatting as expected.
Verify that downtime reports print as expected.	1. From the list of functional or clinical areas, go to each area. 2. Select the downtime report for that area. 3. Print downtime reports and verify reports print as expected, content is as specified, and time to print is acceptable.	Rachel Medina and each IS clinical Lead	05/15/19—see Downtime Report Inventory checklist. "OR Downtime Report" did not print. "Radiology Downtime Report" printed but was garbled. All other reports printed as expected. ESCALATED OR and Radiology reports to Kyle Gressel for resolution.
[Other validation/ verification steps, as needed]			

1. Measure response times for various transactions in your system. Your EHR vendor may have tools you can use for this activity. Some of these metrics may be defined in service level agreements with your EHR (or other systems) vendor contract, so be sure to check what was agreed to at this time. If you're paying for enhanced response times for systems you're renting (a.k.a. cloud services, for example), check at this juncture to make sure you're getting what you paid for.
2. Simulate very high load and high volumes. Simulate everyone logging in at shift change or month end, for example. Anticipate peak load times on the system and simulate those loads to get an idea of how the real environment will behave. Again automated scripts drive consistent testing processes.
3. Measure time between screen refresh, mouse clicks, report generation requests, table or graph generation, etc. If you have system tools that can measure these elements, that's great. If not, use a stop watch to time events. It may not be 100% accurate, but it beats a user's perception of "slow."
4. Perform, simulate, and/or measure time to perform backups or data migration. If these activities exceed the allowed timeframe, you'll have a problem managing the operational aspects of the system. If it takes longer to back up your system than the organization can tolerate, you'll have unscheduled or unacceptable downtimes right from the start. Many solutions provide near real-time backups so that an actual downtime is not required. However, don't assume that's the case.
5. Test your backup process. Assuming your solution provider (or your systems team) has developed a backup solution, be sure you test it. Just because your data are backed up doesn't mean you could easily come back up and run from those data. Test your recovery processes and then document them.
6. Simulate real-time operations activities (to the extent possible) that network, systems, or storage engineers may need to undertake in the standard management of these systems.

One important item to keep in mind is the performance testing in a non-production environment will not exactly replicate your environment on go live day or beyond; so if you see warning signs at this juncture, investigate more fully. One organization who upgraded to a new EHR version had purchased all new server and storage hardware to meet vendor requirements. Performance testing sailed through, but when go live launched, the system was sluggish. Further investigation indicated the hardware was more than capable of handling the load (processor usage below 50%, storage IO [input/output] well within tolerances). The root cause ended up being the new software code itself. The organization worked with the vendor to improve code. This is something that might not have been discoverable during the testing phase, despite the best efforts of the team. So, if you run into issues, don't jump to conclusions; seek root cause. The answers aren't always the most obvious ones.

Super User Considerations

Let's start by defining the term *super user*. In healthcare EHR terms, a super user is a clinical or business person who is well versed in the work of the department and who is assigned to become very knowledgeable about the functionality of the software as it relates to their area of expertise. There are specific, defined duties assigned to super users. These roles are typically filled with frontline staff and/or supervisors. It's less effective to have managers in these roles because the way managers need to work is typically very different than how frontline staff work within the EHR.

Super user programs can be an incredibly effective mechanism for engaging clinical users and ensuring the eventual (and ongoing) success of your EHR initiative. There are many upsides to having a strong super user program in place, but there are key considerations to make it successful as well as organizational constraints you'll need to address. A study in 2009, at the early end of EHR adoption, conducted by the U.S. Department of Health and Human Services Agency for Healthcare Research and Quality, stated that there was a positive correlation between super users and the perception (and success) of the clinical information system (CIS), which we now refer to as the EHR.

> The researchers found that more hours devoted to carrying out the super user role was associated with positive employee perceptions about the CIS. They also found a positive correlation between super user attitudes toward the CIS and employee attitudes. How super users perceived their qualifications was also significantly associated with employee outcomes. According to the researchers, the effects produced by super users are far reaching within the health care organization. These individuals

> enhance the perceptions among employees about the usefulness and ease of use of the CIS. Super users also provide clinical staff members with supplementary development of informatics competencies in the form of just-in-time training at the point the staff are doing actual work. The study was supported in part by the Agency for Healthcare Research and Quality (HS15196). (US Department of Health and Human Services, Agency for Healthcare Research and Quality, Publication # 09-RA010, July 2009, Number 347, https://archive.ahrq.gov/news/newsletters/research-activities/jul09/0709RA26.html).

The effectiveness of super users has continued to show positive results. However, many organizations struggle to gain the needed commitment of clinical time to develop and sustain a super user program. This is unfortunate since the payoff is primarily on the end-user side of the equation. Strong super user programs promote

- More effective use of the EHR
- Higher productivity of end users who use the EHR
- Higher satisfaction with the EHR due to familiarity
- Higher satisfaction because local resources (super users) are available to answer questions
- More positive attitude about the EHR (aptitude follows attitude)
- More reliable and consistent input back to the IT department for optimization requests

If you were to ask organizational leaders what dollar value they would place on these attributes, they might be hard-pressed to come up with a specific number. However, if you pose it differently—perhaps asking if they would support bringing in a consulting firm at $X cost to significantly enhance the usability and satisfaction with the EHR—you might be surprised at the response. The real challenge is that it requires clinical resources, which are almost always in short supply. If you can make the business case first and then quantify the clinical resources needed (time and subsequent cost), then you may be able to develop a robust super user program. A link to one super user program is included in the Resources section at the end of this chapter to get you started on defining your super user program requirements.

In addition, identifying the right people to be super users is important. Here is a list of attributes you can start with in identifying potential super users:

1. Excited about technology in healthcare
2. Computer literate
3. Able to learn quickly and share that learning effectively with others
4. Natural leaders, willing to speak up and assist in problem resolution
5. Has been with the organization long enough to fully understand their current role

In developing super users, you may engage your communications or marketing team to not only help advertise the opportunity but also communicate the super user program as an opportunity to enhance a career, assist others, and make a positive difference to the organization. Healthcare is filled with people who passionately care about improving patient care, so this is an opportunity to pull those people into a very important aspect of EHR deployment success.

User Acceptance Criteria

User acceptance criteria are a standard part of most software development projects, but they're not always incorporated into healthcare IT projects, especially EHR-related projects. However, projects that do include user acceptance criteria or conditions tend to be more successful. Success can be measured by project metrics such as on time, on budget, and in scope, but success is also measured by end-user satisfaction. Developing user acceptance criteria will help inform building, testing, and training activities.

Many aspects of user acceptance are part of testing activities. If users participate in testing, successful user acceptance is typically more likely to be achieved.

User acceptance criteria typically are derived from functional requirements. These criteria should list a set of features or functions that must be present in the final product. For an EHR, these are often listed by module and are defined at the outset of the project. Though features and functions may evolve in the initial stages of the project, they should be agreed upon and documented before build or configuration begins.

User acceptance criteria should include acceptance criteria for errors and defects. It's hard to go into a project agreeing to accept defects, but few software products are ever 100% defect-free. Therefore, you may want to agree ahead of time with your user base about what types of defects are acceptable and what types are not. In most instances, critical- and high-priority defects are unacceptable and must be resolved before user acceptance sign off. However, medium- and low-priority defects may be acceptable and may be placed on a list of items to address after go live, during the first phase of optimization efforts. A critical error would include things like the wrong data being written to the patient's record or a critical alert failing to fire at the appropriate time. A medium or low error might be the placement of a component on a page or a workflow not working as expected. Defining what *critical-*, *high-*, *medium-*, and *low-*priority defects are in advance of your project work is important. If it's not done by the time you begin testing, you'll spend a lot of wasted time and effort defining them while trying to use them.

User acceptance may include expectations regarding system performance. We've all experienced systems that worked as designed, but they were so slow as to be unusable. That's a really unfortunate scenario to run into because in most cases it's avoidable, which is why performance testing is a vital part of your testing plan. User acceptance criteria might include acceptable performance metrics such as time to log in, time between screen refresh, or time from click to action, screen or system timeouts, etc. Though these can be difficult to measure when you're sitting with the user staring at the screen, many EHR vendors can provide behind-the-scenes metrics to help you measure these elements. And if you can easily measure these things while sitting with the user, it probably means systems are running far too slowly. Define these elements as part of your technical requirements so that your systems are up to the job of running your EHR within acceptable limits.

Training Tips

Training is always challenging in a clinical environment because it needs to be delivered to all end users and it needs to be delivered in a timely fashion. If you train staff too early, they'll forget what they learned. Train them too late, and you may be short-changing training and time to familiarize the staff with the end product. It will always be a challenge, but there are a few things to keep in mind that will reduce these potential problems.

1. *Make training timelines part of your project schedule and protect that window of time.* Often project schedules start tightening up at the end of a project. Time is squandered early in the project, and compression happens at the tail end. This is common in many projects, so having a strong project management process is important. It's pretty typical to see a training project plan that ties into the larger EHR project plan. Be sure the dependencies are clearly marked and understood. The training plan breaks out different types of training and different types of users, and sets timelines and schedules for training. The organization needs to commit to expending the resources for this training and to avoid compressing training because other timelines have slipped.
2. *Ensure you train super users to train end users.* Training the trainer is crucial and many organizations overlook this. Just because a nurse or a supervisor or a tech knows how to do something does not mean they make an effective trainer. Spending time training your super users on the basics of training will make them far more effective. Don't just toss them into the deep end of the training pool and expect to get good results.
3. *Make sure your end users are trained using methods that work for them.* A one-size-fits-all training approach is actually a one-size-fits-some. The rest will be left behind. Some learn by doing, some learn by reading, some learn by seeing. You'll need to accommodate different learning styles along with varying computer skills. You may want to provide basic computer user classes on a recurring basis to help end users who are not yet comfortable on computers. This is also true when you migrate platforms from Windows 7 to Windows 10, for example. Most end users need to interact with the computer as well as with the EHR, so having basic computer skills can reduce stress and increase confidence as a support for EHR learning.
4. *Understand your end user's work context.* Registration for inpatient areas may not be the same as registration for surgical or special procedure areas, for example. Don't make blanket assumptions (hint: this is where your super users are vital to your training plans).
5. *Perform the minimum amount of needed training as close to go live as possible.* Keep it simple; make sure people know how to use the system to do their specific job. Additional skills workshops can be conducted, either by super users or by trainers, after go live.
6. *Perform a gap analysis.* Segment your users into those with moderate to strong computer skills and those with low to no computer skills.

These groups will learn at different rates and will need different types of training in order to help them be successful.

7. *Develop standardized curriculum.* As basic as this sounds, some organizations leave curriculum development to each trainer, so training across EHR modules may be inconsistent or completely useless. Be sure to develop curriculum using standard practices. Many EHR vendors provide starting curriculum; just be sure it is focused on end users and not your applications teams. Applications teams need training, but it is vastly different from end-user training. That said, your applications teams could stand to go through your end-user training if you really want a powerful feedback loop.

Lean Process and Product Testing

Throughout this chapter, we've discussed a relatively traditional approach to the topics of testing, super user testing, user acceptance, and training. These approaches can certainly be used, but if we look at them through the lens of Lean thinking, we can make noticeable improvements in our testing and acceptance processes. As we've learned in previous chapters, standard work and visual management are foundational Lean concepts that can be readily applied to the testing and user acceptance phase of your EHR deployment.

One way to help make things more visual is to create an Obeya room. Obeya translates literally as "big room" from Japanese. It's used in Lean organizations as a place for the organization (and/or department) to meet on a regular basis to discuss improvement activities, track True North Metrics, update leaders on key A3 projects, and for leaders and peers to ask questions and offer assistance. It's not a place for bragging about accomplishments, rather for discussion about items that are "red" and what can be done as a team to get them to "green." The Obeya concept is different from a Central Command Center or war room. In the next chapter, we will discuss the importance of creating a Central Command Center for the go live phase of your EHR deployment. The Obeya process is also more commonly used as an operational improvement tool, where high-level organizational goals and strategies are deployed to the frontline level of the organization. The same thought process can also be used for the testing and user acceptance phase of your implementation.

If we start by looking at Unit and Functional Testing, we may ask

- Are all major functions present?
- Do they perform as they should?
- Do the screens appear as they should?
- Etc.

How can you make the status of each topic more visual? Lean thinkers would likely create a white board and update it with an erasable marker. Of course, this approach usually drives the IT team crazy. The IT department would probably create an electronic dashboard that can be placed on the organization's internal website. For the Obeya process to work, the format does *not* matter. It can be electronically projected, on a white board, or on a napkin, if you prefer. What really matters is that the status can be conveyed simply and easily and that it is communicated in person in your Obeya room on a regular basis. Virtual communities and online tracking mechanisms rarely work, and you miss the opportunity to learn from your colleagues and build relationships that will be vital as the project gets closer to go live and its associated stress levels. An example of an Obeya Room is shown in Figure 9.2.

The standard work of a typical Obeya process flows as follows:

- Representatives from your functional areas will present their status to the leadership team at a scheduled time in the Obeya room. This may be weekly or daily, depending on your particular needs and phase of deployment. The presenter should be close enough to the work to truly understand the problems and issues associated with the topic. For clinical areas, this would typically be a nurse manager or nurse supervisor.
- Only the "red" items will be presented. For instance, 10% of the major functions are not performing as desired.
- *What* are the details and background of this problem?
- *Who* is working on the issues, and what is being done to solve them?
- *When* do we expect to have resolution?
- At this point, leaders and colleagues from other functional areas would ask additional questions and offer ideas to help close the gaps.
- Each topic only gets 5 to 10 minutes, and you should have a designated time keeper. This is basically a stand-up meeting.

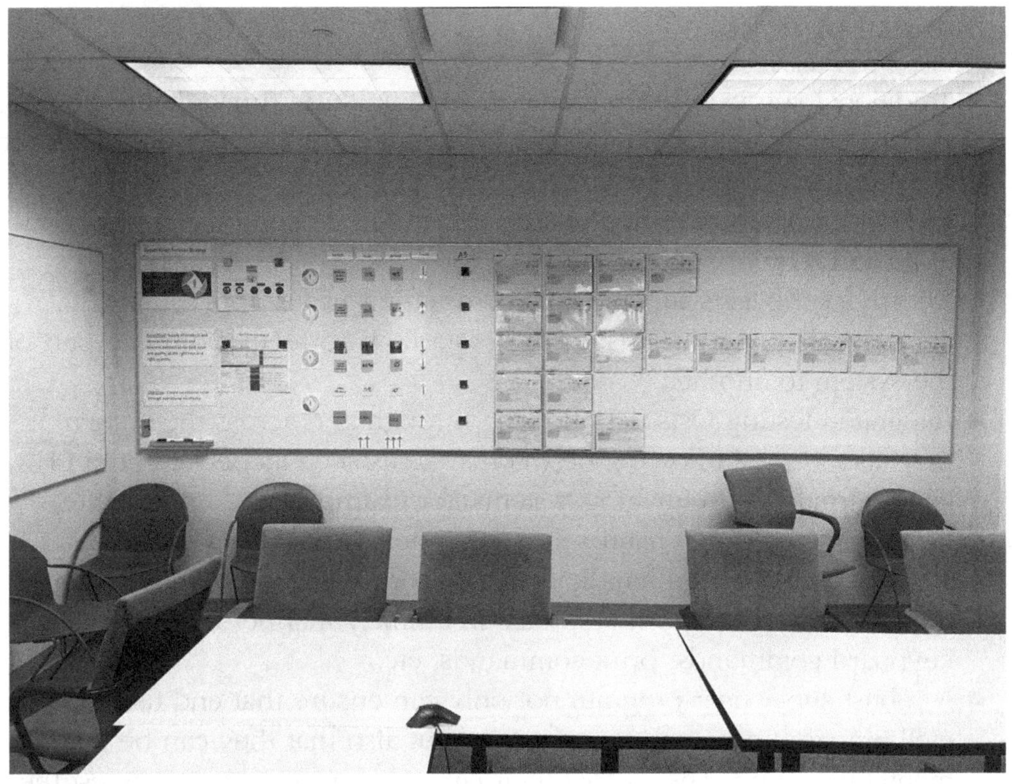

Figure 9.2 Obeya room.

- As with any large project, there should also be standard work around escalating issues that could potentially impact your implementation timeline.

This same process can be used for system testing, integration testing, performance testing, and user acceptance. Remember that the format of visual management isn't nearly as important as personal interactions and teamwork that result from using the Obeya process.

As you can see, the same standard elements for testing, user acceptance, and training are present in both the traditional and Lean approach. By using the Lean methodology, we can make these processes more visible and, therefore, more effective. Working from checklists is certainly a basic approach; making work progress visible for all and routinely reviewing status of at-risk ("red") items is the Lean approach. From this discussion, you can see how you can easily migrate your standard testing processes to Lean processes to achieve better results.

Chapter Summary

- Traditional software testing tasks include unit and functional testing, system testing, integration testing (sometimes called "end-to-end" or "go live" testing), and performance testing.
- Unit and functional testing ensure that the basic build meets specifications and requirements.
- System testing tests functionality across the various applications that comprise the system. This ensures data flow correctly from one part of the system to another.
- Integrated testing tests data flowing through and across the system. It may also test data flowing between systems such as between the EHR, lab, pharmacy, and imaging systems, for example.
- Performance testing ensures that the system infrastructure (servers, storage, network) can handle the data load of the EHR. It also ensures that the application itself responds in a timely manner (to mouse clicks, keyboard commands, print commands, etc.).
- A robust super user program not only can ensure that end users are well prepared to use the new system but also that they can be instrumental in testing. They know their clinical workflows and can test the system (from unit testing to performance testing) to ensure the system is working as expected.
- Developing complete user acceptance criteria, based on agreed upon requirements, will help focus efforts during the testing process.
- Training is always a topic of discussion in healthcare because it's challenging to get clinical staff out of the patient care areas and into classroom training. Additionally, when there are large numbers of people to train, it becomes a challenge to schedule everyone in an appropriate timeframe. Train too early and knowledge is lost. Train too late and it's likely to short-change staff training time. An Obeya room and the associated standard work can help you use visual controls and teamwork to quickly resolve gaps and at the same time cultivate relationships that will be invaluable as the project moves toward go live.
- Standard testing, user acceptance, and training activities have to be undertaken, but using a Lean approach can improve outcomes by reducing waste, improving visibility, and accelerating results.

Further Reading

Guerrero A. "Five best practices for training staff on using a new EHR," May 17, 2013. http://profitable-practice.softwareadvice.com/five-best-practices-for-training-staff-on-ehr-0513/ (accessed November 20, 2016).

Kaner C, Faulk J, Nguyen HQ. *Testing Computer Software, 2nd Edition*. New York: Wiley & Sons, Inc., 1999.

Stratis Health. "Testing plan—Physician office," https://www.stratishealth.org/documents/HITToolkitclinic/2.Utilize/2.1Implement/2.1Testing_Plan.doc (accessed July 6, 2017).

University of North Carolina Health Care. "Super user partnership agreement," http://news.unchealthcare.org/epic/super_user_partnership-agreement (accessed November 20, 2016).

U.S. Department of Health & Human Services, Agency for Healthcare Research and Quality. "Staff 'super users' who train others on clinical information systems help shape positive employee attitudes.", Research Activities, July 2009, No. 347, Publication # 09-RA010, https://archive.ahrq.gov/news/newsletters/research-activities/jul09/0709RA26.html (accessed November 20, 2016).

Further Reading

Chapter 10

Go Live

Overview

Through the previous chapters, we've described the processes and work needed to deliver a more Lean EHR to your organization. In this chapter, we'll discuss how to prepare for and implement your go live plan so that you achieve the objectives you've defined.

We use the term "go live" to indicate the point in time at which the code, development software, and corresponding processes are moved into a live production environment. Typically, that is a "point of no return" where the previous production environment is overwritten or taken down and the new environment is the only thing users can access. Sometimes this is almost invisible to end users, such as when software is updated, but most of the changes are behind the scenes. Other times, such as when you deploy a completely revised (or new) EHR, the change will be dramatic. How you handle the go live activities will dictate the overall success of the project, so these final steps are crucial to get right.

Planning the Go Live

If you've been working through the elements in this book, you should be pretty well set to plan and implement your go live processes. As with all other aspects of deploying a Lean EHR, go live activities need to be well aligned to the organization and be structured to provide the most value to your customers. If the work done up to now has been focused on reducing waste and increasing value, then your go live should be relatively straightforward. You should double check that your post–go live processes (that have been optimized using Lean tools) are aligned with your objectives. In other words, it would be a wasted opportunity to go live on a new or updated EHR without having examined your processes to ensure they are adding the highest possible value to your customers—who ultimately are your patients and your care providers.

Readiness

It's important to assess your readiness before go live. The information in the following sections will assist in reviewing organizational readiness.

Application Readiness

The EHR is, of course, the most important application in terms of reviewing your readiness, but it's not the only one. We'll start with your EHR and then discuss some of the ancillary applications that might come into play in your organization.

1. *Unit testing and integrated testing are completed satisfactorily.* Your results should support your readiness. If you find during testing that things are not working as expected, you must assess whether or not you are actually ready for go live. If there are minor adjustments to be made, you probably can safely proceed. However, if you found large gaps or large problems, you should step back and analyze the impact. Many organizations consider large gaps irrelevant. The timeline becomes the most important thing. After all, we are paying staff and integrators and trainers a lot of money to work through the configuration and technology issues. Delaying the launch adds expense to the project. This thinking leads to a poor launch and consumes a lot of emotional capital with the staff. It ultimately leads to suboptimal results or failure, which is pure waste from any perspective.
2. *End user and super user training have been successfully conducted.* Training is critical to the proper and safe use of the EHR. Whether your organization has opted to pull everyone into classroom training or provide training in the working environment, you should have data that support your training is substantially complete. You should also have a

plan for assisting during go live since no training can adequately prepare a person for all scenarios one might encounter in a clinical setting. Keep in mind that functionality changes also impact the workflows and processes. Both training and support are needed for success.

3. *Physicians are engaged and trained.* If you have not had success with physician engagement and training, you are facing an uphill battle in your go live. While the organization's leadership team may have worked to get physician engagement, if you believe there is insufficient physician leadership and participation, you should escalate this early to your leadership team for evaluation. This may not stop your go live, but it may influence it, and you should address this head on if it is the case.
4. *Interfaces are tested and working.* If your EHR is dependent upon data inputs from other systems (and just about every EHR is), you should be certain that data are flowing as expected. That means that the data fields have been validated, the data coming across have also been validated, and the locations to which the data are flowing have been inspected to ensure data are arriving in the right place, at the right time, in the right manner. While this is part of unit and integrated testing, it is worth calling this out specifically to ensure it is not overlooked. The corollary to this is that you must also validate any data coming out of the EHR for input to other systems or for direct use. This is particularly true if the data have any impact on patient safety or on the transfer of information for continuity of care. For example, discharge summaries, prescription information, or after-visit instructions provided directly to patients should be closely inspected for accuracy and usability. All documentation provided to physicians or provider offices should also be checked for accuracy and usability as well as timely delivery. If these data are provided via secure electronic access, check that they are working as expected.
5. *Financial charges are as expected.* Coding and billing are essential to every healthcare organization. Though it is likely part of your testing process, it's worth calling out that test charges should be reviewed so that the organization's leaders are confident that charges will be captured appropriately and that billing will continue uninterrupted. Inaccuracies and delays in this area of the EHR can cripple an organization, so it's important this is also called out as a discrete element of testing and readiness. Most organizations expect (or hope) to improve charge captures or reduce days outstanding on receivables. If these are expected improvements, then these should also be tested. At worst, you should not see these get *worse* than the current state.

Staff Readiness

We've discussed training as a key component, but there are other aspects of readiness worth reviewing before your go live. As we've discussed throughout the book, the objective is not to simply automate the processes you have in place today (that's true whether your updating/optimizing an existing EHR or installing a new one). To do so would be to miss a rare opportunity to make improvements in physical and logical workflows, which in turn could improve productivity, satisfaction with the EHR, and ultimately, patient care. Before you get set to pull the trigger on your go live, be sure everyone is in alignment with respect to the desired outcomes.

- Have you adequately addressed the naysayers in the organization?
- Have you completed required tasks from your Lean project plan?
- Have the critical milestones been met?
- Are you really ready to go?

Pushing out a go live is often considered a near-catastrophic event, so we're not suggesting you casually push it out; but, if tasks are not complete, milestones have not been met, and your organization is not ready, the go live will launch poorly or even fail. It's better to delay than to fail altogether, so be sure to take a hard look at the overall organizational readiness.

Of course, if you're like most organizations at this point, everyone is pretty tired from the efforts thus far, and they're more than ready to go live. This is your last opportunity to check in, so make full use of it. Don't let all the hard work (and fatigue) leading up to the go live cause a default decision to blindly go forward with the go live. If you're not ready, call it and then figure out how to get ready. You can figure out the root cause later (and you absolutely should), but don't bow to pressure if things are not set for success.

Process Readiness

A corollary to staff readiness is process readiness. Typically, with a new (or optimized) EHR, many processes will be changing. Super users and training should have helped users get a basic understanding of what will change, but the organization should also have new standard work defined that will enable the adherence to the newly defined or modified standards. In anticipation of go live, while some standard work may not be able to be created or finalized until the very end of testing, each area should be targeting the creation, validation, and training of standard work processes in parallel with the go live activities.

It's also important to remember that downtime procedures need to be developed for those times when the EHR has a scheduled or unscheduled downtime. This task should be one of your major tasks in the readiness for your go live milestone. Most EHR vendors provide numerous options for downtime procedures including access to read-only data or access to reports that contain key patient data for a period of time that are automatically created every 15 or 30 minutes, etc.

If you haven't yet developed any contingency plans or any downtime processes, now is the time to think this through. You should work with organizational leaders to develop scenarios that you can use to walk through your processes to ensure you are able to provide safe, effective patient care regardless of the availability of EHR or other electronic systems.

Though a full discussion of business continuity and disaster recovery (BC/DR) is outside the scope of this book, it is vital to have these kinds of plans in place. Many organizations view BC/DR as an infrastructure problem to solve, and to some degree, it is. Do you have high availability architecture that provides redundancy of core components? Is your network highly reliable? Is it hospital-grade? Is it up 99.999% of the time? What about servers and storage? Do you have reliability issues you need to address? Do you have defined patch windows for patching applications and servers, and do you have methods for notifying operations of these downtimes?

Finally, are your patient data going to be stored safely in a usable format somewhere else? If you have neglected to create sufficient backup and recovery plans, if you believe that storing tapes off-site is the extent of your need, you may want to take another look. If you're working in a small organization, this might suffice. In most cases, it will not be an adequate business continuity solution. If you are not certain if you have taken appropriate measures, your EHR vendor likely has strong recommendations that you can use as a baseline. Hopefully, this topic came up much earlier in your deployment schedule, and your work now is to validate and test your capabilities and then to ensure the organization is ready.

Organizational readiness for business continuity includes things not related to the EHR such as ensuring you have backup communication methods if your network or phone system (especially if using network-based VoIP telephony) fails. If your network fails, you won't have your EHR and other electronic systems. How will you care for patients in this scenario?

Technology Readiness

Finally, you want to validate that all hardware identified as required for the go live is installed and working. This will also be a task in the project plan, but it is a good practice to *triple*-check. You also want to ensure you've "stress-tested" your overall network infrastructure to verify that it can handle the anticipated load at go live and beyond.

During a "big bang" go live of an EHR a few years ago, a large organization dispatched a team that included desktop support staff as well as volunteers from the IS department—from analysts to directors. Everyone was assigned an area of the hospital, and they were tasked with ensuring every PC, printer, bar code scanner, and document scanner called out on the plan was installed, labeled, plugged in, and functioning. They were expected to print something from each type of printer (laser, label, and wristband) to ensure each worked and had the appropriate supplies loaded in it (paper, label roll, wristband roll). They had checklists they used to check each device type and each device. These sheets were collected, validating the hardware was working. Volunteers were given new assignments, and the process repeated.

If any equipment was missing or malfunctioning, it was reported and repaired immediately. This "all hands on deck" last effort (it went on throughout the Saturday and Sunday prior to the Monday morning go live) resulted in zero defects with respect to missing or malfunctioning equipment at go live. This, in turn, supported the organization and helped drive a very favorable first impression for the EHR. When the only problem users encounter is navigating a still unfamiliar system, the perception of the system and its success skyrockets.

Strategy

Determine your rollout strategy. Are you going to roll this out by application? By department? By location? It can be challenging to do a limited go live because systems can quickly get out of sync. However, it can also be easier to manage a go live that is limited in scope or geography. Typically, organizations do one of three things:

1. Go live throughout the entire organization simultaneously (often referred to as "big bang").

2. Go live with the entire application in one location (one hospital, one region, one clinic, etc.).
3. Go live with a portion of the EHR (one or more applications) at all locations (such as an OR module or an ambulatory module across all such departments in the organization).

If you have designed the workflows and the functionality using the model cell approach, part of this question may already be answered for you. It is also recommended to discuss the approach with your EHR vendor, and use their expertise in assisting with go live events. They want you to be successful, and they have performed many more go lives than you have. Be sure to assess their advice, though, to ensure it is appropriate to your organization.

1. Does it apply to an organization of your size and type?
2. Is there anything about your organization that is truly unique?
3. Is there anything about your organization that the vendor believes would influence the decision about the go live one way or the other (timing, scope, etc.)?
4. Are there differences in your provider population that would cause you to choose one type of go live over another?

Based on the EHR vendor's assessment, and your own internal discussion with subject matter experts, you should develop a go live strategy. Developing a go live strategy will be one of your tasks in your project plan. The strategy should be written down and discussed at a formal meeting. It should be formally approved by all executive stakeholders as an interim milestone.

Data Management during Go Live

Your technical teams will no doubt be discussing these processes in meticulous detail in the months leading up to the go live. However, it's worth mentioning that as part of the overall improvement, you will possibly be migrating some data from your existing systems (EHR and other), so you need to ensure you have identified those data as well as a method to prevent duplication of records. You will be leaving some data behind, and you will be archiving other data. Your go live plan should have this spelled out in detail so that your technical team can implement the plan, and your super users and other testers can validate the data as they are migrated.

This also includes decommissioning systems, interfaces, VPN connections, and any other activities related to ensuring that only the new system and the new processes can be used. It would be pretty devastating to have a group of users continuing to enter data into an old system, causing data to get out of sync and requiring manual efforts to remediate the problem. Ensuring all older systems are at least unavailable, even if not fully decommissioned, when you go live will keep things organized.

Go Live Staffing

Before we discuss the Command Center itself, let's talk about go live staffing. Who do you need working when? What resources will you need? The short answer is *everyone*. The longer answer is that you'll need to develop a schedule of the go live day and the duration of intensive support you will need to provide after go live. Most organizations find that 1 week of intensive support is required and a second week of somewhat less intensive support is helpful—but again, this varies greatly by organization. If you are optimizing your EHR, your go live support needs will be vastly different from an organization that is going live on a new EHR or going live on an EHR (i.e., no prior electronic system existed) for the first time.

You have probably already identified staffing issues you have within the IS department. During your project work, you may have had to (1) train staff in new skills, (2) hire new staff with needed skills, or (3) hired consultants to fill gaps (and hopefully, perform knowledge transfer as part of the engagement), so you are likely painfully aware of your go-forward staffing needs. That said, you should ensure you will have the skills and expertise on hand during go live that you need to be successful. This often includes consultants as well as the vendors EHR support team in conjunction with your own in-house staff.

Once you've determined the skills you need and have performed a gap analysis, (do you have the vendor, consultant, or internal staff to support the entire organization at go live?) you can take the necessary steps to fill those gaps through your EHR vendor or a competent consulting or staffing agency. You can determine whether these staff are needed only for go live support or for slightly longer-term support. You'll have to make a staffing plan to address gaps for the long term, but that's outside the scope of our discussion. Completing the staffing gap analysis and developing the go live staffing plan will also be a task in the go live readiness phase of your project plan.

Another task in your go live readiness phase is to create a go live schedule by estimating need by support role (provider, biller, scheduler, nurse, PCT, etc.). For example, your physician offices or clinics may only need assistance during normal business hours (and perhaps a few hours after closing in order to complete the day's work and prepare for the following day). Obviously a hospital's inpatient areas, as well as procedural areas, will need to have resources available 24/7. If you need to provide 24/7 support, and you only have two people who can fill the role, they'll become highly ineffective after a day or two. Go live support is more stressful and demanding than day-to-day work, so you're better off slightly overestimating the amount of support that will be needed.

You may find that creating a schedule similar to the example shown in Table 10.1 will help you get started in creating your own Go live staffing schedule.

Central Command Center

Most organizations choose to stand up a central command center for their EHR go live. This facilitates effective communication, as well as fast decision-making and rapid issue resolution. In this section, we'll describe a few different scenarios that might work for you, but of course, each organization is unique and the specific needs of your organization will vary. The key elements for a successful command center are the following:

1. Decision-making leaders are present.
2. Clear, organized communication methods are in place (phones, radios, wireless, and cellular options).
3. IS teams have been assigned clear roles and responsibilities.
4. Escalation procedures have been defined, agreed to, and published.
5. Teams not directly involved in the go live have been assigned support roles.
6. A schedule has been published indicating how the command center will be staffed.
7. Computers, printers, and phones are installed and working in the command center and possibly in nearby locations.

Table 10.1 Go Live IS/Super User Staffing Schedule Example

Date	*Role*	*Location*	*Skills Needed*	*Staff Needed*
Friday, 3/20/2020	Physician support	Hospital—all locations	Physician order entry, physician documentation	19
8 a.m.–8 p.m.	Martina, Cathy, Jose, Katrina, Mary, William, Farad, Lucien, Lisa, Kit, Bobby, Lawrence, Jessica B., Lauren, Pete, Manny, Sarah			
8 p.m.–2 a.m.	Cindy, Jessica M., Tamika, Lourdes, Chris, Roberto, Darrell			
2 a.m.–8 a.m.	Jim, Paul, Tina, Lisa, Scott, Kevin, Michelle			

Date	*Role*	*Location*	*Skills Needed*	*Staff Needed*
Friday, 3/20/2020	Nursing—inpatient	Hospital—all locations	Nursing workflows, including specialty areas (cardiac, neuro, Peds, PICU, NICU, L&D)	44
8 a.m.–8 p.m.	Melody, Chauncey, Chris, Lucy, William, Marc, Flory, Justin, Natalya, Loren, Angelica, Maurice, Fernando, Alicia, Marcus, Lola, Nancy, Cathy B., Sebastian, Lisa M., Kim, Hoyt, Vincent, Grant, Joe, Mina *(see roster for specific area assignments)*			
8 p.m.–2 a.m.	Jessica (Vendor), Larry (Vendor), Charles, Erin, Adam, Chris, Ricardo, Buzz, Loi, LuAnn, Brian			
2 a.m.–8 a.m.	James, Katherine, Lester, Vince D., Spector, Wayne, Willow, Roxanna, Freeman, Ellis, Karla			

Roster Friday, 3/20/2020	*8 a.m.–8 p.m.*	*8 p.m.–2 a.m.*	*2 a.m.–8 a.m.*
Unit 1000	Melody, Chauncey, Chris, Lucy, William	Larry (Vendor), Charles	James, Katherine
Unit 2000	Marc, Flory, Justin, Natalya	Jessica (Vendor), Erin	Willow, Roxanna
Unit 3000	Loren, Angelica	Chris, Ricardo	Freeman, Spector
Command center	Maurice, Fernando, Alicia, Marcus, Lola	Adam, Buzz, Loi	Lester, Vince D

8. Restrooms, breakrooms, copiers, and supplies are nearby or easily accessible.
9. The space is large enough to accommodate the expected staffing levels.
10. Chairs and tables are configured to meet the need.
11. The location is booked well in advance for a period of time that includes 2 weeks prior to go live through 2 weeks beyond go live (or whatever timeframe the organization designates).
12. The location is central enough to be convenient.
13. The location is accessible 24/7 for all authorized staff.

The command center itself should have these items in place:

1. A central phone number that is well publicized. You will receive all calls in through this number, and you will want to track these calls. You may utilize your service desk function, but be sure you don't handle your go live like an ordinary service request.
2. Phones should be able to route calls to the appropriate application team—your ED application team, your OR application team, or your clinical documentation team, for example, should be able to get calls routed directly to them for immediate attention.
3. An incident or ticket tracking system. Whether you use your service desk software or another system, all incidents should be tracked electronically. Key issues may be written by hand on a whiteboard for visibility, but an electronic tracking method will ensure all issues are addressed (resolved, closed, escalated, etc.).
4. A diagram of critical information for routing calls and managing escalations. For example, you might diagram your information flow as shown in Figure 10.1 so that everyone in the room knows key data points at a glance. These are internal data, so if a physician calls for assistance, he or she will be calling the published number. If you choose to have special numbers for various roles, be sure that is clear when you publish your main numbers. In this example, physician and nurses are all calling the same single phone number, but the calls are internally routed according to this chart. Escalation phone numbers are provided so that critical issues can be escalated 24/7 throughout go live without trying to figure out who is on call or who should be covering. By pre-establishing these key contacts, you will reduce errors and gaps in coverage.

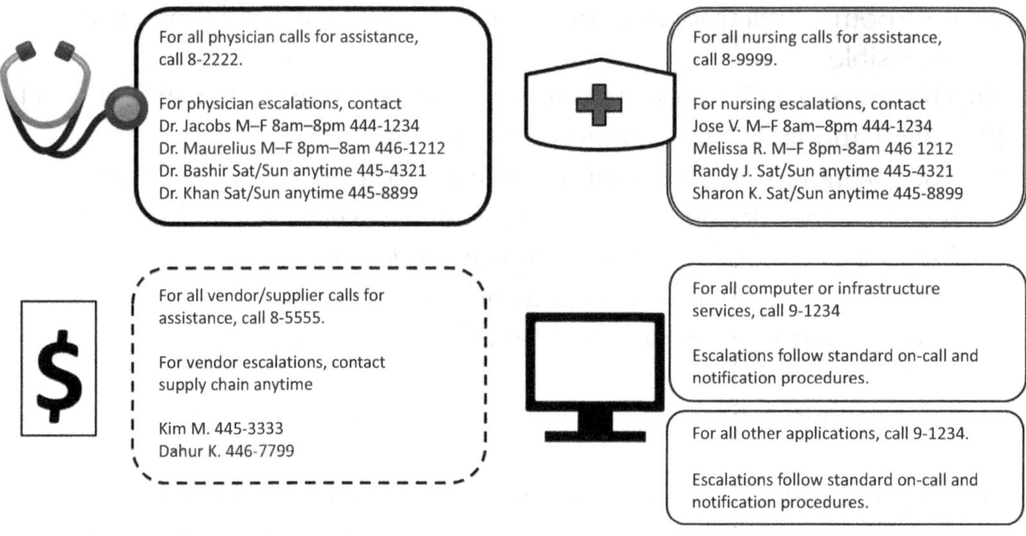

Figure 10.1 Sample information chart for go live.

Go Live Statistics

It can be helpful to track statistics for evaluating the number of "defects" in your process. These defects can be defined as anything that did not go as planned, and therefore required a remedial action of some sort. Some helpful statistics you may want to consider, especially if you have an existing EHR and are optimizing/upgrading or transitioning, include

1. Number of service desk calls received.
2. Number of service desk calls dispatched. *(This is also known as First Call resolution—how many tickets the service desk resolved vs. how many they had to send to another team for resolution.)*
3. Number of severity 1, 2, or 3 calls received (must be predefined by the organization).
4. Number of issues identified as patient safety, "showstoppers," etc. (be sure these are predefined by the organization).
5. Number of requests received to fix something that seemed to be broken (not working as expected).
6. Number of requests received for "enhancements" (things work fine, but it's not what the user wanted or expected).
7. Number of issues reported by physicians, by criticality (severity 1, 2, 3, etc.).
8. Number of issues reported by [insert stakeholder], by criticality.

In addition, usage statistics can be helpful, depending on how easy (or hard) it is to collect them. These may include

1. # Physician logons per hour.
2. # Nursing logons per hour.
3. # Electronic tasks (define what these are, such as electronic orders) completed per hour.
4. Total # of logons in 24-hour, 7-day, 30-day period. Track trends.
5. Total # of complaints or escalations initiated by providers.
6. # of issues reported as broken that were fixed.
7. # of issues reported as broken that were training issues.
8. # of issues reported as broken that were enhancement requests.
9. # of patient records created in [insert timeframe].
10. # of problems found per patient record reviewed in [insert timeframe].

These kinds of statistics are not only fact-based, but they also support your efforts to better understand the go live—what worked, what didn't work as well, and where gaps in your process might be. Without data, you'll be dealing with a swarm of anecdotal information that may or may not reflect the reality of your situation at and after go live.

In the spirit of visual management, a whiteboard can be used to track this information in real time with complete transparency. The reason transparency is needed to rapidly shift resources from one area to another to address problems in as close to real time as possible.

Support "At the Elbow" for Providers

Regardless of whether your care providers work for your organization (employed physicians, for example) or are independent providers who work for multiple organizations (community physicians, for example), you will need to develop a plan for ensuring physicians and other care providers are properly supported during the go live. In many instances, it's difficult to schedule training time in advance of go live with these providers. You might find that getting providers in for 1 to 2 hours of training is the maximum tolerable, for instance. When there are significant changes to the EHR, you should plan on providing "at the elbow" support for all providers for some period of time. In many large organizations, this might be for 2 to 3 weeks. In smaller organizations, it may be 2 to 3 days. How long this support is needed depends on how much the EHR is changing and what type of training (and attendance in training) has been provided. It's always better to plan on more support than may be needed rather than stopping early and leaving your users in the lurch.

One of the most effective ways to do this is to understand each of the potential provider workflows. Hospitalists will have a different workflow than cardiologists, for example. Ideally, creating a visual map of the workflows for each type of provider may help in providing at the elbow support during go live.

You will also need to have your clinical informatics specialist or a team of physician super users available to answer questions and assist. If your organization has a chief medical information officer (CMIO), he or she can be invaluable in identifying potential workflow challenges and potential physician champions and reviewing go live support plans to ensure there are no critical gaps.

If you've been successful in working with physician champions throughout the model development of process and functionality, you should find this support model easier to implement. Below are some things to keep in mind when doing this:

1. Think about all physician and provider (from here forward, we'll refer generically to "providers") types that may need go live support services.
2. Identify those providers that were involved in model development and/or in testing. Determine if they might be willing and able to assist their peers in particular workflows or to be points of contact for escalations, if needed.
3. Schedule clinical informatics and/or clinical application support analysts according to their specialties, provider needs, and patient demand. For example, if you have the greatest demand for behavioral health providers in the ED on weekend nights, make sure your strongest support personnel are scheduled at that time.
4. Develop a clear, concise, and simple process for providers to receive immediate assistance during the first week of go live. For example, it might be a text to a particular command center smartphone or a phone call to a special service desk phone number. Whatever it is, make it simple, make sure it works, and make sure you have a process for responding *immediately* when called.

5. Develop a triage system so you can determine the relative priority of provider support requests. Patient safety requests should come first. For example, an erroneously placed order should be a higher priority than how to document a rounding note. Granted, in an ideal scenario, all requests for at the elbow assistance result in a person showing up to assist the provider in a very short period of time. Since that may not be a realistic goal, you should be able to clearly articulate priorities so everyone is in agreement and is aware of how issues will be handled.

Hopefully your CMIO, chief medical officer, chief nursing informatics officer, and chief nursing officer, or whatever combination of these executives exists in your organization, are actively engaged in planning support services, establishing processes and procedures, and developing documentation and escalation plans so that all issues can be resolved quickly and effectively during the go live window.

You may also consider having an established method for capturing optimization requests during go live. As mentioned, sometimes things work as expected, but not as desired. These may be defects that occurred during the project cycle, but they also might be great ideas to further advance quality, improve timeliness, reduce the cost of care, or enhance the patient experience. Oftentimes, these suggestions cannot be resolved during the go live unless they pose a serious threat to patient safety. In all other cases, you should have a process in place for capturing these requests, the requestor, the date, and the relative urgency of the request. You may use a simple piece of paper with these fields on it that a clinical informatics or application analyst could fill out as they are assisting the provider. They would capture the information and let the provider know that the request will be submitted for review. This can potentially prevent getting sidetracked by issues unrelated to the expected functionality and also respects the voice of your customer by capturing this request.

A word of caution about taking requests for optimization during go live: Often the requests for change are caused by a simple lack of familiarity with the new system (versus really needing different functionality). One possible method for addressing this is to capture these requests, as discussed, but simply put them in a list to be reviewed with provider leaders after 90 days. After this period of time, many of the items will likely be closed with no further action needed. Some items may warrant additional analysis and action; but the providers can make these decisions once they become more familiar with the EHR.

Leveraging Super Users

We've discussed super users a number of times, but it bears repeating in this section. Your super users should be expected to provide support throughout the go live process and beyond. In some organizations, super users are enticed and rewarded for stepping into the roles with additional training, additional perks, and sometimes additional pay. With this comes additional responsibility. Whether the super user is assigned to a particular unit or is expected to support all users across the environment is an organizational decision. For example, a nurse super user should be able to assist any nurse in any unit with support on basic nursing workflows. Specialized super users such as in special procedure areas (ORs, cath labs, GI labs, nuclear medicine, etc.) many only be expected to support all workflows in their assigned area(s).

The key to success with a super user program is to give the super users the tools, training, and support they need to be successful and to hold them accountable for success. The super users should also be intimately familiar with process/clinical standard work they are supporting and demonstrate proficiency in following this standard work. (Ideally, your super users were involved in the creation and validation of standard work prior to go live.) To be an asset to the organization, the super user needs both pieces of the equation. Sometimes super users are not given the tools, training, and support needed to be successful, but they are held accountable. Sometimes super users are given all the resources needed, but they are not held accountable for results. Be sure you have both in equal measure.

Clearly defined standard work for the role of super users will help ensure everyone understands fundamental expectations. Processes and templates for super users to utilize during go live (and beyond) can help facilitate the flow of information. From capturing issues to noting observations from being at gemba, the super users are your eyes and ears in the go live environment, and they can contribute significantly to the success of the project and the organizational knowledge captured for future improvements.

Triaging Requests for Changes

You may receive a number of requests for optimization that at first appear to be requests for support or reports of system issues. However, if you have a good process in place for reviewing *functionality* against *requirements* (in the testing phases and then in the go live process), you will be able to determine the following:

1. Does the system function as designed?
   If yes, the request is likely an optimization request.
   If no, the request is related to a defect in the system and must be triaged and addressed accordingly.
2. Does the system do what is needed?
   Sometimes the system is functioning as designed, but the way it is designed was in error. If you designed it to do X, but it should actually do Y, then it may be functioning as designed, but it's not working as needed. This a change request, so it is technically an optimization request, but it may need to be treated as a defect and be repaired during this go live period.

Of course, all patient safety-related items should be addressed immediately and your triage system should make sure those are visible and addressed quickly and effectively. Documentation about the problem and the change made should be preserved for review later. Other issues reported should be prioritized according to criticality and handed to the proper build team for review and remediation. Each issue should be assigned a unique number (most service desk ticketing systems do this by default) so that each item can be easily tracked. An hourly, daily, and weekly report of issues resolved should be provided to the command center team and to the team leaders to ensure all critical issues are being addressed in a timely manner. It will also enable statistics to be developed regarding time-to-resolution or other relevant data that may help you determine the overall success of the project's processes. In other words, were functional specifications well developed, or did you find a lot of unmet needs at go live? Were critical issues related to one specific area (your emergency department? ORs? Clinical documentation? Order sets? Admitting? Billing?)? Or one type of system functionality? Was testing performed well or were there areas that were missed in the testing phase, and these errors showed up at go live? These data can be analyzed and used for future improvements in your processes.

Validating Critical Issues

It's helpful to have criteria in place for determining critical issues prior to your go live. What is a showstopper? If patient data are being somehow mixed together (patient A's data show up on patient B's file; patient A's medical record number gets associated with patient B), then you have a huge issue that testing missed. You may have to make a hard decision to stop and roll back to prevent patient harm. Those massive decisions aside, you should have some method for assessing criticality for addressing reported issues. For example, does the problem hit one or more of these areas?

1. Data reliability
2. Data integrity
3. Data usability
4. System response time
5. System integration/data flow (images are getting to the right place at the right time, for example)

Table 10.2 shows an example of a criticality matrix you can use to determine the overall criticality of the issue and how quickly you may need to address it. Many IT organizations already have some sort of criticality matrix established (for instance, "Patient safety issues will be addressed immediately and moved into production as soon as the fix has been developed and tested.") and those should be leveraged here. If you don't yet have a system in place, you can develop a matrix based on the level of risk and the relative ease of fixing the issue. For example, a patient safety issue just has to get

Table 10.2 Sample Issue Criticality Matrix

Description	*Patient Safety (5)*	*Data Integrity (4)*	*Usage (3)*	*System Responsiveness (2)*	*Annoyance (1)*	*Criticality Score*
Face sheet prints in wrong location for Unit 2000			3		1	4
System slow when clicking on Images tab				2	1	3
Medication alert for possible interaction between drug A and drug B does not ever work	5	4				9

fixed, whether that means modifying the software or implementing a temporary workaround. A misspelled word or the wrong order of items in a drop-down list also needs to be fixed, but they may fall under the "Annoyance" category, meaning they annoy people when they come upon them, but they don't impact the ability to provide care.

Your list may have more (or more detailed) criteria than those shown, or you may have different sets of criteria for different parts of the business. Patient safety will always be the top priority in the clinical parts of the application, but there are also the business and finance parts of the application to consider as well. For example, in your revenue cycle application, the inability to assign the proper codes to procedures may be deemed as critical. If you cannot code correctly, you face regulatory and financial penalties, which can be extremely detrimental to the organization. So, those issues in the revenue cycle application may be deemed the most critical.

It's important to define what your criticality headers mean. Using our example in Table 10.2, we would want to use specific language to define what we mean by "Patient Safety" and "Data Integrity," etc. We would likely include a few common examples to ensure a shared understanding of the criteria. This leads to a more systematic and data-driven approach to addressing issues that arise.

Clearly, you can run some samples of your own through your matrix to ensure the results are as expected. Once you have a solid scoring matrix, you remove (or at least, reduce) emotion and politics from the equation and begin relying more on semiquantitative data for evaluation and resolution of issues.

These critical issues should be reviewed against the test plans later (after go live is complete, during the project review phase) to see if these areas were missed. These go live issues are often errors that were not detected earlier and are impacting your end users. The team should make an effort to review errors against the project scope, requirements, and build. Was the EHR built substantially to requirements? If not, ask questions to get to the root cause (Lean "5 Why's" or A3 can be helpful). Also review test plans to find ways to improve test scripts and the testing process to prevent errors on your next EHR go live (whether that's a version upgrade or a software update). If the issue is an end-user error, determine if the problem is training (and review against training plans) or whether it was simple human error. Each issue that arises is an opportunity to see your process in action and determine where you can make improvements. Embrace these opportunities.

Decommissioning Command Center and Go Live Support

Once all critical items are resolved and no new critical items are being opened, you can consider closing your command center and scaling back your go live support. You should be seeing system users becoming more confident with the use of the system, the reported issues start becoming optimization requests instead of defect reports, and the overall environment in the command center begins to wind down. At the elbow support, requests may be dwindling and the daily rhythm of work seems to be back to normal. You may select specific metrics for your organization to use as the point at which you decommission your command center. Many organizations select a predetermined timeframe, such as 3 weeks, and will decommission sooner or stay open longer, depending on outcomes from go live.

Prior to decommissioning the command center, the core team may want to take some time to compare the requirements to the results—in other words, requirements validation. Did the system deliver what was required? If this is not done prior to the decommissioning of the command center, it may be pushed down the road so far that it never occurs. Making this the last requirement for the command center may help ensure that your executives, your user representatives, and the IS team leads are all engaged in this review prior to close out. If you choose not to do this prior to closing the command center, you should schedule a date for review within the following 2–4 weeks at latest. It's important to ensure the project delivered on expectations, that requirements have been met, and that everyone is substantially satisfied with the outcome. This helps in two ways. First, it validates for everyone that requirements *were* met. That way, there can be no backtracking later to complain that core functionality was not, in fact, delivered. Second, it is a way to acknowledge that the system is up and functioning as designed. The teams did their work and achieved a successful outcome. Subsequent requests for new features, functions, or changes can be viewed in that light—of optimization, rather than remediation.

Once the decision is made to decommission the command center, operations should be normalized. Standard work, regarding how service requests are opened and reviewed, should be invoked (assuming these processes were in place prior to the go live). Normal operational processes should resume.

Chapter Summary

In this chapter, we discussed preparing for and going live on your new (or dramatically revised) EHR.

These topics will help ensure you cover key aspects of your go live:

- Ensuring you have reviewed your post–go live processes to optimize value creation for your customers, from your patients to your care providers to your other business stakeholders.
- Verify the readiness of your applications, staff (both IS and organizational—hospitals, clinics, etc.), providers, processes, and technology.
- Technology readiness indicates all needed hardware is deployed and working and that the overall infrastructure is capable of handling the anticipated load at go live.
- Determine and document your go live strategy and ensure you have organizational agreement.
- Define the status of older systems so they can be decommissioned, or at least made unavailable, at the appropriate time during the go live. This will prevent errors by staff who may accidentally (or intentionally) log into old systems out of habit.
- Go live staffing is a key to success, so be sure you know what resources you have, what you will need, and how you will fill any gaps. This may entail asking people to work extra shifts or extra days, or hiring temporary staff to assist during go live.
- Define, plan, organize, and deploy your command center. A well-run command center can greatly enhance the go live process and reduce stress for everyone.
- Plan for very strong "at the elbow" support using standard work for physicians, nurses, and other care providers. Strong support during go live typically translates into faster, more effective adoption of technology.
- Leverage super users in every care area. This enhances user engagement, facilitates strong and correct use of the EHR, and provides an ongoing conduit for cost-effective training in the future.
- Use your issues from go live as a guide to reviewing your project. Were errors due to scope, build, test, training, or use? Identify opportunities to improve your process for your next upgrade or update.
- The decision to decommission the command center should be made using metrics such as number of new critical issues reported, number of

critical issues open and resolved, and number of new noncritical issues reported, etc.

- If possible, take time to perform a requirements validation prior to closing your command center. This may be your last, and best, chance to have all the key players in the room to review the requirements and how well the project delivered on those requirements.

Further Reading

Danaher S, Felt P, Sirois ML. "Lessons learned: Avoiding some of the common pitfalls of EHR activation." 2013, http://divurgent.com/wp-content/uploads/2013/12/EHRLessonsLearned.pdf (accessed July 10, 2017).

The National Learning Consortium (NLC). "Electronic Health Record (EHR) Implementation Go-Live Planning Checklist.", https://www.healthit.gov/sites/default/files/tools/nlc-ehr-implementation-go-live-planning-checklist.docx (accessed July 10, 2017).

U.S. Department of Health & Human Services, Centers for Medicare & Medicaid Services (CMS), EHR Go Live Planning Checklist, 2006, https://healthit.ahrq.gov/sites/default/files/docs/workflowtoolkit/ehr_go_live_planning_checklist.pdf (accessed July 10, 2017).

Chapter 11

Optimizing the Electronic Health Record

What Is Optimization?

Congratulations! If you made it this far, your system is now operational. You defined requirements including software considerations, key interfaces to third-party applications, and alignment with upstream and downstream vendors. You defined your hardware, infrastructure, analytics, and measurement needs.

You engaged stakeholders and system users to design the system. You used current state and future state workflows, and a lot of Lean thinking to remove waste from tasks and operations. Lean project management approaches allowed you to design, project-manage, and implement the new system in the "least waste" way.

You used some more Lean thinking to navigate through the testing phase and gain user acceptance. If you engaged stakeholders in the design phase, this job was made infinitely easier. Lean project management principles and standard work supported the development of training materials designed to optimize user understanding, while supporting best practices and evidence-based care. Super users were trained to support the upcoming start-up phase and minimize timelines for getting system functionality questions resolved by the clinical and administrative staff.

And you finally made it through the start-up phase. The go live phase of the project was also developed and delivered using Lean project management approaches. The necessary support resources were made available to ensure proper training support and correct navigation of the new system while ensuring patient care and business operations were able to operate effectively and safely.

Many organizations are flat out exhausted at this point. There is no doubt that it has been a monumental task to get the new EHR deployed. And you should celebrate your achievement!

As discussed in Chapter 4, a Lean organization designs processes and systems using Lean attributes. These attributes include the principles of flow, pull, defect-free, and visual management. The Lean EHR uses these principles both in the processes used to deploy the system, as well as in the design of the system in support of the clinical and administrative processes. However, there is a fifth and final principle: the principle of kaizen or continuous improvement. Now that we have deployed the new EHR, we must now pursue perfection in our processes, and the EHR has a front and center role in this pursuit.

As much as we desire to take a break from EHR-related tasks following our design and deployment of our new system, we must now pursue optimization of both the system and of our clinical and administrative processes. Lean organizations know continuous improvement is a journey and not a destination. What is great today is mediocre tomorrow. What is a best practice today is obsolete next month. Both the practice of medicine and the use of technology are changing at a more rapid pace than any other time in history; this change is exponential! Our EHR must be redesigned and optimized *continually* to keep up with these changes.

Hopefully the initial stages of this optimization are not simply rework from a faulty design or poorly implemented launch. Some organizations, when speaking of optimization, are fixing “poor” decisions around lack of standardization and failure to design Lean workflows; this body of work does not meet the true definition of optimization. This work is simply defined as rework, one of the seven operational wastes. In a large-scale EHR deployment, there will be some things that will be missed and will need to be fixed. We hope to anticipate as many of these things as possible upfront. And the use of Lean tools and approaches will uncover and remove many of these hidden problems. Nonetheless, work of this type has unintended consequences, and we can expect to encounter some design changes and fixes post go live.

After this blitz of rework activity, we want to move our system to a steady state and then begin our continuous improvement phase. I’d like you to consider the optimization phase from three lenses. The first lens is maintaining the clinical integrity of your system. Over time, evidence-based care changes and order sets, protocols, and care plans become obsolete. Updating order sets and care plans in the system is not the problem. Having a mechanism to keep the evidence current is the problem. A best practice strategy will be covered to help you keep the evidence within your system current. The second lens is repeatedly improving your system through the use of managing for daily improvement (MDI) techniques. This approach leverages visual management and is used to make small incremental improvements to the system and to simply maintain the system. World-class organizations have a systematic approach to setting and maintaining standards that allow the organization to end each day in a better place than where it started. The final lens is that of continuous improvement. If your organization has truly embraced continuous improvement through Lean, then there will continue to be value stream improvement work, and kaizen improvement work, in support of delivering compelling value to your customers. A Lean organization is always seeking to remove more waste and change the ratio of value-added activity to non-value added activity. Your EHR, and the support processes used to run the system, must keep pace with the ongoing workflow and process improvement needs. And it must be done in a way that enables system-wide standardization. Strategies to engage IT system support resources in continuing to develop solutions that deliver the highest quality, in the shortest time, with the lowest cost, will be explored.

Optimization through the First Lens: Keeping the Evidence Current

The single biggest problem we routinely find in healthcare systems is that organizations have poor processes and systems to keep order sets and evidence-based care practices current. What happens over time is that when the system is no longer current with the latest evidence, clinicians deviate from the use of order sets. This deviation leads to personality-based care with wide degrees of variation in practice. One of the biggest benefits in going to an EHR is to leverage the latest and best standards and evidence. This helps ensure that every patient gets the best possible medicine.

It was surely a lot of work to get everyone to agree on the order sets for the first IT system load. Perhaps you can recall when you were on paper charts. How hard was it to change a form? How many months did it take to get an order set change or evidence-based care change through forms committee or professional practice? How many revisions did the work go through? These challenges won't go away simply because you are now electronic. In fact, electronic changes can take even longer, because these changes have to be tested and validated. We must ensure any small change does not negatively affect another part of the program or a report.

One best practice is to establish a change control committee to manage both changes in evidence and upgrades and recommendations to optimize the system. The art is not in simply having a change control committee, as many, if not all, organizations have such a committee. The opportunity is to get the change committee to make decisions in *real time*. A change control committee is not any more effective than a forms committee if it takes a year to make a decision.

The role of the committee is to keep current of the latest evidence and *quickly and effectively* collaborate with affected clinicians to maintain and update clinical standards in real time. The frequency of the meeting is recommended to be *weekly*. The meeting length is scheduled for an hour. Anyone should be able to submit evidence for consideration not just a committee member.

The often seen structure of sending proposed changes to "everyone" for review and then voting at the highest levels of the medical advisory council and quality or professional practice council is outdated, time consuming, and simply not nimble enough to keep up with the growing body of medical knowledge. Yet this is what is frequently in place in many healthcare organizations.

If you'd like a validation of why the change control committee is endorsed, here is an example. I recently left a client that had not updated their evidence in their EHR in over *6 years*. There was no formal process to request a change, and what did get submitted for review and made it to the physician leadership level took over 9 months to get approved. Updating the system and testing took another 2 months. So the medical community simply ignored order sets and placed individual orders by patient. A review of diagnostics for one common patient diagnosis found eight different order patterns by eight different physicians. The outcomes varied moderately, and the treatment costs varied by a greater amount. None of the variations in the outcomes or of the costs were "extreme," but variation in clinical outcomes and cost is not a behavior found in world-class healthcare organizations. Physicians wanted to do the right thing, but the systems were not in place to enable those behaviors.

Aside from order sets, there are ongoing improvements to the standards of care that are implemented by nursing. There are new therapies for physical therapists, occupational therapists, and respiratory therapists. New evidence-based standards of care in home health and long-term care are continuously released. Having a mechanism in place to ensure that evidence is current, and can be changed quickly and efficiently if warranted, is a must in optimizing an EHR. Addressing this core issue will go a long way in ensuring the best patient outcomes and in keeping the system users satisfied with the EHR.

Let's discuss how to operationalize the change control committee. The committee has the following makeup (note: different organizations have different titles for these positions):

Core Team:

- Director of IT—chairs the committee
- IT manager
- Case management manager
- In-patient nursing leadership (representative)
- Nursing charge nurses (representative)
- ED director or ED manager
- OR director or OR manager
- Materials management director or materials management buyer
- Health information management director
- HIM coder (representative)
- Registration director or manager
- Patient financial services director
- Charge master manager
- Outpatient (clinic) leadership (representative)
- Director of radiology and/or laboratory or manager(s)
- Lab IT system lead
- Pharmacy IT system lead
- Clinical documentation specialist
- Physician IT system liaison

As needed (if the system or process change affects these people):

- IT staff experts in the various system modules
- Physician medical director or chief from affected area
- Frontline case manager representative
- Inpatient and outpatient frontline staff
- Education coordinator

- Radiology system administrator
- Quality improvement leadership
- QI and risk management director allied leadership (occupational, physical, speech, nutrition, respiratory, etc.)
- Professional practice leadership
- Finance director

Generally, the list of changes for review goes out a minimum of a week in advance of the meeting. The committee members then self-select and attend if there is something that affects them. A typical meeting will have about 15 team members in attendance.

Physician Change Control

Physician-related changes to the EHR will likely be handled slightly differently depending on the size of your organization and the types of physician relationships you have. There are many different types of physician relationships in healthcare—some are employed, some are independent, some own their own practice or clinic, some are contractors, etc. So there is no one-size-fits-all answer to how to engage physicians in EHR discussions on features, functionality, or optimization. However, we'll explore a few common methods in this section that you might consider for your organization.

Physician Participation in the Change Control Committee

As we discussed prior, some organizations have a change control committee (or similar) that is charged with overseeing all requests for significant changes to the EHR. It is also responsible for reviewing changes for upgrades and approving the major elements of the upgrade to ensure the development of the EHR continues to align with the work and needs of the organization. In this committee, changes are reviewed and approved to move forward for IS teams to work on, or they are put on hold or declined. In some organizations, physicians or providers participate in these committees; in other organizations, the CMIO or the clinical informatics teams represent the interests of the providers and may take significant changes back to a physician advisory group for review and approval as needed. More and more organizations are moving away from the silos of physician work groups and leveraging the change control committee practice. A Lean organization has one known, standard, best way to do things, and having two structures in place for EHR change control does not meet this definition. We believe having physicians and physician liaisons as part of the change control committee to be the best practice for EHR optimization.

Physician EHR Advisory Group

In this model, the organization has a group of physicians, often led by the chief medical information officer (CMIO) or chief medical officer (CMO). This group directly provides input, decisions, and guidance on the ongoing design and maintenance of the EHR. This group is involved with developing high-level requirements for a new EHR (or transitioning from one EHR to another) as well as steering activities around optimization from a provider perspective. The direction they set, and changes they approve, are then implemented under the guidance of the CMIO or the informatics teams responsible for physician build.

Physician Input through Medical Executive Council or Service Line Advisory Groups

Other commonly used vehicles for ensuring physician/provider participation or input into the development and maintenance of the EHR are existing council or advisory groups. These groups meet on a scheduled basis and some organizations leverage this structure for vetting proposed changes or for discussing strategic topics related to the future direction of the EHR. This can be a very efficient method of routinely engaging your physician or provider population, but the downside can be that the agendas of these meetings are often already packed with other practice related topics, and getting airtime for EHR discussions may be difficult. However, if you can carve out a dedicated timeslot for review and discussion, you may be able to keep the time commitment to a minimum while maintaining high engagement and awareness.

Physician Builders

Some EHR vendors recommend (or require) physician builders to participate in the EHR development. These providers attend EHR training and learn to build within the application. While they may not address the more complex build of the EHR, they often will become well-versed in the use of the EHR through this training and become better advocates for the overall development of the EHR as a result. These builders may be responsible for things like building order sets or other changes specific to provider or physician workflows. Leveraging the physician builder skill set post EHR deployment is another way organizations maintain system optimization.

The key to keeping your system current and optimized is to make decisions in real time or as close to real time as possible. The first principle of improvement is to enable work to flow. We want to handle issues and improvements as they come up. Creating an inventory of issues moves us away from Lean thinking. As such, action items are never deferred. *The change control committee is a decision-making body, not a recommendation making body.* Chiefs and C-Suite members do not have veto power over the committee's decisions. If a committee member cannot be present, the committee member is responsible for sending a representative in their place. Each committee member is responsible to meet with their affected stakeholders prior to the decision-making meeting taking place. It is important to note that not everything that gets recommended is approved. This can be a source of frustration for the person making the recommendation, but the system functionality must be optimized from the broad system perspective, not in small increments. Decisions made from the meeting are communicated broadly across the organization. When functioning well, optimization decisions will be flowing to the organization on a weekly basis.

Optimization through the Second Lens: Managing for Daily Improvement

Every organization is concerned with results. In optimizing our EHR, we also want to ensure the system is operating at an elevated level. In a broad sense, results are how we measure success, and in most businesses, compensation and promotions are linked to the ability to deliver consistently improving performance. In a Lean organization, results are the outcome of developing and using great, waste-free processes predicated on standard work that is managed visually. In a traditional work environment, leaders/managers get monthly reports, budget summaries, and statistics, then try to make sense of the prior period's activities. But correlating cause and effect from historical data is often very difficult. Lean leaders manage at the process level and guide the recipe of the process to great outcomes.

The system used to get better every day is known as managing for daily improvement or MDI. Great Lean organizations use visual management to create transparency in both process and results. Recall from Chapter 4 that visual management is a combination of visual and audio signals that allow everyone (staff, physicians, and management) to discern normal from abnormal conditions at a glance so that real-time interventions can be taken to get the process back on track.

The MDI system is a key component of visual management. This system visually tracks the key measures of a department or key process, identifies and prioritizes variances from plan, and develops and implements plans for improvement. This work is done *daily* by the entire staff. While management has the responsibility for the MDI system, everyone is expected to contribute toward the data capture, tracking of results, prioritization of the variances from plan, and implementation of improvements.

To illustrate the power of MDI, imagine your organization for a moment. If you are a large healthcare organization, you might have 10,000 staff and another 400 providers. What could your organization look like if all of these staff members were engaged in improving their core processes daily? Would this daily engagement help change your culture? Ten thousand staff and 400 providers marching toward a shared vision can make a significant amount of change in a brief period of time. Now compound this daily change over 30 days, 6 months, 1 year, and 5 years. This is Lean healthcare in action! While MDI can be used anywhere across the organization, we want to leverage the MDI system to continually optimize the EHR.

Our role as a leader is to establish the vision, allocate the resources to accomplish the vision, and inspire people to act toward this vision. In optimizing our EHR, we want to align the staff towards a common goal: improving clinical and process outcomes. The MDI system establishes the local level vision, creates the infrastructure to accomplish the vision at the unit level, and inspires the staff to meet the vision.

The tools used for MDI include a performance board, a daily huddle, and a project management system for managing the improvements. An illustration of the performance board is shown in Figure 11.1.

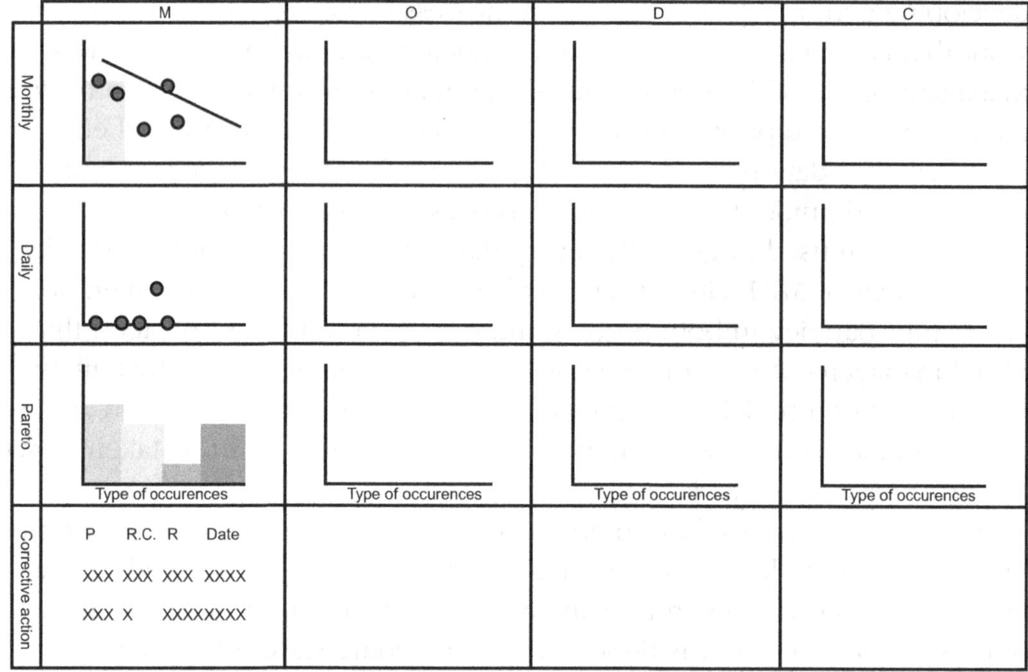

Figure 11.1 MDI performance board.

Each individual column represents a different true north dimension. The operational true north dimensions include staff engagement/morale, quality, access (delivery), and cost. In Lean organizations, this is known by the first letter of each dimension: M, Q, D, and C.

In our performance board, each column has a set of four charts. The top chart in the series of four charts will always display the year to date performance updated monthly with both targets and actual performance. We want to show target and actual performance so we can discern normal conditions from abnormal conditions at a glance: a key tenant of visual management. Our dimension for our example chart will be quality. We are measuring the effectiveness of the help desk. The target line in our chart is the solid line running from the top left of the chart to the bottom right. This chart is shown in Figure 11.2. Getting first call resolution is important to our customers (clinicians and administrative staff). Call backs, in a Lean organization, represent a service failure regardless of the reason for the call back.

The second chart is month to date performance updated daily with both targets and actual performance. Assuming we are tracking the month

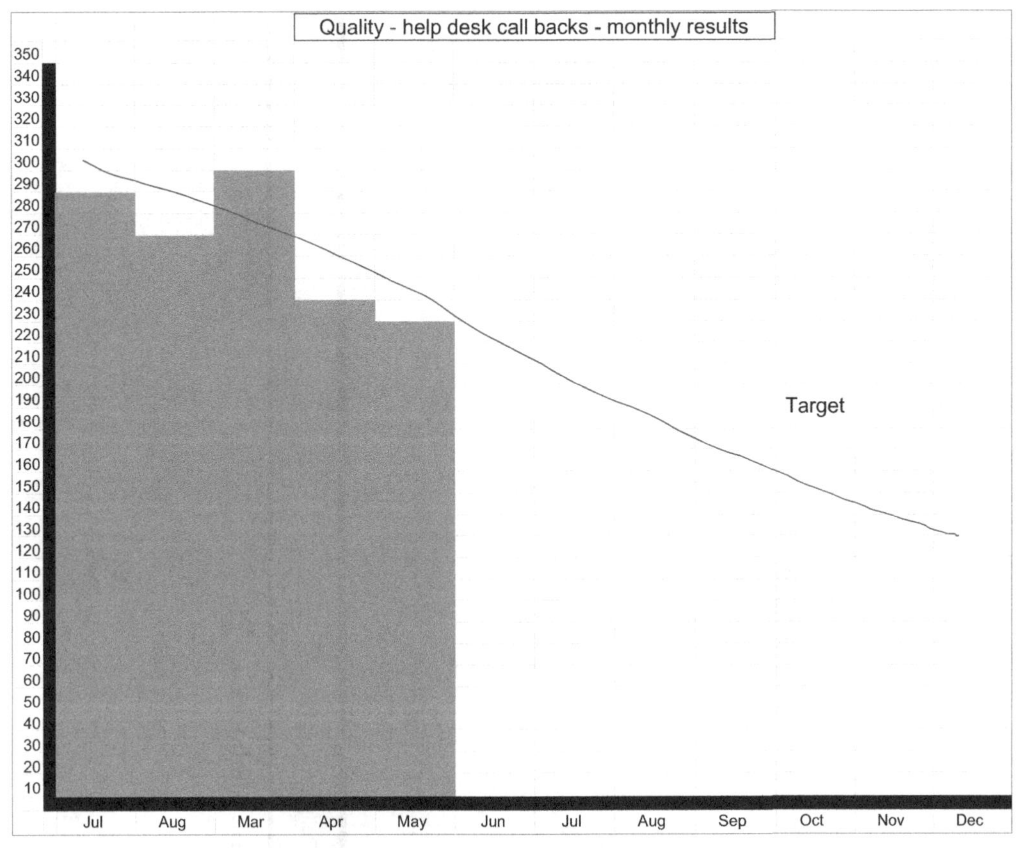

Figure 11.2 Year to date performance chart for help desk call backs.

of June, we aspire to be fewer than 210 call backs. Since June is a 30-day month, our daily target is 210 (plan) divided by 30 days = 7 call backs per day. If we trend at 7 calls or less during the month of June, we will meet our planned reduction in call backs and get closer to our goal of first call resolution. Figure 11.3 provides an illustration of what the month to date chart would look like.

The third chart is a histogram of the sources of variation between the month to date (daily) plan and actual, and the fourth chart is the improvement plan. Some organizations call the improvement plan the kaizen newspaper, because it summarizes the kaizen (improvement) activity planned to ensure the daily target is met. An example of the histogram chart showing the sources of variation is provided in Figure 11.4.

The histogram when prioritized from high frequency to low frequency can be turned into a Pareto chart. The Pareto principle holds

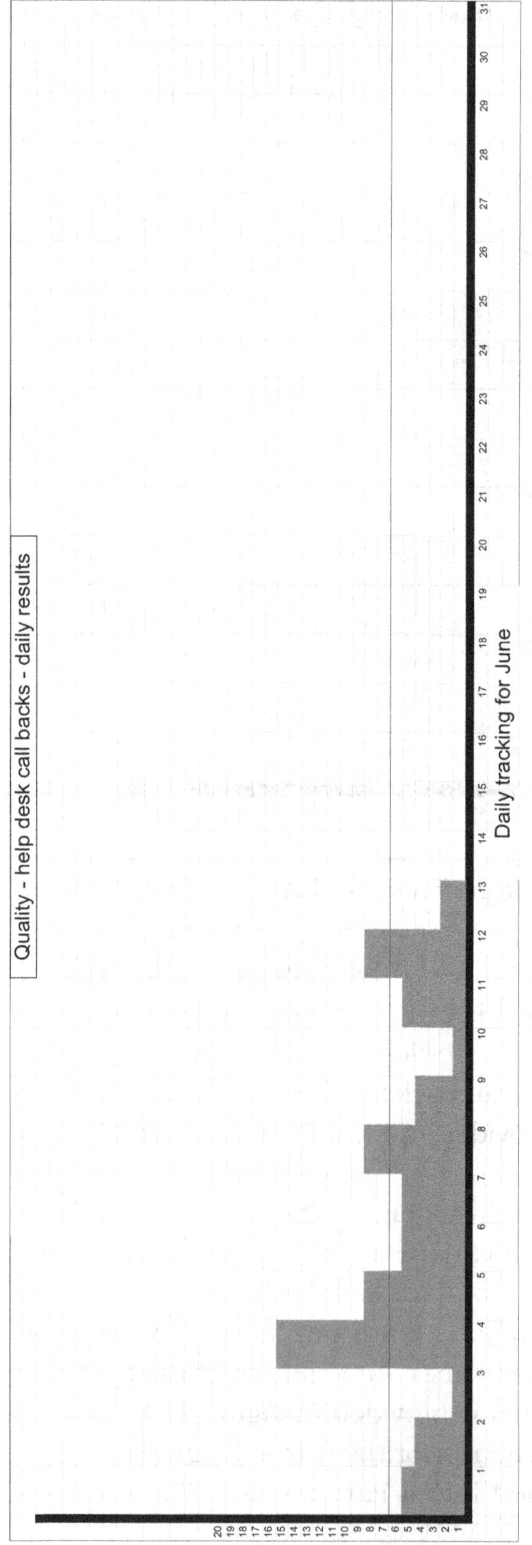

Figure 11.3 Month to date performance chart for help desk call backs.

Frequency chart - June

Frequency	Password help	Functionality question	Frozen system	Forgot login name	Hardware wouldn't power up	Workstation on wheel trouble	Cannot print	Printer format question	Wi-Fi connectivity issue	Other
28										
27	X									
26	X									
25	X									
24	X									
23	X									
22	X									
21	X									
20	X									
19	X									
18	X									
17	X									
16	X									
15	X									
14	X									
13	X									
12	X									
11	X									
10	X									
9	X								X	
8	X								X	
7	X								X	
6	X	X					X		X	
5	X	X					X		X	
4	X	X		X			X		X	
3	X	X	X	X		X	X		X	
2	X	X	X	X	X	X	X	X	X	
1	X	X	X	X	X	X	X	X	X	

Reason for variance

Figure 11.4 Histogram of sources of variation—reasons for help desk call backs.

that 20% of the sources of variation contribute to 80% of the overall sources of variation. Our Pareto chart would look like that shown in Figure 11.5.

The Pareto chart makes it obvious at a glance that the two largest opportunities to reduce call backs would be to address password help issues and Wi-Fi connectivity. If we eliminated these two issues, we would reduce the callbacks by 58%.

So thus far we have established and tracked annual goals reported by month, and we have established and tracked monthly goals tracked by day. We also have established a daily reporting mechanism to capture the reasons

Pareto Chart

Frequency	Password help	Wi-Fi connectivity issue	Functionality question	Cannot print	Forgot login name	Frozen system	Workstation on wheel trouble	Hardware wouldn't power up	Printer format question	Other
28										
27	X									
26	X									
25	X									
24	X									
23	X									
22	X									
21	X									
20	X									
19	X									
18	X									
17	X									
16	X									
15	X									
14	X									
13	X									
12	X									
11	X									
10	X									
9	X	X								
8	X	X								
7	X	X								
6	X	X	X	X						
5	X	X	X	X						
4	X	X	X	X	X					
3	X	X	X	X	X	X	X			
2	X	X	X	X	X	X	X	X	X	
1	X	X	X	X	X	X	X	X	X	

Reason for variance

Figure 11.5 Pareto analysis.

for return calls. This is what many organizations do. They track performance. However, Lean organizations don't simply track performance; they drive improvement. The data is helpful so we all know the score, but getting results is the ultimate goal. The final chart is where accountability for improvement is assigned. Action plans are documented in our fourth chart, the kaizen newspaper. An example of the kaizen newspaper is shown in Figure 11.6.

You can see from the trended results in the year to date graph that the solutions deployed were making a difference; the number of call backs has been trending downward since the beginning of the year. This shows that our solutions have been effective. We can correlate the cause of the problems and the effectiveness of the targeted solutions.

But what if our solutions were not effective? I liken the MDI system improvement to using your Global Positioning System (GPS) for navigating your vehicle to a new location. What happens with your GPS when you miss a turn? It simply recalculates the direction and route, re-sets the time, and

Kaizen newspaper (action plans)

What (activity to address opportunity)	*Who*	*When*
Develop online capability for system users to be able to reset passwords without calling help desk.	*Janine*	*23-Jan*
Perform a wi-Fi connectivity analysis to determine poor coverage spots	*William*	*20-Feb*
Add signal boosters to CCU and ER south wing	*Avijit*	*5-Mar*

Figure 11.6 Kaizen newspaper for help desk call backs.

keeps working to show you the shortest and easiest path toward your destination. Your GPS will never give up and never quit as long as it is turned on and has power.

In improvement, you will try things, many things that will not work or will work marginally well. This generally implies you did not get to the true root cause of the problem you are trying to solve. But most organizations don't operate like a GPS and recalculate and continue pressing on. *They simply quit trying to resolve issues.* Perhaps the issues are too hard: too time consuming, too difficult to navigate through the personnel issues, too difficult to work through system and functionality challenges.

Would you be able to get to your new destination if you turned your GPS off? Perhaps you will get lucky and make your way. Your problems may also miraculously go away in the workplace, but the odds of that happening are not very high. So don't turn your MDI system off. Keep generating and deploying countermeasures and action plans. Seek out root causes and eliminate the wastes that prevent you from hitting your target outcomes. It is in this manner that you keep your EHR operating in an optimized manner.

Operationalizing the MDI System

Now that you have seen the four charts and how they are used as a complete improvement system, let's review how to get the MDI system up and running. One key requirement of this process is that data in the MDI system is updated daily. The measures must be something that is accessible every single day. Measures that are only available once a month or once a quarter do not lend themselves to *daily* improvement. Staff members are accountable to update the data, as they are thus able to engage in the process, because they now own these numbers. Accountability for data collection and reporting encourages staff to understand both the measurement system and the supporting data. In a Lean organization, the assignment for who updates the performance boards changes weekly on a rotating calendar. Once a shift, the *entire* staff huddles in front of the board for a 6–10 minute meeting. The meeting agenda is scripted. The typical agenda is as follows:

- Morale/human development measurement results, variances, and action plans—1 to 2 minute discussion
- Quality measurement results, variances and action plans—1 to 2 minute discussion
- Lead-time/access measurement results, variances, and action plans—1 to 2 minute discussion
- Cost/productivity measurement results, variances, and action plans—1 to 2 minute discussion
- Unit level communication update—2 minute discussion

Total time for the huddle: 6–10 minutes

After a short review for each of the different measurement dimensions, daily results, and understanding variances from the target, ideas for improvement should be solicited and documented on the kaizen newspaper. Results of improvement projects from the earlier assignment should be briefly discussed as well. It is important that the successfully implemented ideas be incorporated into standard work and used by everyone. The improvements can be as simple as a suggestion that can be tested, to a more formal PDCA (plan-do-check-act) project, all the way through a project documented and deployed using A3 thinking. As you learned earlier in this book, an A3 is a form that contains all the elements of the scientific method. On this form, the team will apply Lean thinking to an area of focus. A3 thinking is the application of the scientific method used in a Lean improvement project.

The key is to be continuously engaging staff in improvement of the targeted measures of the unit. Total transparency from the MDI system gives everyone an opportunity to be informed and to participate. It is through engagement and participation that the culture is changed. In our case, we need to constantly be improving our EHR process to ensure that it stays optimized.

One important question we need to think about is, what topics should we try to improve on our MDI system? Since we have four dimensions of operational excellence, there are many topics in each domain you might consider measuring and improving in an information technology environment. Table 11.1 shows some of the candidates for improvement. This list is not comprehensive, and your unique environment might spur other important areas of improvement.

To develop your own list, I would start by looking in a couple of places. First, ask your customer what they would like to see improved. The clinicians and the administrative staff will let you know where your service is not meeting their needs; this is the best place to begin in developing opportunities for improvement. The second group of stakeholders I would ask would be your IT staff. They will know the areas that frustrate them and also have the pulse of their customers. Between these two stakeholder groups, you should be able to identify several areas of improvement to get you started.

Table 11.1 Sample of MDI Dimension Measurement and Improvement Candidates

Morale/Human Development	*Quality*	*Delivery/Lead Time/Access*	*Cost/Productivity*
Number of ideas submitted for improvement	Help desk call backs	Time to respond from the help desk	Staff hours per help desk call resolved
Number of compliments received	Service ticket first time resolution	Time to respond for a help ticket	Staff hours per help ticket submitted
Cross-training hours for application specialists	Daily system uptime/downtime	Turnaround time for a change request (including new evidence)	Staff hours per new report request generated
	Daily percentage of rework associated with system changes	Turnaround time for hardware/ software installation	Staff overtime
	Reported number of software "glitches"	Turnaround time for a report request	Compliance to monthly hardware budget
			Rework hours for system changes

The MDI system is a key piece of keeping your electronic medical record optimized. The content within the EHR and the actual operation of the system both need to be operating at a peak level to run a world-class healthcare system. MDI utilizes the skills of the entire IT staff to monitor key areas of both system and process to make improvement. When standard work is in place, visual management systems that show variance between expected and actual performance are utilized, and interventional strategies are deployed, daily improvement is possible.

The MDI system creates a framework and process to make daily improvement possible. World-class organizations leave the organization in a better place than they found it at the beginning of their work shift. This is the essence of daily improvement and living a culture of improvement.

Optimization through the Third Lens: Continuous Improvement

If you are a Lean organization, regardless of the status of your EHR, you likely have a series of ongoing improvements related to quality, access, and cost improvement. In a world-class Lean organization, improvement is best done in the context of a value stream. And if you have ever done value stream improvement, you will likely have run into a host of EHR opportunities. For those of you who do not know about value stream improvement, an overview is provided for you.

A value stream is made up of all the process activities (both good and bad) used to deliver value to a customer. A value stream typically begins with a customer's need and ends when the customer's need is met. Likely, the work will span many different departments, so a value stream is *not* a department.

For example, if a patient arrives for a preadmission surgical consult, this patient will meet with registration, a preadmission nurse, and an anesthesiologist. In addition, there may be a lab test required and perhaps a chest x-ray. This is after agreeing to surgery with a surgeon. At the end of the visit, the area is cleaned by environmental services, and supplies are restocked by materials management. This work spans at least six departments. However, even the preadmission surgical consult is not a value stream. The value stream begins with the customer's need: the patient's need to have surgery. It ends with the customer's needs being met; in this example, let us assume this will be a day surgery and that our process ends when the patient leaves recovery. So how many other departments will the patient's surgical experience touch? Surgical consult, booking, insurance verification, pre-registration, pre-op, surgery, post-op, health records, coding, billing, sterile processing, bio med, environmental services, pharmacy, etc. The entire suite of these people, processes, and departments and their corresponding work make up the value stream.

To make an improvement in isolation, like a change within only the OR suite or patient registration, would only make marginal improvement. Waste can be pushed upstream and downstream in these types of improvements. Breakthrough improvements are made across the entire value stream by engaging and transforming all departments, staff, and processes in delivering compelling value to the patient. In improving the value stream, waste is eliminated from the system, and not simply moved from one department to another. Spot department improvements, while holding some promise, rarely add up to revolutionary change. This is the power of value stream improvement over departmental improvement.

To develop an improvement plan within a value stream, we apply the value stream mapping and analysis (VSMA) tool. The VSMA tool is designed to deliver an action plan for improvement across a value stream. Also known as "product and information flow mapping," the VSMA tool provides a structure and process that identifies waste within a value stream, identifies the sources of the waste, develops a vision for the future, and generates an action plan to deliver the future process.[1] Coming out of a VSMA session, you will identify multiple small, medium, and large projects for improvement. In each of those projects, your organization will use the scientific method (A3 thinking) to deliver incremental improvement to a portion of the whole value stream.

It is certain that several, if not all, of these projects will involve some type of IT system enhancement affecting the EHR. When there are several improvements happening simultaneously across an organization, the IT resources associated with implementing these changes can and do become severely taxed. *Rarely are these changes budgeted, or planned for, so this frequently compounds the IT resource challenge.* Clinicians and staff are frustrated because the IT-related changes to the EHR are slow to come about, and simultaneously the IT staff is buried in unplanned work and wonders why the organization cannot prioritize the EHR optimization activity better. The organization is set up for a lose–lose proposition.

To best manage the EHR optimization process, while coexisting with the process improvement activities of your organization, there are four best practice steps that can be followed.

1. Plan on changes
2. Assign an IT optimization resource to the value stream steering team
3. Do not lead with IT solutions
4. Minimize hand-offs before automating

Let's add some detail to the key steps.

Plan on Changes

In modern medicine, IT is at the core of many workflows and healthcare processes. Obviously, we understand order entry and clinical documentation as a couple of basic functions in our clinical work. Virtually every improvement activity will include some combination of work that people perform and information that people either access or create. So while we cannot always know what the change requests are going to be from our process improvement activities, we have a high likelihood of knowing that changes to how we access and how we create information are going to touch our EHR. A sound Lean organization will have valuable information on the areas of focus (value streams being improved) within the organization and the timelines at which these areas of focus are improved. Figure 11.7 shows the value stream improvement plans for 2018 for a medium-sized hospital.

We can see from the chart that while we don't know what the exact EHR optimization recommendations from the team will be, we do know we will be touching the EHR in surgical services from February 2018 through February 2019, ambulatory care (specifically, neurology specialty care) from April through October 2018, and bed management from July 2018 through April 2019. And we know this several months in advance for resource allocation and planning purposes. So be proactive, and plan on EHR changes in these areas.

If your organization jumps from project to project and doesn't follow a strategic value stream approach to improvement, then your visibility into projects will be less transparent. Unfortunately, since many organizations do not use a value stream approach to improvement, this is more the norm

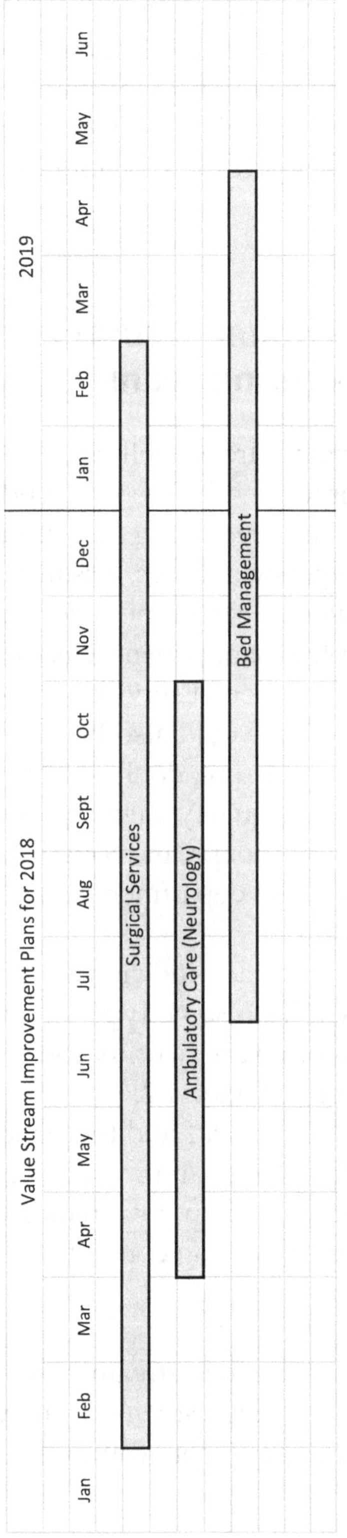

Figure 11.7 Annual value stream improvement plans.

than the exception. One way to offset this lack of transparency into upcoming projects is to have someone from the IT department be part of the team that selects projects. This way you will have some visibility of the upcoming work and be able to allocate available resources to support the work. Being on the selection committee enables some control of both selection and timing of new work.

Assign an EHR Optimization Resource to the Value Stream Steering Team

As previously discussed, a value stream will cut across departments of an organization. It will cover processes from end to end, spanning from the customer need to the customer need being met. An example of a clinical value stream would be emergency services. Assume a patient arrives with a kidney stone. This patient would impact the following departments at a minimum: the ER staff, the ER physician, patient registration, diagnostic imaging, laboratory services, and environmental services. If you follow the patient health record, coding and billing would also be involved. So to transform the value stream, that is to improve by double digits in the key measures of staff engagement and morale, quality, delivery, and cost, we would need representation from all of these groups. In modern healthcare, it is nearly impossible to improve all of these departments and processes without touching the EHR in a meaningful way.

In a world-class organization, each individual value stream that a Lean organization is improving will have some type of value stream governance. This governance is in place for a variety of reasons. But, most notably, it has the accountabilities as shown in Table 11.2.

To ensure that the needs of the staff and the patient are met pertaining to the EHR, the best practice is to have a representative from the EHR optimization team be part of the value stream governance. The traditional makeup of the value stream governance steering committee is as follows:

- Executive sponsor
- Administrative leader for the value stream
- Physician champion for the value stream (if the value stream is clinical)
- Key managers that lead departments within the value stream
- Lean internal expert

- Professional practice and/or educator
- Representative from accounting/finance
- Representative from the EHR optimization team

Note: For a more detailed explanation of Lean governance at both the organizational (enterprise) level and the value stream level, please review *Lean Leadership for Healthcare: Approaches to Lean Transformation* (CRC Press).

The EHR representative has a role to ensure that the improvement needs of the value stream are met timely *without* sub-optimizing the EHR system as a whole. This resource also has the accountability to prioritize the improvement/changes within the overall IT improvement plan. Said differently, the resource needs to assist in managing the improvements while taking into consideration the broader IT/IS strategy for the organization.

Table 11.2 Value Stream Governance Accountability

Preparation	*Improvement Review at the Strategy Wall*	*Follow–Up*
Update measures	Review kaizen A3 measures	Execute action plans
V.S. action plans are current	Discuss kaizen follow-up plans	Update resource board
Kaizen follow-up plans current	Discuss barriers including EHR issues or concerns	Capture results
Ensure availability of resources	Repeat for each open kaizen A3	
	Review value stream action plans (improvement plan)	
	Review value stream measures	
	Document actions needed	
	Staff engagement issues and stories	
	Area tour to review visual management and sustainability issues	

Do Not Lead with IT Solutions

One of the most common mistakes organizations make is to pursue IT solutions to problems that are not clear or not well understood. Organizations apply technology as solutions in search of a problem. In a Lean thinking organization, you might hear the phrase "creativity before capital." This is a phrase used by Lean thinkers to explore all types of solutions *before* spending resources to solve a problem. Many work-related issues can be resolved with a low-cost, commonsense approach. Unfortunately, with an "app" for just about everything today, many forward thinkers leap to automation to solve many of today's problems.

An urgent care clinic had a challenge knowing when a patient care exam room needed to be cleaned, and subsequently, knowing when the room was cleaned. One potential solution identified was to add a bed tracking software system to flag when the room was ready to be cleaned and to flag when the room was clean. The software had an added feature of tracking the time the room was waiting to be cleaned and the time it took to clean the room. Many healthcare organizations have this type of system, and it works very well when used appropriately for a hospital. But a hospital has hundreds of beds, all out of sight from those that need to know what is going on in those rooms so that the rooms can be assigned, prioritized, and cleaned in a timely and appropriate manner.

This urgent care clinic had eight rooms total, and all were in the line of sight of everyone that worked in the clinic. Can you think of a lower cost solution? A significantly lower cost solution? I am sure you have seen the door flags that many clinics use to inform the clinic team of the status of the patient. These simple plastic/metal door flags that sit near the top of the door frame utilize distinct colors to signal to the team that there is something to do. Black, for example, means ready for the physician and similarly, dark gray means ready for the nurse. How about adding a light gray flag to signal a room needs to be cleaned? And perhaps a white flag that means the room is clean and available for the next patient? Figure 11.8 is an example of a patterned flag system.

As of June 2017, this solution has a top end expense of about US$75 installed with no further system maintenance or training required. The start-up and maintenance expenses to set up the IT solution, train the staff, maintain the licenses, etc. would be significantly higher.

When working on a process improvement, *always* try to spend a little time thinking through what non-technology alternatives exist prior to an IT solution or EHR modification. Often for a few dollars, or even no cost, a simple solution can be found. This is using creativity before capital. The best

Figure 11.8 Flag system in a clinic.

practice is to explore many alternative solutions to existing problems before thinking about automation. A lot of money can be saved in the ongoing optimization of the EHR when the organizational and improvement team thinking chooses not to lead with IT as the initial solution set. As a bonus, the non-IT solution will generally be faster to deploy and easier to maintain.

Minimize HandOffs before Automating

Along the lines of using creativity before capital, it is frequently thought that automation can streamline communication. In many instances this is true, but not in all instances. Let's demonstrate this thinking with a simple case study. Figure 11.9[2] shows a communication circle. A communication circle is used to show how information is exchanged between people. Each line represents communication between one party and another. Figure 11.9 shows the communication that takes place for a multidisciplinary team when managing the care of a patient that has a 5-day length of admission.

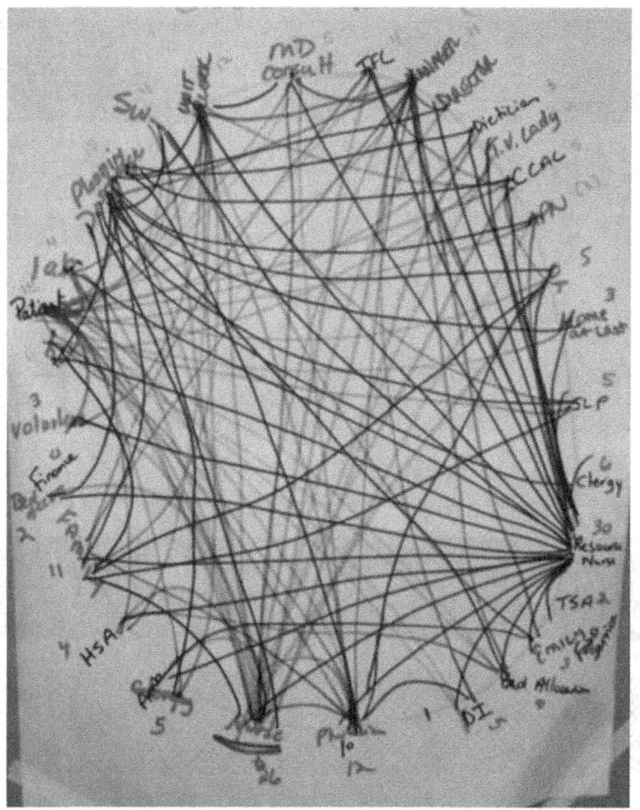

Figure 11.9 Communication circle. (From Bercaw, Ronald, 2012, *Taking Improvement from the Assembly Line to Healthcare*, CRC Press, Boca Raton, FL, p. 85.)

If you were in charge of the EHR, where would you start your automation of electronic communication? Most organizations fail to understand the complexity of the problem and root causes of the problem before jumping to IT solutions. In this example, you might say, we need a better way to communicate and complete transparency of the communication. Candidly, this type of streamlined communication is one of the areas where the EHR excels.

But what would a Lean thinker say about the communication circle shown in the example? Let's understand a couple of things about handoffs of communication. First, no one is generally sitting around in the work environment. So anytime information goes from one person to another, it is likely going to sit in a queue for a while. Odds are very high that when this many handoffs occur, there is going to be some waiting involved. Waiting is wasteful to a Lean thinker. Waiting takes time but delivers no value to the customer. Waiting can contribute to delays in patient care and a longer length of stay or clinic visit.

Odds of work being communicated properly through step 1 = 90%
Odds of work being communicated properly through step 2 = 90%

Odds of work going through two steps accurately:

0.90 (step 1) x 0.90 (step 2) = 0.81
0.81 x 100% = 81%

Figure 11.10 Reliability of accurate information making it through two steps.

Second, information that gets exchanged is frequently one-way communication. So it is subject to misinterpretation leading to errors. From a statistical standpoint, if there are two handoffs in a process, and both are handed off correctly 90% of the time, the odds of the work being handed off correctly twice is not 90%. Rather, the odds of the work going through both handoffs correctly is 90% multiplied by 90%, or 81%. The mathematical formula for this analysis, known as rolling throughput yield, is shown in Figure 11.10.

If we have 25 handoffs all with 90% accuracy, our reliability plummets. Let's do the math: $.90^{25}$ = 7.2%. That means that a 25-step process, with each step being 90% accurate, has a rolling throughput yield of just 7.2%. So, we can quickly understand that by reducing the number of handoffs, the quality of the process automatically improves.

To answer the question posed at the beginning of the previous paragraph, "Where would you start your automation work to streamline the handoffs/information flows shown in the communication circle?," a Lean thinker would say that before we automate the communication flows in the current state communication circle, let's first eliminate 50% of the workflow handoffs and then automate. Even with the real-time automation benefits of the EHR, the myriad of handoffs will still contribute to waiting and will still contribute to lower than expected quality of information. Reducing the number of handoffs will reduce the overall time for the process, increase the quality of the information, and simplify the EHR automation requirements. A win–win–win solution!

Why Is Optimization of the EHR so Difficult?

After all the pain and effort of the initial development and deployment of the EHR, rarely do organizations want to plan for and quickly discuss optimization of the system. Most organizations want to take a deep breath and say "thank goodness we are operational". Great organizations think differently. They use the initial EHR deployment simply as the baseline for further improvement. Just as we expect our clinical practices and outcomes to continually get better, and our operational practices and business results to continually get better, we should also expect getting our EHR better.

The places organizations most often fail in optimization include: not planning adequately for any further changes to the system from Lean process improvement activity, not leveraging and linking the appropriate IT optimization resource to the ongoing Lean improvement efforts, having IT be the lead solution for most problems, and failing to minimize handoffs before automating. Hopefully a few of these ideas can help you in avoiding these common mistakes.

We discussed in detail the importance of planning for future changes and having a team in place to manage these changes with a sense of urgency. Having an IT resource in place while making value stream change is critical. The organization must balance making timely value stream change while not sub-optimizing the system as a whole for a local improvement. Lean thinking and "creativity before capital" should always lead our solution approaches. Automation is expensive and takes a long time to deploy. A "creativity before capital" mind-set can lead to the discovery of solutions to simplify work without design, programming, training, display monitors, keyboards, and mouse clicks. Finally, be sure and reduce the workflow handoffs before you automate. This simple step reduces waiting while improving the quality of your information flows. These four steps will greatly enhance your success with optimizing your EHR and keeping your system current. Make your system an asset and not a liability. Make the system an enabler of greatness for your organization.

Chapter Summary

- EHR optimization contains three major sets of activities:
  - Maintaining the clinical integrity of your system.
  - Improving your system and processes with MDI techniques.
  - Planning for ongoing system changes coming from breakthrough continuous improvement work.

- Evidence changes more rapidly today than at any time in history. Having a change control committee in place that can rapidly review and approve, modify, or reject system changes will greatly enhance your organization's chances of keeping the system current.
- The MDI system is a key component of visual management. This system visually tracks the key measures of a department, identifies and prioritizes variances from plan, and develops and implements plans for improvement. The system measures, tracks, and improves key measures aligned to the true north dimensions.
- The content within the EHR and the actual operation of the system both need to be operating at a peak level to run a world-class healthcare system. MDI utilizes the skills of the entire IT staff to monitor key areas of both the system and the process to monitor and create improvement in support of this journey to excellence.
- Many organizations fail to plan for any EHR change from process improvement work, although it is known that Lean value stream improvement is planned and occurring.
- To best manage the EHR optimization process, while coexisting with the process improvement activities of your organization, there are four best practice steps that can be followed:
  - Plan on value changes from the Lean value stream improvement work occurring within your organization.
  - Assign an IT optimization resource to value stream steering team.
  - Do not lead with IT solutions. Use creativity before capital.
  - Minimize handoffs before automating.

Further Reading

1. Rother M, Shook J. *Learning to See*, Brookline, MA: Lean Enterprise Institute, Inc., 1998, pp. 4 and 5.
2. Bercaw R. *Taking Improvement from the Assembly Line to Healthcare*, Boca Raton, FL: CRC Press, 2012, p. 85.

Chapter 12

Optimizing Your Legacy System—Standardize by Specialty

The final chapters of this book are for those of you who already have an electronic health record. If this describes you, your organization does not need to acquire an EHR as you already have an operational system. If you are like many healthcare organizations, you face the following on a daily basis:

- Dozens and dozens of help tickets are waiting for action.
- Constant demands for new system functionality.
- Constant demands for new reports and report capability.
- Requests for additional bolt-on applications to your system, or new applications outside of your system altogether.
- Request for upgrades to your legacy systems.
- Requests for interfaces between existing legacy systems.
- Difficulty in getting consistent documentation compliance with various modules and screens within the system.
- A real or perceived shortage of IT resources to maintain and improve your system.

In Chapter 11, we talked about maintaining your newly deployed EHR system. There will always be challenges with keeping your system in top form. Technology continually advances and people's expectations of their technology is constantly changing. But what if you have deviated far from the original intent of your EHR? Incremental maintenance will not get your system back to its baseline. You will need to transform your existing system into a system that meets your needs in today's complex healthcare environment.

Three Steps to Transforming Your Legacy System

To transform your legacy system, we suggest you consider three important tasks. As Lean thinkers, anytime we speak about tasks, we want to deploy Lean thinking and Lean culture into the implementation of those tasks. The three tasks to transforming your legacy system include standardizing by specialty, developing the model line, and finally spreading the model. Usually, when the EHR drifts far from the baseline, it is because the organization allowed too much variation on system operation on a unit-by-unit basis, a clinic-by-clinic basis, or on a provider-by-provider basis. Sometimes this variation started right at the beginning of your original EHR deployment. Another common cause of the EHR not being in top shape is a failure of the organization to keep the evidence of practice current with the tables loaded in your system. A different possibility is your organization continued with Lean workflow improvement, and the EHR no longer works well with your simplified processes. A final possibility is you failed to keep up with the periodic updates and software releases to your legacy system. If you find yourself here, Chapters 7–10 discussed earlier in this book will apply. Assuming your organization has funding, you can use Lean project management approaches and go through the applicable milestones in upgrading your system to the latest release.

Standardize by Clinical Specialty

The first step in transforming your legacy system is to standardize by clinical specialty. This chapter will be devoted to this topic. The second step in transforming your legacy system is to create the model area to pilot and optimize the changes. By creating a model, you allow yourselves an opportunity to complete controlled experiments with the combination of both functionality and process to deliver the best possible outcomes. Lean principles and Lean design can be used to develop the best combination of people, software, space, and process to enhance your ability to deliver compelling value to your patients. Chapter 13 will cover this topic.

As a third step, you will need to spread your best practices. Taking the solutions developed at your model area of focus, you can systematically move these solutions from unit to unit, or clinic to clinic, and/or provider to provider. What will be spread is a standardized process and standardized system functionality to ensure everyone in your organization is performing at your current best standards of excellence. Chapter 13 will cover spreading solutions.

To demonstrate a simple example of deviating from clinical and system baseline, we'd like to share a common observation we find within healthcare organizations. In our travels, we have seen many times where clinicians, programs, units, and clinics were allowed to create/modify their own intake screens or assessment screens. The reasons for the deviations aren't always clinical in nature or even evidenced based. Many times the deviations were for personal preference. Unit A wants to assess falls and unit B wants to assess for mental health issues. Dr. A wants to ask these questions; Dr. B wants to ask a different set of questions. The majority of time, this is what was happening in the paper-based system and the variation in practice was then migrated to the EHR.

So what are the challenges with this deviation? The problem is when someone wants to make a system change, the proposed change cannot be taken to a review committee for discussion and quickly resolved. Why? Because at this point, you are no longer working with one EHR; you are working with many versions of the same EHR. Changing one screen, or text field, or drop-down menu will now require many different versions of approvals, development time, and test time if you want to make an organizational change because each clinician, clinic, and/or unit has a different variation of intake on their computer/tablet.

Making a change in this environment is very time consuming and frustrating to both the clinicians who want to make a system change and to the IT engineers and application specialists who must work through all the technical aspects of the change. Having a standard platform to work from makes the speed of the change and the work content of the change considerably easier. User satisfaction increases, evidence-based changes can be implemented faster, and the constrained IT resources can be more productive. This sounds like a win-win-win solution.

Why is standardization so important? Let's start to answer this question with the dictionary definition of a standard. According to http://www.dictionary.com, a standard is defined as "something considered by an authority or by general consent as a basis of comparison: an approved model."* In its simplest form, a Lean organization would define a standard as a basis for comparison. We all know the common standards for time (seconds, minutes, hours), weight (pounds or kilograms), and volume (liters or gallons). Because we have standards, we can consistently and accurately declare that something weighs more than something else or that one item has a greater volume than another. So as we start to make changes to the EHR, how do we know that one change is better than another? If we do not have a baseline established, then we cannot measure the effectiveness of a change. The baselines, known as standards, are what make this evaluation possible.

If you work in a Lean organization, you understand the importance of standards. *Having a waste-free standard that is consistently followed is likely the single most important factor to improving an environment.* Without a standard, improvement is not possible, because there is no way to compare one work method versus another or one outcome versus another. The standard becomes the baseline for further improvement. Now we don't want to standardize for the sake of standardization; this is a common and faulty misconception held by many clinicians. A guiding phrase heard in Lean organizations is, "Don't standardize for the sake of standardization, but don't deviate for personal preference."

It would be simply amazing to have the EHR run perfectly in your organization right out of the box. If it were only that simple! Each department and organization has different terminology, definitions, libraries, practices and protocols, etc. And as everyone is aware, the body of medical knowledge is exponentially growing every year. So the variation, organization to organization and unit to unit, etc. creates quite a conundrum. Because of the complexity of patient populations, we know universal standardization is out, at least for today, yet we also know the serious challenges caused by too much variation. What we have seen in the best run Lean organizations is a nice compromise. Some standardization is helpful, but not at the expense of compromising the needed variation in clinical specialties. So the best practice today, for system and process standardization in a Lean organization, is created by clinical specialty.

There are lots of ways to slice up healthcare services. We could divide the healthcare services by population. We could also divide healthcare into acute services and preventative services. Organizations wrestle with this

* www.dictionary.com/browse/standard?s=t

division every day when trying to define their leadership and organizational structures.

By clinical specialty, we are implying that you standardize your EHR by clinical program. So we may look at standardizing the EHR within cardiology, oncology, laboratory medicine, for example. If your organization has multiple cardiology clinics, multiple inpatient units, or multiple cardiology service providers, the cardiology service workflows and EHR functionality can and should be standardized to this level. At a higher level, multiple hospitals within the same system can also standardize at the clinical specialty level. So each hospital within the system will have the same workflows and system functionality for their cardiology services. That way, an EHR change to cardiology services will impact multiple hospitals and minimize the variation in your EHR system.

The differences between clinicians, organizations, clinics, and units are well known. There is variation in the physical footprint, organizational structure, support resources, technology, standards of care, practice patterns, clinician/staffing availability, etc. The authors of this book are not naive. *Standardizing the workflows and functionality will be a difficult process.* However, unless you want to end up with a number of workflows and EHR processes, this is a necessary first step. Think about your legacy EHR and the challenges you face today. Now be completely honest with yourself. Aren't there a substantial number of issues that you face today that would be infinitely easier to resolve with some standardization?

So what might this look like in practice? Let's walk through an example using a patient population of adults with the chronic disease of heart failure. This particular clinic has four practicing cardiologists and two nurse practitioners. The clinic is also supported by seven nurses in the clinic, two nurses handling the phone triage function, a pharmacist, and a receptionist. In the current state, the doctors could customize the intake screens and choose which questions would be asked and answered by the nurses taking the history and by the providers themselves. When the EHR was originally installed, the vendor recommended this practice not be followed; the explicit recommendation was to standardize the clinic assessment process. For this organization, candidly, the doctors mutinied and said they would leave the hospital if they were forced to go in this direction. No one in leadership wanted to upset the providers by making the decision to standardize. Prior to the introduction of the EHR, the doctors used paper forms to document. Stocking various paper forms was a nuisance, but with only four doctors, stocking and using the various forms was manageable. When the system was designed and deployed, the paper-based processes were then replicated into the electronic environment. This process of trying to maintain the paper-based workflows and simply layering those practices into an electronic system is an all too frequent occurrence in healthcare. And it usually ends poorly over time.

So let's fast forward 6 years from the original deployment of the EHR. Now there are eight doctors in the practice and four nurse practitioners. Since the precedent was set to allow intake customization, each doctor, upon starting in the organization, went through a process to determine how they wanted their workflow and intake questions/screens to be formatted. This is quite a burden on the IT resources and required a fair amount of training for the nurses each time a new doctor was added to the practice.

When a change in heart failure care evidence occurred, the assessment screens needed to be updated by having a few common intake questions removed and a few new, evidence-based questions added. Had there been workflow and functionality standardization in place, the change would have occurred relatively quickly. However, since the non-standardized precedent was already set, each provider decided on a case-by-case basis how to add (or not add) the questions to the intake screen. A decision and system change that should have taken 30 days took 18 months, and the resulting variation took the organization even further from standardization. New evidence was not deployed quickly and while not leading to a bad outcome, likely limited some patient's ability to get the best possible care. This simple example is how organizations end up with what we call "multiple EHRs." Once the erosion from standardization occurs, then the complaints about how long it takes to get a system change start to surface.

It would appear this might be a physician issue. Actually it is not. This is an organizational leadership issue. The challenges to standardize or not standardize arise daily between clinics, clinicians, units, and hospitals. What is typically lacking is both a philosophy to standardize and a process to then carry it out. By having a philosophy to standardize, the organization needs to believe that the fundamentals of best practice and evidence-based standardization of workflows and system functionality outweigh the pain of requiring clinicians and administrators to set and maintain standards. This philosophy is engrained in a Lean organization. It is not challenged, and it is not subject to debate. Standard work is embedded in all activity. Standard work is followed, and standard work is not optional.

To standardize, we mean having a standard structure *and* process in place for standardization issues to be brought forward and discussed and for decisions to be made quickly. Earlier in the book, we discussed the role of the change control committee in maintaining the system. This same forum can be effectively used in vetting and setting organizational standards. Once the standards are set, the change control committee can keep the standards current by continuing to meet and optimize the system as discussed in Chapter 11.

The best approach to getting started with standardization is to create a model area of focus. The model area can be used to "experiment" in a controlled environment with different standards to come up with the optimal combination of people, process, technology, workflow, information, equipment, and supplies for a given process. The model approach is the topic covered next in Chapter 13.

Standardizing by Subspecialty?

Regarding clinical standardization, the question arises from time to time of whether we should specialize by clinical specialty or clinical subspecialty. For example, if we are working on standardizing neurology as a clinical specialty, there are several subspecialties to consider, such as epilepsy, concussion, neurogenetics, pain management, neurosurgery, sleep, etc. In our known experience with EHRs, there may not yet be a perfect answer to this question. In a very limited sample size, one approach we have seen to be effective in this space is the rule of 80% standardization. By this we imply that ~80% of the system functionality be standardized for all the specialty and ~20% of the functionality be tailored to the subspecialty. The rule of 80% is a guideline. In practice, this 80% can vary based on clinical need and variation in core processes within the subspecialty.

One last thought on standardization: we have seen many, many times in our travels where leadership did not have *the will* to require standardization. In western culture, people following standards are not generally recognized or rewarded. People that innovate are recognized and rewarded. So the value in having and following a standard is frequently not well known or appreciated. Not in a way that would be mandated. The decision to standardize, and to what level, has to be determined and supported by top leadership. Pursuit of standardization has to be a top priority if you want to become a great organization.

Lean organizations clearly understand the benefits of standards. Standards are inherent in all work being done. How well does your organization support clinical and process workflow standardization and functionality standardization? What are the benefits to your organization in standardizing? What are the risks? How much time, energy, effort, and rework are caused with your documentation by either lack of standardization or lack of following the standards?

Step 1 in creating a new system out of your legacy system: Standardize by clinical specialty.

Chapter Summary

- Many organizations have an EHR. Their challenge is not to purchase and install a new system, but to get and keep their existing system optimized.
- There are three key steps to optimization: First, standardize by clinical specialty (Chapter 12); next, develop the model area; and finally, spread the model to other areas (Chapter 13).
- A standard is a basis for comparison. Your EHR system needs to get to a standard to allow you to compare one change against another to see if the change is measurably better.
- The longer you have gone without setting organizational standards, the more difficult this task will be.
- Organizations that have *not* standardized will need to maintain more process and system functionality than those that have. Lack of standardization creates a phenomenon known as "multiple EHRs."
- The same resources that make up the change control committee can be used to set the clinical standards.
- For the EHR, the best place to start to standardize is at clinical specialty level.
- Standardizing to the clinical subspecialty is best accomplished by standardizing ~80% of the process and system functionality at the clinical specialty level and tailoring the remaining ~20% at the subspecialty level.

Chapter 13

Optimizing Your Legacy System—Create and Spread the Model

What Is a "Model" Area?

As you learned in the previous chapter, the first critical step in optimizing your EHR is to standardize by clinical specialty. Repeating again for emphasis, the definition of a standard is a basis for comparison. As an organization, we need to get to a standard baseline so we can compare (measure) if one idea is better than another. With a standard and a measurement system in place, we can move quickly to deployment as we do not need to debate variation in workflows, mouse clicks, screen views, reports, etc. throughout the deployment process. Having a standard in place limits rework and maximizes human talent, while minimizing deployment expense. Before we can get too far down the deployment road, we need to test our standardization and create documented evidence that our known standards are measurably better. The process we use to operationalize our new standards is called *creating a model*. In a Lean organization, the phrase you will hear is *creating a model cell*. A cell is a physical place, or construct, where we optimize people, process, equipment, and information together through standard work and visual management. Steps 2 and 3 in the legacy system optimization are to create and spread the model.

Create the Model

Lean improvement systems are developed on the principle of deciding very carefully and then deploying quickly. "Deciding carefully" implies using all the stakeholders in the process in evaluating many alternatives, testing those alternatives, and then making a *fact-based*, informed decision on the best approach. Not many organizations operate repeatedly in this manner. Frequently, organizations and teams rush to solutions and deployment of solutions without any robust structure to generate solutions, leading to subpar results or results that require a lot of massaging and rework in the deployment stage. In optimizing the legacy EHR, we want to create a model area that will serve as a laboratory for experimentation. Great Lean organizations consider themselves a community of scientists, where everyone is involved in small experiments to see and eliminate waste in their work. In the model space, for example, we can decide what is the best method to capture intake data, what is the best method to capture patient demographics, what layout is easiest to enter an order set, what evidence-based order sets create the best outcomes, what set of standard tasks make patient care the safest, etc.

The model area in healthcare is generally a subset of a program or a department. For example, in one hospital we worked with, there were 11 discrete inpatient units: cardiology, general adult medicine, critical care, medicine, oncology, orthopedics, neurology, etc. To optimize the legacy EHR, the desire was to come up with the best workflows and processes to support inpatient care and the documentation of that care. Our example hospital has decided that cardiology will be the model area for inpatient care and documentation in the EHR. This means that the standards discussed in Chapter 12 will be operationalized first on a single cardiology unit.

In the model cardiology unit, workflows would be mapped, Lean thinking would be applied to eliminate waste from the workflows, and the EHR would then be optimized to support those improved workflows. The design, experimentation, and measurement capture of these changes would occur *only* within cardiology until three conditions are satisfied. First, the standards are followed. Second, the resulting process shows improvement. And third, the process has stabilized and the results have been maintained (generally for a period of 60–90 days). Once cardiology is optimized, we would then proceed to spread these best practices (standards) to the next unit, or units depending on the implementation plan. Many organizations attempt to optimize their EHR from an organizational perspective: in other words, to design the inpatient care work using the perspective of *all* inpatient units. We have found that the variables are too complex and the dynamics of making this scale of change across the organization are monumental, both structurally and culturally. The model area concept allows you to design, test, and improve in a controlled environment. This will allow your organization to be nimble and get to design and test much faster. We have seen first-hand where organizations that take an organizational perspective to designing their EHR end up with a consensus process and system. That one size approach standardizes the workflows and system functionality across the organization, but the resulting process and product work for no one. Worse, we have seen where organizations end up with a system-wide process and functionality that not only doesn't work between units but also doesn't work between hospitals. These system hospital wide and system standardization examples are the polar opposites of the "multiple EHR" phenomenon. With mass levels of variation, change becomes very difficult because getting to a standard is extremely difficult. Overstandardization also leads to a process and product that don't work optimally for anyone. So, the process and system do little to add value to the clinical and administrative staff. The model area concept mitigates both challenges.

Using Rapid Cycle Improvement

One approach to optimize the EHR and corresponding workflows within the model is to use rapid cycle improvement. Rapid cycle improvement has many names, including kaizen event, kaizen blitz, rapid process improvement workshop, and rapid improvement event. The names, while different, generally apply the same methodology. Rapid cycle improvement is common to many Lean organizations and serves two purposes: to minimize the time for results and to develop the team members in their ability to see and eliminate waste. In the rapid cycle improvement for our model area, the optimization team will be applying Lean thinking to a specific workflow. By applying Lean thinking, we mean taking a workflow through the scientific method.

Some of the people reading this book are clinical. If so, you are familiar with the scientific method. The same approach that is used in clinical trials to develop evidence-based care and to develop and market new pharmaceuticals is used in Lean organizations to create a culture of improvement. If you are not clinical or new to Lean, the scientific method is the standard

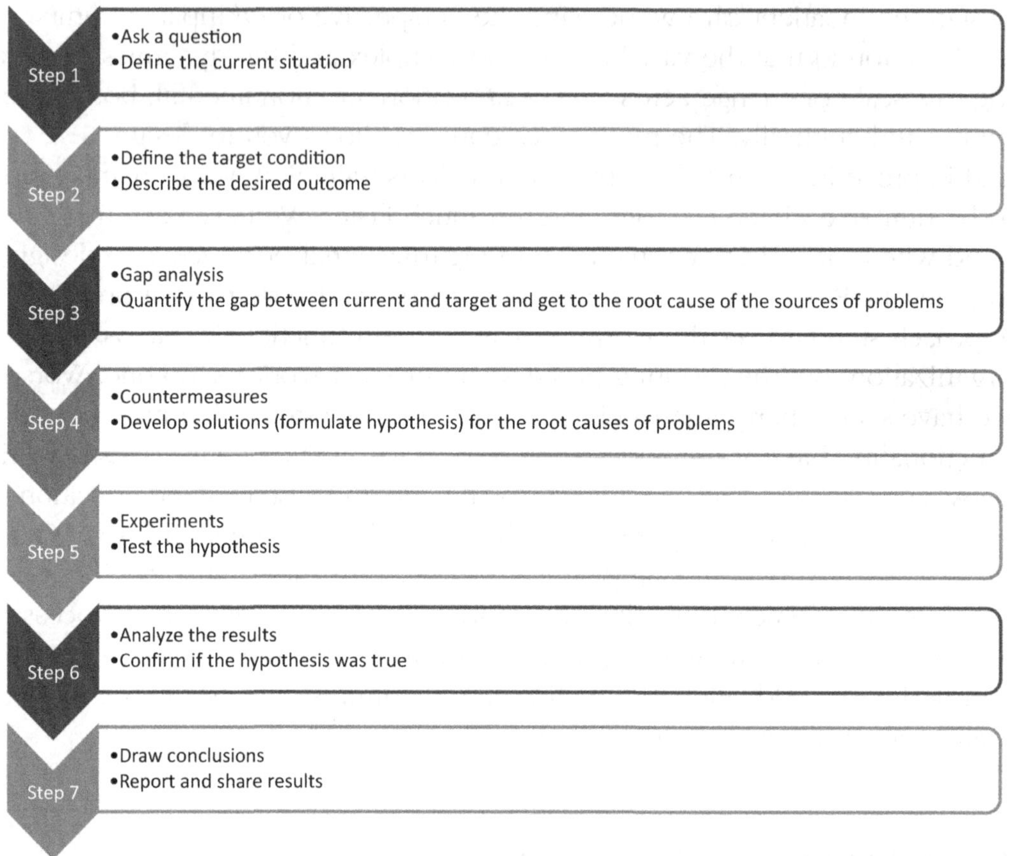

Figure 13.1 Scientific method.

approach Lean thinkers use for both problem-solving and improvement. In the case of the EHR, we will be using the scientific method to optimize the process and system functionality of our model. The key steps of the scientific method are shown in Figure 13.1.

Applying the Scientific Method and the A3

A Lean organization would apply the scientific method using an A3 form and A3 thinking. An A3 form is named as such because it describes the size of the paper that the form is written on—11 inches tall by 17 inches wide. When the A3 form was created, it was placed on 11 × 17 paper because that was the largest size paper that could be faxed given the technology available at the time. The A3 is written in story board form. The document tells the story of the improvement activity, and the story follows the scientific method. There are distinct types of A3 forms. The most common A3 is the problem-solving or improvement A3 form. Other variations of the A3 form include approval of justification of resources A3. This A3 is like presenting a business case. A final type of format for the A3 is for documentation of organizational strategy. In our model, we are trying to improve the process and the supporting system functionality to deliver the best possible healthcare, in the shortest time, at the lowest cost. This type of A3, shown in Figure 13.2, will follow the problem-solving format.

In a Lean organization, one way to apply the scientific method via the A3 process is through rapid cycle improvement. Rapid cycle improvement is not required to complete the scientific method but does afford a couple of major benefits. The first benefit is it will compress your timeline for results. Bringing the team together for a consecutive period will get you to your model state faster than meeting for 1 hour a week over 6 months. The second benefit of the rapid cycle event is that the rapid cycle event experience is designed to change organizational culture. When team members have an opportunity to go through the scientific method to optimize a workflow and to see the entire process from current state through implementation, their perspective on improvement and your EHR will change for the better. Having user input in real change to both process and functionality is a fantastic morale builder.

The time of a rapid cycle event is variable. Enough time needs to be given to get through all the steps of the scientific method; the general range of duration for most organizations is 3 to 5 days. A sample agenda for a 4-day rapid cycle event in optimizing an EHR is shown in Table 13.1.

During the rapid cycle event, the team will go through all the steps of the scientific method to optimize a core process and workflow and optimize the EHR functionality to support the workflow.

Rapid Cycle in Action—A Case Study

Let's continue with our cardiology inpatient model to demonstrate an example of where the scientific method was applied in a rapid cycle event to optimize the EHR and deliver sustainable, measurable results.

At our organization, it was determined that the inpatient length of stay (LOS) for patients in our unit exceeded the benchmark LOS by one full day. This has cost implications, and it caused a backup in the emergency department each day by not having an available bed for both ER patients with heart

A-3 Theme: <Title> | **Date:** <insert date> **Revision #:** <insert revision #>

Team Members: <insert team member names and positions>

Reason For Improvement:

- <3-5 bullet points tied to high level business objectives>

Current Performance and Reflections on Current Performance:

- <Describe attributes of current performance and culture>
- <include good and bad>
- <include reflections on current performance>
- <Look from today backward>

Target Performance:

- <Attributes of desired performance and culture>
- <Think Lean (flow, pull, defect free, managed visually, standard work, leveled work)>

Dimension	Measure	Current	Target
Morale/HD			
Quality			
Delivery/Access			
Cost/Productivity			

Anticipated Hard savings: <budgetary changes>

Anticipated Soft Savings: <non budgetary changes like hand-offs or steps reduced, also includes cost avoidance>

Gap Analysis:
<Quantify or Qualify the gap between current and target conditions>
<This is usually the "waste" (over production, over processing, waiting, inventory, motion, transportation, defects)>

Waste Theme	Root Cause
Summarize the key wastes	Identify their root cause
Summarize the key wastes	Identify their root cause
Summarize the key wastes	Identify their root cause
Summarize the key wastes	Identify their root cause

<Note: nine out of ten times, the root cause is as follows: there is no defined standard, the standard is not followed, or the standard is not adequate>

1

Countermeasures and Action Plans:

Waste Theme	Root Cause	Countermeasure	Expected Result
Copy from Gap Analysis	Copy from Gap Analysis	<Solution to the root cause>	<result of our test>
		<should be obvious>	
		<often "lean" related (flow, pull, defect free, standard work, etc.)>	

Follow Up Plans:

What	Who	When
<activities/plans to institutionalize the change>	<person responsible>	<due date>

Measurement Tracking:

Dimension	Measure	Current	Target	Week 1	Week 2	Week 3	Week 4	Week 5	Week 6	Week 7	Week 8
Morale/HD	From targets	From targets	From targets	actual	actual	actual	actual				
Quality	From targets	From targets	From targets	actual	actual	actual	actual				
Delivery/Access	From targets	From targets	From targets	actual	actual	actual	actual				
Cost/Productivity	From targets	From targets	From targets	actual	actual	actual	actual				

Verified Hard Savings: <insert actual budget changes>

Verified Soft Savings: <insert actual results>

Reflections:
<insert team comments on what you learned from the process to capture organizational learning>

2

Figure 13.2 Blank problem-solving A3 form with completion instructions.

Table 13.1 Rapid Cycle Event Daily Agenda

Day 1 Define Current Conditions (See Waste)	*Day 2 Develop Solutions (Eliminate Waste)*	*Day 3 Implement/Test Solutions*	*Day 4 Document New Standard Work*
• Team training • Review measures and targets • Use appropriate tools to see waste • Gather time observation data • Generate 50 to 100 forms of waste	• Prioritize wastes • Develop countermeasures and action plans to eliminate waste • Use Lean principles to design a new work flow	• Implement countermeasures • Train team members on new process • Verify effectiveness of solutions by measuring	• Document standard work • Document event results • Deliver final presentation • Recognize team

conditions and not having a bed to step down any patients from critical care. We also know the longer a patient is in the hospital, the more susceptible they are to getting a hospital-acquired condition. This avoidable day for these patients created an opportunity to optimize the EHR and to optimize the corresponding processes in providing ideal care in the shortest inpatient visit.

The solution approach was to complete a 4-day rapid cycle event with three deliverables:

1. Reduce the LOS by 1 day on the model unit
2. Optimize the EHR functionality of the discharge planning process
3. Create standard work for the discharge planning process to enable the spread of the process and EHR functionality to other units and sister hospitals

To ensure good clinical outcomes, readmission rates were also evaluated to ensure that the LOS was not impacted by sending patients home before they were ready to be safely discharged.

The baseline measures and targets were as shown in Table 13.2.

The A3 form was initiated and the team was assembled. Figure 13.3 shows what the first few boxes of the A3 looked like in preparation for the rapid cycle event.

Table 13.2 Cardiology Inpatient LOS Reduction and Discharge Planning EHR Optimization

Measure	*Baseline*	*Target*	*% Change*
Cardiology inpatient LOS	4.3 days	3.3 days	Decrease 23%
Optimize the EHR discharge planning functionality—time spent documenting d/c plans	138 minutes across all disciplines for the entire patient stay	45 minutes across all disciplines for the entire patient stay	67% reduction
Create standard work for the discharge planning process	Not standardized	Standardized	N/A
Readmission rates (%)	7.8%	<5%	34% reduction

The team then assembled and went through the scientific method to deliver their improvement to the measures identified in the A3. At a high level, the team completed the following activities: (For a more detailed description of running a rapid cycle event, please see *Taking Improvement from the Assembly Line to Healthcare*, Bercaw, 2012, p. 61, CRC Press).

Monday:
- Map the current state patient care workflow and the information flow
- Visit gemba and gather direct observation data
- Complete a value-added/non-value added analysis
- Complete a current state communication circle
- Identify 50 to 100 discrete wastes

Tuesday:
- Prioritize wastes
- Determine root causes of the wastes
- Develop countermeasures for the root causes
- Create the future state workflow and information flow
- Develop products and artifacts to support countermeasures
- Write standard word to support the future state process
- Build templates and screen designs to support information flows

A-3 Theme: *Reduce Cardiology I/P LOS*	**Date** *7 Oct 2017* **Revision** *1*
Team Members: *Jill Smith—Charge RN, Stacy Jones—RN Manager, Fred Smith—Case Manager, Owen Vicks—Application specialist, Ron Gatling—Cardiologist, Jane Kluber—Pharmacist, Elise Weiss—Nurse tech*	
Reason For Improvement: • *The provide cardiology patients the best care at the best value* • *To optimize staff resources by streamlining their clinical documentation*	
Current Performance and Reflections on Current Performance: • *Median LOS = 4.3 days* • *Readmission rates = 7.8%* • *Variation in D/C planning goals and implementation of the goals* • *Excessive time spent doing clinical documentation*	**Target Performance:** • *Standard work for all disciplines* • *Evidenced-based best practices in place for care delivery and clinical documentation* • *Time freed up the deliver more dare at the bedside* • *Patients and care givers have the knowledge to continue care in home environment*

Dimension	Measure	Current	Target
Access	*Cardiology inpatient length of stay*	*4.3 days*	*3.3 days*
Productivity	*Time spent documenting d/c plans*	*138 minutes*	*45 minutes*
Quality (%)	*Readmission rates*	*7.8%*	*5%*

Figure 13.3 Cardiology inpatient LOS reduction A3.

Wednesday:
- Train the model area on the standard work and the new functionality (in sandbox)
- Trial the new process
- Record results
- Debrief and modify the standard work and EHR functionality

Thursday:
- Retrain on the amended standard work and amended EHR functionality

- Trial the new process
- Build visual management systems
- Finalize standard work
- Create the follow-up plans
- Develop formal rollout and communication plans
- Create and deliver final results in a presentation format

For this organization, it took 2 weeks to finalize the design and test the system functionality. The cardiology unit underwent system and process training the third week post rapid cycle and went live with the new discharge planning process the following Monday. Sixty days after going live, the results shown in Table 13.3 were reported.

Some of you will immediately pick up on the fact that not all the goals were met. One of the goals was to reduce the documentation time to 45 minutes. After 60 days, the documentation time was sitting at a median of 52 minutes. You will not hit every goal in a Lean improvement event. What you should always expect and achieve, though, is a double-digit improvement (10% +). Even though the goal was missed by 7 minutes, 86 minutes of patient care were returned to the clinicians. Think about picking up ~90 minutes of staff time per patient, for every patient on that unit, forever. And the other goals were comfortably met.

The key point here is that optimizing your EHR should lead to business improvement. Making the system navigation easier and more intuitive is important. But the core business of healthcare is...well healthcare—taking care of patients. The EHR should enable quality and operational improvement, not impede it.

You should expect, when completing an EHR optimization workflow rapid cycle event, to deliver measurable results. As you saw in the case study, in a workflow optimization event, we would expect several operational measures to improve simultaneously. This is what happens when you see and eliminate waste from a process. In a Lean environment, operational measures come from five different dimensions. These dimensions include staff engagement and morale, quality, timeliness, cost, and growth. Table 13.4 lists the different measures of operational excellence and what types of measurable benefits we might expect to see from optimizing workflows in the EHR.

Aside from the measurable benefits of optimizing the EHR, another major benefit is the standard work and functionality standardization that comes from applying the scientific method to improving workflows. By focusing

Table 13.3 Cardiology Inpatient LOS Reduction and Discharge Planning EHR Optimization Results

Measure	*Baseline*	*Target*	*% Target Change*	*Results*	*% Actual Change*
Cardiology inpatient LOS	4.3 days	3.3 days	Decrease 23%	3.1 days	28% decrease
Optimize the EHR discharge planning functionality—time spent documenting d/c plans	138 minutes across all disciplines for the entire patient stay	45 minutes across all disciplines for the entire patient stay	67% reduction	52 minutes	62% decrease
Create standard work for the discharge planning process	Not standardized	Standardized	N/A	Standardized	N/A
Readmission rates (%)	7.8%	5%	34% reduction	4.3%	45% decrease

Table 13.4 Measures of Operational Excellence

Dimension	*Measure*	*Results Realized through Process and EHR Optimization Efforts*
Morale/people development	Staff morale or staff engagement measures	Improved staff and provider morale created by a better process and better functioning EHR
Quality	1. Clinical outcomes and patient safety measures 2. Measures of process quality 3. Service quality—measures of patient experience and patient satisfaction	1. Improved patient safety and improved quality outcomes 2. Less rework and fewer clerical/ information errors 3. Improved patient experience and patient satisfaction
Delivery/ access	Lead times for goods and services from "customer need identified" to "customer need met"; expressed in minutes, hours, or days	Decreased LOS, decreased clinic visit length, and decreased wait times for information, procedures, transportation, disposition, services, orders, results, etc.
Cost	Resource hours or dollars consumed per unit of service	Reduced operating cost, improved productivity, improved throughput, and capital avoidance
Growth	Increases in volumes or revenues	Growth in volumes or growth in revenues

our changes in the model area, we can quickly move, unencumbered, to standardizing the process and the workflows supported by the EHR to set our baseline for further improvement in the future.

In our example, the inpatient cardiology unit had been chosen as the model for inpatient workflow optimization. After applying the scientific method to core processes, workflows can be optimized to transform your legacy EHR and build your model EHR. There are a handful of core processes that are commonly seen in an inpatient unit. Table 13.5 shows a small sample of some inpatient core processes where model processes and workflows can be created. Many of these same areas will apply for clinic processes. An example is shown in the table.

Table 13.5 Healthcare Inpatient Core Processes

Core Process	*Standard Work Created*	*Results Realized*
Admission order	Standard work for generating an admission order Standardized computer screens for admitting a patient	Reduce time for documentation, streamlined/standardized order entry, and reduction in errors
Nursing admission assessment	Standard work for completing the nursing admission assessment Standardized computer screens for completing the nursing admission assessment	Reduced time for documentation/screens that flow with the logical order of completing the nurse assessment/standard approach to documenting the initial nurse assessment/reduction in assessment data errors
Physician admission assessment	Standard work for completing the physician admission assessment Standardized computer screens for completing the physician admission assessment	Reduced time for documentation/screens that flow with the logical order of completing the physician assessment/ standard approach to documenting the initial physician assessment/ reduction in assessment data errors
Physician order entry	Standard work for documenting physician orders Standardized computer screens for documenting orders	Reduced time for order entry/better compliance with standardized order sets/fewer phone calls regarding questions on physician orders/fewer medication errors
Discharge planning	Standard work for discharge planning Standardized computer screens for documenting discharge planning	Reduced time documenting discharge planning/fewer redundancies in the discharge planning process/clearer discharge instructions leading to fewer clarification phone calls

Nursing and/or physician handover	Standard work for physician and nursing handover Standardized tools and screens for physician and nursing handover	Reduced time in completing handover/fewer risks left undiscussed in the handover process/less redundancy in documentation between the progress notes, assessment documentation, and the handover process
Patient education	Standard work for patient education Standard approach to documenting episodes of patient education	Consistent patient education practices/better retention of education by patients and families/less redundancy in patient education between clinicians/and fewer readmissions
Medicine administration	Standard work for medicine administration Standardized screens for documenting medicine administration Standard screens for managing the Medicine Administration Record (MAR)	Less time spent to deliver medicines/fewer adverse events/higher patient safety/less time spent documenting medicine administration
Allied health assessment and progress notes • OT • PT • SLP • RT • Nutrition • Infection prevention and control • Care management	Standard work to completing allied health assessments, reassessments, and therapies Standardized screens for documenting allied health activity	Less time spent documenting/easier access and visibility to notes and orders/more time spent with patient therapy vs. documentation/less time spent looking for information within the EHR system

Daily nursing reassessment	Standard work for completing the nursing reassessment Standardized computer screens for completing the nursing reassessment	Reduced time for documentation/screens that flow with the logical order of completing the nurse reassessment/ standard approach to documenting the nurse reassessment/reduction in reassessment data errors
Medication reconciliation	Standard work for completing medication reconciliation Standardized screens for documenting medication reconciliation	Less time spent completing the medicine reconciliation/higher quality medication reconciliation/fewer errors/better clinical outcomes
Writing the discharge summary	Standard work for completing the discharge summary Standard screens for documenting the discharge summary	Less time spent completing the discharge summary/ better quality discharge summary/fewer phone calls with questions regarding the discharge summary

The outcome themes of a well-done EHR optimization remain consistent process to process. We expect the quality of the process to improve. When this occurs, we see better clinical outcomes and fewer questions for clarification caused by interpretation considerations. The timeline to complete the documentation should go down. The least waste way to document should take the shortest amount of time. This gives valuable minutes back to the clinicians to deliver more patient care and to be able to leave work at a reasonable hour. Fewer errors will occur resulting in better patient safety and less rework. And finally, we get the most important thing in improvement, standardization. Standardization is our platform for further improvement. If we can get to standardization, we can move from good to great! Standards can be continuously improved to continue to move the organization to better and better outcomes, in the shortest lead times, at the lowest cost. This is the very essence of Lean improvement.

Summarizing the chapter to this point, once you have optimized your workflows and made the EHR an enabler of these workflows in the least waste way, you should both expect and realize double-digit improvement in your model area. By double digits, we mean 10% plus improvement in the outcome measures you have specified before beginning the work. On top of that, you have made progress in optimizing your EHR for a portion of your system.

After the model area leadership has ensured all the staff and providers have been trained, have stabilized their processes by ensuring everyone is following standard work, and have realized the measurable impact of the optimization work, you are now ready to spread these improvements to the next area! The learning from the model development, the standard work from the model area, the measurable results from the model, and the optimized EHR will all greatly enhance your ability to spread your solutions quickly to other areas of your organization.

Spreading the Model

Recall from our example that we chose to improve processes and optimize the EHR for our cardiology service. We have other units to improve and optimize: general adult medicine, critical care, oncology, orthopedics, neurology, etc. What spread implies is taking evidence-based, documented, proven solutions from our model (cardiology) and applying them to the other departments/services. While it was mentioned previously, there are three conditions that must be satisfied before attempting to spread a solution.

1. The model area has been trained on the standard work and system functionality for the new process.
2. Standard work is followed by everyone.
3. There is a documented measurable improvement in the new process.

All model area staff, leadership, and physicians need to be trained in the new process. Without ensuring everyone is trained, it is doubtful the results expected will be realized. If standard work is not followed, then variation will be found in outcomes, and the ability to sustain any improvement or further improve the work will be quickly lost. Without documentation of measurable results, there is no business case to spread any solution. Why would you invest more time and resources into spreading a solution that has no impact for the patients, the staff, and the organization? More importantly, the staff will ask why this "new" approach is better and it is easier to have the conversation on how the new process, workflow, and functionality enhance their value-add with improvement data in hand. Assuming these three things are thoroughly entrenched in the organization, you are ready to start spreading solutions.

Yokoten

Spread in a Lean organization is called *Yokoten*. Yokoten is a Japanese phrase that is shortened from its true spelling, which is yoko ten kai. Yoko translates to horizontal, lateral, or sideways. This is the word that means "spread." Tenkai means to develop, deploy, or advance. The two words put together translate to best practice sharing (wisdom) and deployment, so our definition of spread is the deployment of best practice.

Great Lean organizations *always* approach improvement through the model-spread approach. The model is used as an area of the organization that can constantly be experimented with to develop innovative approaches to work. Spread systems are used to quickly translate learning throughout the organization, when the results have proven to be defined as a best practice. When we optimize our EHR, we want to ensure we leverage this proven practice to design, develop, test, implement, and stabilize the development of improved processes in the model area, followed by a period of quickly deploying these proven solutions to other areas. It is rare we find this practice in place within healthcare organizational. Most healthcare organizations do not have a model area but rather have councils and workgroups that look at improving processes and system functionality from an organizational perspective. What does your organization look like?

With an understanding of what is meant by spread, let's review the most common approaches to spread that Lean organizations deploy when optimizing an EHR. A Lean spread approach involves the replication tools, processes, and artifacts and translating them from one area to another to yield comparable results. What we are spreading here is tested solutions. In our model cell, we have created new standard workflows supported by standard work. We likely have standardized some or all the work, we have tested the work, and we have demonstrated measurable improvement. Our mission is to rapidly deploy these new processes and workflows into a new environment. In optimizing an EHR, we will likely have to do some system customization to support the variation in clinical practice. The assessment for a patient coming to a unit following heart surgery will be answering different questions than the assessment on a patient coming up to the unit following a hip replacement. As always, we anticipate that 80% of the process and system functionality will be the same when spreading solutions, but 20% will appropriately need to be changed to support the clinical variation in the patient populations.

The advantages of spreading a known solution include the following:

- We are leveraging tested and proven solutions with documented measurable results.
- The training key points are well defined.
- Our solutions are based on the Lean principles of flow, pull, defect free and managing visually.
- Spreading know solutions can occur rapidly.
- Limited IT design resources are needed to spread existing solution.

There are, however, some disadvantages to spreading process and functionality using this approach. These include the following:

- Usually we are replicating a product and not the thinking. This limits the organization's ability to learn Lean thinking.
- Within healthcare, there is frequently less buy-in to someone else's solutions.
- This approach can limit novel ideas and innovation.
- The approach is very difficult in "not invented here" environments.

Having a basic understanding of some of the advantages and disadvantages of spreading solutions, you can use this knowledge to formulate your communication strategy to leverage the strengths while managing some of the challenges. Having your team understand the "what" and the "why" of the change will help when spreading solutions from your model area. Knowing there might be challenges with buy-in, be sure to clearly communicate the features and benefits of the new solution set. What is the win for the patient and families? What is the win for the staff and physicians? What is the win for the organization? What are the measurable outcomes achieved by the new processes and functionality?

Having covered our definition of spread and the advantages and disadvantages of spreading products and process to other areas of our organization, let's discuss the Yokoten deployment model used by Lean organizations. There are four steps to Yokoten in spreading process and functionality solutions:

1. Create and stabilize the model for spread
2. Ensure preparedness and readiness of the location/team to spread to
3. Deploy the best practice
4. Take the learning back to the model

1. *Create and stabilize the model for spread.* We covered step 1 in detail in previous portions of this chapter. Hopefully you can recall the three conditions required to stabilize the model: everyone is trained, standard work is in place and followed, and measurable results have been realized and documented. One of the points of failure in many organizations' attempts to optimize their EHR is that they move quickly in deploying solutions that are not stable. Usually stability breaks down because the standard work is not followed consistently. You are once again encouraged to not spread any new process or functionality until all three conditions are satisfied.
2. *Ensure preparedness and readiness of the location/team to spread to.* Mandating everyone change to the new process and system will almost assuredly fail. The area you will be bringing the innovative solutions to must be prepared and ready to accept the changes. Some of you might be thinking, "I am the CEO/CNE/CIO/CMO. I can mandate that everyone get on board." You would be right 20% of the time. It is possible to muscle through system change about 20% of the time, but this is not a recipe for long-term success, and it doesn't meet one of the two pillars of Lean improvement—respect for all people. One of the most common mistakes organizations make is assuming that everyone will jump onboard with change. It is true that the model will have created an improved process. There will be standard work in place to support the new process, and the system functionality will be optimized in support of the new workflows. And you will also have documented results you can share. But to ensure the spread efforts go smoothly, you will want to make sure the area you are coming to optimize next is both prepared and ready.

   Readiness should come first. To ensure the area is ready for spread, you can address many change management needs. The place to start is to develop a business case for change, which can be documented on a spread A3. Will the project have a reason for improvement? Is there a current condition and a target condition? Can success be measured? These questions can be answered by completing the first three boxes of the A3 form using A3 thinking. The people case for change will also have a current condition and target condition. These reasons for change can be documented on the A3 form as well. The training plan and the communication plan will be actions that will be created and monitored by documenting them on the follow-up plans section of the A3 form. An example of a spread A3 is shown in Figure 13.4.

Readiness comes next. Once we have prepared the receiving area for change, we must now ensure they are ready for change. The main way organizations get the receiving area ready for change is by introducing elements of managing for daily improvement (MDI). Introducing MDI, at the receiving unit level, will accomplish a couple of key things. First, we begin getting staff engaged in process improvement. Engagement will be necessary to optimize the EHR when the solutions are spread to the receiving area. Second, improvement from the MDI system will be driven by the creation of standards and by testing innovative ideas. Both skills will be needed when the process developed in the model area is spread.

Depending on how mature your organization is in Lean improvement, there are other management system techniques that can be deployed as part of readiness for change as well. These techniques include *Kamishibai* task audits, leader standard work, 5S, and implementing a suggestion system. Kamishibai is an audit and sustainability system that uses cascading and peer audits to ensure standard work is followed. Leader standard work is a technique where management at all levels is given core tasks and responsibilities each day that focus on sustaining and improving operational standards. Rather than standard work for completing a task, think of leader standard work as standard work leading improvement in an area. 5S is a system for creating a high-performing work area to enable flow and standard work while building discipline among the team members. The suggestion system is an ideas board that empowers staff to generate and implement ideas daily. Each of these approaches will help ensure readiness for change by helping create a culture of improvement and migrating your organization away from fire-fighting.

3. *Deploy the best practice.* Once you have taken the necessary steps to ensure that the receiving area is prepared and ready for change, you are

A-3 Theme: Adult Medicine Inpatient Process and EHR Optimization Spread

Date 5 Mar 2018 **Revision** 1

Team Members: Amy Sinsich—Charge nurse, Emma Long—Nurse manager, Will Smith—Case manager, Julie Wilson—Application specialist, Carlee Smoker—Hospitalist, Elizabeth Hankins—Pharmacist, James Phelps—Nurse tech, Robbie Jackson—Unit secretary, Josh Summers—Performance improvement

Reason for Improvement:

- To spread process and functionality improvements generated in the Cardiology Model
- To provide inpatients the best care at the best value
- To optimize staff resources by streamlining clinical documentation

Current Performance and Reflections on Current Performance:

- Median LOS = 5.3 days
- Readmission rates = 14.6%
- Variation in D/C planning goals and implementation of the goals
- Excessive time spent doing clinical documentation
- Variation between hospitalists on the application of evidence and selection or orders.
- Variation in clinical documentation between all clinicians
- Variation in discharge planning between clinicians

Target Performance:

- Standard work from model leveraged for all disciplines
- Evidence-based best practices in place for care delivery and clinical documentation
- Time freed up to deliver more care at the bedside
- Patients and care givers have the knowledge to continue care in the home environment

Dimension	Measure	Current	Target
Access	Adult medicine inpatient length of stay	5.3 days	3.3 days
Productivity	Time spent documenting d/c plans	123 minutes	45 minutes
Quality (%)	Readmission rates	14.6%	5%

Figure 13.4 Spread A3.

now ready to deploy (spread) the best practice. We learned the Lean project management approach in Chapter 6. And it is this approach we see as the least waste way to spread our solutions and best practices. What might the milestones look like for a spread project? We can suggest four, and the milestones' names are identical to the model for Yokoten deployment: stabilize the model, ensure preparedness and readiness, deploy the best practice, and take the learning back to the model.

In the deployment phase, you will be adopting the solutions or adapting the process and functionality to meet your specific clinical or administrative needs. Then you will test your solutions to ensure effectiveness. This work will be followed by training all the staff and a formal rollout of the new process and functionality. Deploying the best practice will end with a stabilization period and validation that the measurable results have been met. Then you will be ready to spread to the next area. Follow the project management technique of moving task by task through the deployment phase, and hold your milestone review meeting to ensure you capture lessons learned to improve your spread process when you go to the next unit.

4. *Take the learning back to the model.* The last step in the Yokoten deployment model is to take any new learning back to the model area. Lean organizations are a community of scientists. Everyone is engaged in small experiments to see and eliminate wasted time and activity. The model area has done some heroic work. The model area has improved workflows and functionality and created a best practice to be spread throughout the organization, but that doesn't mean there isn't room for improvement. It is highly likely that the area receiving the best practice can take the new standard and enhanced functionality and make it even better, especially if you are a mature Lean organization. This behavior should be encouraged and recognized. Now we want to ensure this learning can go back to the model so they too can benefit from the improvement.

Follow your Lean project management plan and move area by area throughout your organization until everyone is using the new process and functionality. While you are spreading your best practices, the model can be working on improving even more, and this process can repeat itself over and over. It is through repeated cycles of improvement that the processes are made waste-free and the EHR remains optimized.

Chapter Summary

- Lean organizations use a model area to develop and test different approaches and solutions. In the model space, we can decide the best methods to deliver the best possible care. For example, we can determine the best methods and functionality to capture intake data, to capture patient demographics, to determine what layout is easiest to enter an order set, what evidence-based order sets create the best outcomes, what set of standard tasks make patient care the safest, etc.

- In healthcare, models are usually created along clinical specialties. Models are further decided by geography and are best contained to a single unit, department, or clinic.
- Improvement work within the model includes improving both process and system functionality to deliver operational improvement.
- Improvement work in a Lean organization follows the scientific method. The A3 form and A3 thinking are used to apply the scientific method. One prevalent way to apply the scientific method is through a rapid cycle improvement event.
- Rapid cycle improvement is designed to change the culture of an organization while shortening the timeline for results.
- The standards that come from an improvement are critical, since they serve to both hardwire the solution and set the baseline for further improvement.
- EHR workflow and optimization rapid cycle events can be run for each of the core processes a department or a unit uses. True North Measures can be used to evaluate the effectiveness of the rapid cycle events.
- Within the model area, when all of the system users have been trained, standard work is in place *and* followed, and the measurable outcome objectives have been realized, the organization will be ready to spread solutions to other areas.
- Spreading solutions from the model area is known as Yokoten, which means best practice (wisdom) sharing.
- There are four steps to the Yokoten deployment model: stabilize the model, ensure the receiving area is prepared and ready, deploy the best practice using Lean project management, and take any new learning back to the model.
- The model, spread approach, is used by Lean organizations because it is ultimately faster and contains less rework than other deployment approaches. The model area can continue to improve while the solutions are being spread to other areas.

Book Summary

We started this book looking at the patient's perspective, and why it's vital for healthcare to figure out how to improve our use of the EHR to improve patient outcomes. There is a direct connection between how well we architect our care workflows and how we build our EHRs. Many organizations around the world have seen dramatic improvement in quality, safety, cost, and access through the application of quality improvement approaches using Lean. Yet when it comes to linking quality improvement to the EHR, healthcare organizations are coming up short of ideal.

Healthcare is under increasing scrutiny and pressure to provide better care, better outcomes, and lower costs. This can be achieved, but only by looking at where waste exists and removing that waste. There are compelling cases, discussed throughout this book, demonstrating that modifying processes and workflows with Lean thinking can lead to substantial improvements. These improvements must be undertaken with a clear, consistent commitment to making these changes or we'll end up endlessly repeating the same tasks over and over without making progress. Indeed, this is where many organizations find themselves today. They have implemented an EHR based on existing workflows and sometimes antiquated processes around care. Unfortunately, automating poor processes only allows us to do poorly more quickly (or perhaps less quickly, depending on how the workflow was built). Repeating the current state will simply keep us where we are, at best, and we know that is not an acceptable state of being. Even worse, organizations oftentimes implement their EHR without attempting to standardize clinical practice. These create an electronic environment with copious amounts of variation leading to waste and varying outcomes. The organizations that did standardize up-front in their EHR deployment struggle to keep the evidence current.

Early in this book, we looked at some of the current problems facing healthcare organizations. Inefficiencies run rampant—not because people are oblivious to these issues, but because they lack a systemic approach to solving the problems. We read stories about provider burnout, though these stories sometimes don't mention the state of work for these providers pre-EHR. In fact, much evidence points to provider burnout related to how care is provided rather than the use of an EHR (or not). We cited examples of providers modifying their workflows to gain efficiencies in their days. These changes lead to more efficient use of time, reducing a sense of burnout. The story of burnout goes beyond just the providers. Clinicians also deal with work burnout. This problem is magnified when we think about the provider and clinician staffing shortages around the world today. Inefficient documentation practices and redundancy of documentation simply extend the work day, and this has negative repercussions on work–life balance influencing burnout.

Of course, many provider offices and healthcare organizations have already deployed an EHR, and many are now facing optimization challenges. The financial implications of upgrading, optimizing, or replacing an EHR system are significant. We reviewed the financial decisions that organizations face and how to quantify (or justify) the return on investment. There are still carrot-and-stick incentives facing organizations—the carrots are opportunities to reduce costs and improve patient outcomes via an intelligent deployment of the EHR, and the sticks are the penalties now in place for failing to meet certain regulatory requirements, at least in the United States. No matter how you look at the financials of an EHR system, you need to look at how you can create an environment in which you get the most benefit from this massive investment. That typically begins and ends with how processes are developed and how they are improved over time.

For anyone unfamiliar with the basic underpinnings of Lean thinking, we reviewed the fundamentals. While knowledge of the principles and tools of Lean is helpful, having an expert (sensei) guide you through the learning process can help ensure you take the best first steps and create a plan for success. As we've seen throughout healthcare, implementing Lean thinking and Lean processes can be extraordinarily powerful, but it requires a long-term commitment to a culture of improvement. As we've seen, implementing Lean in a healthcare organization can yield some big wins, but it requires care and feeding to sustain those wins. Building in countermeasures to prevent recidivism certainly helps, but it's about sustaining the leadership mindset and commitment to Lean that will drive consistent results.

Whether you're deploying a new EHR or moving from one vendor to another, some fundamental aspects of developing a set of selection criteria apply. We discussed involving stakeholders to ensure that they are not only invested in the outcome but also participants in defining needs. The requirements, both operational and technical, really form the basis of a successful project, so taking time to clearly discover and document needs will help drive the best possible outcome. While the basics follow standard application selection best practices, the EHR is not just any old application, of course. Most EHRs are a suite of integrated applications that function as an enterprise solution. In addition, most EHRs need to interface to multiple up and downstream systems to compile all needed information to run the business. From patient scheduling to patient care to patient billing and revenue management—and everything in between—the EHR requirements are the requirements for the business. Taking time to clearly discuss and define these requirements will absolutely lead to a better result.

We also looked at Lean project management with respect to the EHR deployment process. Using standard project management processes might work, but using Lean thinking in the management of such a critical project can potentially lead to far superior results. We discussed how a Lean project plan differs from a standard project plan and reviewed the benefits of taking a Lean approach. We also saw how EHR, IT, and clinical governance processes are vital in developing and maintaining a Lean EHR. As we discussed, there's a huge opportunity to improve processes while defining a new current state and by building it into the new system, you make it a bit more difficult to go back to the bad old ways of working.

Once the EHR is selected, it's important to develop very specific requirements for the build. While this work varies from vendor to vendor, the key aspects of developing build requirements are fairly standardized. As we saw throughout the book, the more specific you can get with every aspect of your EHR deployment, the better outcome you're likely to have.

Once you've identified the requirements, you can design your build. As we discussed in the design phase, the work includes creating a gap analysis, piloting the physical workflow, configuring that workflow in the EHR, and ensuring your data interfaces are pulling or pushing the data elements required.

Once the build work has commenced, your requirements should be locked. This is the point in many deployments where new or changing requirements create an endless loop of change requests. This can be fatal to any project, but especially to a complex EHR deployment. Testing starts with unit testing by the builder then integrated testing within the module and across modules. Finally, test plans that include end-to-end testing, data validation, and scenarios are run to ensure the system is working as expected in every aspect. Super users are vital to this testing process for two key reasons. First, they are educated members of your end-user population and, as such, they should have a greater awareness and understanding of the workflows in their area of specialty, and they should be able to better assess if the EHR, as built, will meet those workflow needs. These super users often double as at-the-elbow support for their peers during a go live, so having a strong super user program will enhance the EHR on many levels.

We concluded the section specific to the EHR deployment by discussing best practices for go live management. This runs from planning and readiness assessment to the actual go live and command center support functions. Every organization has a different approach to a go live, and there are many valid ways to successfully launch an EHR. Some of the key elements of managing the process were presented in Lean terms to provide a roadmap to using Lean tools and processes for managing the go live process—the handling of defects (errors, omissions) and the handling of optimization requests that inevitably come in on the heels of the go live.

In the final section of the book, we pulled this all together to talk about how to handle post–go live optimization from a Lean perspective and how to standardize by specialty to avoid the "we're special and can't follow standards" argument that is often promulgated by those reluctant to change. We concluded by discussing the model line concept, how to apply it, and how to spread it.

Throughout this book, we've offered examples of how and where Lean principles have been deployed to make significant and lasting change in healthcare delivery. We've also discussed Lean principles to help you gain an understanding of these principles (if you're new to Lean) or to help you see how they might be applied (if you're more experienced with Lean).

Perhaps this book can best be summarized by these statements. The EHR is a reflection of your organization and the way you want to do business. How you manage the configuration and use of your EHR can be done via standard methods, and you'll get the same result you've gotten in the past. If you're looking to make lasting improvements in the delivery of care, you must start with looking at the system from your patient's perspective, understanding what is of value and what is simply waste for the patient. When you begin seeing in this way, you'll begin building in this way. When you begin building in this way, you'll be driving improvements in your care delivery. Only then will your EHR be able to support and enable these improvements. We hope this book has helped you see things in a new light and piqued your interest in breaking the habits of the past that hold you back from permanent improvement and lasting success.

Glossary of Lean EHR Terms

6S: (Sort, Straighten, Shine, Standardize, Sustain, Safety) A process to ensure work areas are systematically kept clean and organized, ensuring employee safety and providing the foundation on which to build a Lean culture.

A3: Both the process and thinking for problem-solving based on the scientific method. The A3 is frequently used to document problem-solving exercises, status reports, and business cases. Named the A3 as the report is associated with the size of paper the report is documented upon.

A4: Like the A3, A4 refers to the paper size that the report is documented on. It is a communication tool used for documenting the problem-solving process. It follows a structured cycle of improvement using the scientific method of Plan–Do–Study–Act. The tool tells the story of problem-solving and includes the following steps: Problem Definition, Problem Statement, Costs, 5 Whys Analysis, Desired State, Plan/Experiments, and Monitor/Updates.

Andon: A visual control device in a production area, typically a lighted overhead display, giving the current status of the production system and alerting team members to emerging problems.

Autonomation: Automation with a human touch, adding "intelligent" features to a process to start or stop operations as needed and emit signals for operators when necessary.

Balancing (work load balancing): The distribution of work units across the value stream to meet *Takt time*.

Bar chart: Way of displaying statistical data using horizontal or vertical bars. The heights or lengths of the bars are proportional to the quantities they represent.

Batch and queue: A mass production approach to operations where large lots of items are processed and moved to the next process where they wait in a line.

Bottleneck: Any resource whose capacity is equal to or less than the demand placed on it.

Business continuity plan: A process of determining critical business systems, their importance, and the processes and technologies put in place to ensure continuous business operations despite disruptive events.

Cells: The layout of machines of different types performing different operations in a tight sequence, typically in a U-shape, to permit single-piece flow and flexible deployment of human effort by means of Multimachine Working. Contrast with functional layout.

Champion: The person that has authority to commit resources of the facility to ensure change takes place. Also referred to as team champion.

Change agent: The catalytic force moving organizations and value streams from the current state to an improved future state.

Cloud-based computing: This type of computing is typically provided by a company that offers software that is accessed via the Internet. In some cases, cloud-based computing simply refers to the method of computing that can be hosted in any location, including on premises in an organization's own data center.

Communication circle: A tool used to show the waste of transactions and hand-offs of information.

Continuous flow: A process's ability to replenish a single work unit or service that has been requested or "pulled" from a downstream process. It is synonymous with just-in-time (JIT), which ensures both internal and external customers receive the work unit or service when it is needed, in the exact amounts.

Continuous improvement: A mindset adopted by organizations to repeatedly identify and eliminate waste.

Control chart: The visual representation of tracking progress over time. Similar to line graphs.

CPOE: Computerized Physician Order Entry, a process that enables physicians to enter orders electronically versus manually writing orders on paper.

Current state: Workflow of the operation as it currently performs. Used as part of value stream mapping.

Customer: The patient/person who requires a service or receives the output of a process.

Customer demand: The quantity of service or product required by the customer. Demand is needed to calculate *Takt time.*

Cycle time: The time it takes to complete a process, as observed through direct observation. Also see *Manual cycle time* and *Touch time.*

Data integrity: The maintenance and assurance of the accuracy and consistency of data over their entire life cycle.

Data interface: The method by which two systems communicate, typically to move discrete data between systems in either a unilateral (one-way) or bilateral (two-way) communication process.

Defect: Work that needs to be redone or clarified. An error that finds its way to the customer.

Direct observation: The Lean approach used to best identify waste. Direct observation involves going to areas and observing the process to identify waste. Direct observation is often combined with capturing time elements of the process to "quantify" waste.

Disaster recovery plan: A process of determining the likelihood and impact of potential disruptive events and steps to be taken to mitigate and recover from such events.

Error-proofing: A technique of preventing errors by designing the process, equipment, and supplies so that a process step literally cannot be performed incorrectly. Also see *Poka-Yoke.*

Flow: Processing one unit of work through a series of steps in a continuous manner, at the rate of customer demand, in a standardized way. Ideally only value-added tasks are linked together.

Flow cell: The location of processing steps for a product immediately adjacent to each other so that parts can be processed in very nearly continuous, one-piece flow.

Flow diagram: A Lean tool used to document a process. The flow diagram is used to show workflow and highlights process stops and starts, hand-offs, and disconnects.

Flow time: Elapsed time (including waiting) of the flow of materials or information.

Fishbone diagram: An analysis tool that provides a systematic way of looking at effects and the causes that create or contribute to those effects.

Five whys: The practice of asking why repeatedly (at least five times) when encountering a problem to discover the root cause.

Future state: Workflow created as a vision for what the new workflow will be. The future state is developed using the Lean design attributes of flow, pull, defect-free, and visual management. Used as part of value stream mapping.

Gemba: "Actual place"; any place where work occurs.

Gemba walk: A scheduled "walk-through" with designated staff to evaluate performance results.

Interface: The point of connection between two or more electronic systems. Typically, this refers to the sharing of data between an EHR system and other clinical systems such as lab, pharmacy, or billing services, for example. Data are formatted in a manner that both sending and receiving systems can process and are transmitted on a periodic basis.

Inventory: Materials and information that accumulate between process steps.

Jidoka: "Not passing defects on." Jidoka can be implemented with the use of technology (*Autonomation*) or without (use quality tools to prevent defects, i.e., SPC).

Just-in-time (JIT): Today's work today. A system of production that makes and delivers just what is needed, just when it is needed.

Kaizen: "Kai" means to "change" and "zen" means "for better." Kaizen is synonymous with continuous improvement.

Kaizen event: Team-based approach to rapid cycle improvement. Spanning 2–5 days depending on the scope of the activity, the scientific method is followed during this activity to deliver an improved process in a portion of a value stream ending with standard work, visual management, and process control.

Kamishibai: Japanese word literally meaning "paper theater." Used as a visual control method to audit and visually manage standard work in the gemba.

Kanban: "Replenishment signal." A card or visual indicator that serves as a means of communicating to an upstream process precisely what is required at the specified time.

Lean healthcare: The application of the Toyota Production System tools and concepts to the healthcare industry. Lean healthcare aims to give the right patient, the right amount of care, at the right time, each and every time, while continuously pursuing the elimination of waste.

Lead time: The total time a customer must wait to receive a service or product after triggering a need.

Leveling: The balancing of work among the workers during a period of time both by volume and variety.

Manual cycle time: The time a person or machine takes to complete all of its operations on one piece. For example, in healthcare, the time it takes to complete a procedure with a patient without interruptions. Also see *Cycle time* and *Touch time*.

MDI: Managing for Daily Improvement, a team-based problem solving system where targets are established, outcomes are reported and updated daily, variances from targets are documented and prioritized and solutions for the root cause of these variances are implemented.

Milestone: A checkpoint in the Lean Project Management approach where confirmation that all activities in a phase have been completed and all necessary questions have been answered in order to move to the next phase. In addition, lessons learned for the completed phase are captured within this milestone for future benefits.

Minimum staffing: Manual cycle time divided by *Takt time*.

Motion: Operator movement in excess of that required to complete a task.

Muda: Japanese word meaning any activity that consumes resources without creating value for the customer. Also see *Waste*.

Mura: Japanese word meaning unevenness; irregularity or lack of uniformity and is also considered waste.

Muri: Japanese word meaning unreasonableness; beyond one's power; too difficult. Muri is also considered waste.

Multidisciplinary team: Team members from different disciplines in an organization that are charged with completing a continuous improvement project or other task.

Network core infrastructure: Network routing and switching management function provided by several network components. An organization will typically have multiple network core devices for high availability and redundancy.

Non-value added (NVA): An activity that takes time, space, or resources but does not directly meet the need of the customer. Also see *Waste* or *Muda*.

Obeya: Japanese word meaning "large room." A mission control room to visually manage a large project, such as an EHR implementation.

Output: The product or service delivered to a customer.

Overproduction: Producing/doing more, sooner, or faster than the next step in the process.

Overprocessing: Doing work-related tasks in excess of value as defined by the customer.

Pareto chart: The visual representation in a bar chart format listing issues in descending order of importance. Also referred to as the 80/20 rule.

Performance board: Tool used to show results from a process. The performance board differs from the process control board in that it details outcome results in lieu of process measures.

PDSA (Plan, Do, Study, Act): A structured problem solving methodology.

Plan: Plan ahead for any change.

Do: Try the change on a small scale under controlled circumstances.

Study: Analyze the results of the experiment.

Act: Take action to standardize the process that produced the desired results.

Phase: A body of work in the Lean Project Management approach where tasks are done to answer input questions necessary to complete the project.

Poka-Yoke: A mistake-proofing device or method to prevent or detect a defect from being made or passed on to someone else during a process.

Pugh analysis: A quantitative technique used to evaluate multiple options against a set of criteria.

Pull: A signal used to link areas of continuous flow together. A method to control work by having downstream activities signal their upstream requirements. Used to reduce/eliminate the waste of overproduction.

Push: The work that is pushed along regardless of need or request.

Quality yield: Percent of time an activity is completed without additional information or rework required.

Rapid improvement event (RIE): See *Kaizen event*.

Red tag: A label used in the 6S process to identify items that are not needed or are placed in the wrong area.

Server farm: A group of computer servers typically in a virtualized environment, meaning the server function is a software function no longer dependent upon a specific set of hardware resources but using shared hardware resources.

Seven wastes: Forms of waste found in operations. These wastes include overproduction, overprocessing, waiting, motion, transportation, inventory, and defects.

Software-as-a-service (SaaS): Software provided via cloud-based technologies accessible via the Internet. This software model is typically subscription-based and is paid for monthly or annually.

Spaghetti map: A diagram used to show the path and distance of travel for a person, supply, or machinery. The map highlights the waste of motion and/or transportation.

Standard work: Work procedures used to define how an operator will complete a task or process. Standard work is based on three elements: sequence of operations, *Takt time*, and standard work in process.

Steering committee: A body designated to govern Lean improvement. The steering committee can be at the value stream or the enterprise level of the organization.

Storage area network (SAN): Typically a large array of disk (SATA, SSD) storage accessible to enterprise systems.

Systems integration: The engineering process of bringing subsystems together to function as a single system.

Takt time: A theoretical calculation used to provide the rhythm of output for a process in time units. The calculation consists of taking the available time to do work divided by the volume of work to be done.

Time observation: See *Direct observation.*

Touch time: The actual time spent performing an activity. Also see *Cycle time* and *Manual cycle time.*

Toyota Production System: A management system for excellence based on providing a customer the highest possible quality, in the shortest time, at the lowest cost by removing wasted time and activity.

Transportation: Unnecessary movement of people, materials, equipment, etc. Transportation is also known as the waste of conveyance.

Trigger: What initiates an activity or process step.

True north measure: Operational excellence comes from five key areas: Staff morale (human development), Quality, Delivery (lead time), Cost, and Growth. A high-level strategic measure of one of the five areas of operational excellence is known as a true north measure. These measures become the compass for the organization to align effort and direction.

Upstream process: The provider of a service or work unit required downstream from a customer.

User interface: The point or method at which a human interacts with a machine. It often is used to refer to the graphical user interface (GUI), which is the arrangement of information on a computer screen with which the user interacts. In healthcare IT, it is most often used to refer to the presentation of visual data on a computer screen.

Value added: An activity that directly meets the need of a customer.

Value-added/Non-value-added analysis: A technique used to identify in each task step whether the step adds value or doesn't. Typically, a value-added task is given a green dot and a non-value-added task is given a red dot. A typical process is nine parts non-value added to one part value added.

Value-effort grid: Grid used to help prioritize ideas into one of four categories:

Easy effort and high value: "Just do it"
Easy effort and low value: "Low hanging fruit"
High effort and high value: "High hard"
High effort and low value: "Kibosh"

Value stream: The activities completed to deliver value to a customer.

Value stream analysis (VSA): A multidisciplinary team event, utilizing the A3 problem-solving model, to develop a future state vision to address a business need, as well as develop a plan for improvement.

Value stream mapping: A tool used to show waste in a value stream and develop a plan for improvement.

Vertical value stream map: A planning approach used for projects used to simultaneously deliver the correct value to the customer in the least waste way. The process begins by defining the milestones and then backward-plans the tasks needed to meet the milestones, thus ensuring the majority of the project is value added.

Virtualized servers: Server software running on shared hardware platform to provide high availability and redundancy for critical systems.

Visual management: A management system that makes normal from abnormal conditions transparent to allow problems to be identified at a glance so they can immediately be corrected.

Waiting: Customer delays caused by the absence of supplies, equipment, information, and resources.

Waste: Any activity that consumes time, space, or resources, but fails to create value for a customer.

Waste walk: The action of going to Gemba to see waste in order to understand the root causes.

Workflow: The series of steps necessary to complete a task or body of work.

Yokoten: "Horizontal deployment." A method to spread improvements from a model line to subsequent work areas.

Zero defects: A mindset based on the premise that while humans are prone to errors, these errors need not make it to the customer becoming a defect. It is possible to achieve a zero-defect system.

Index

M

N

O

P

S

T

W

Y

9781138626584